CLASSICAL

DRAMA

GREEK AND ROMAN

BY MEYER REINHOLD

Fellow of the American Academy in Rome
Formerly Associate Professor of Classical Languages
Brooklyn College

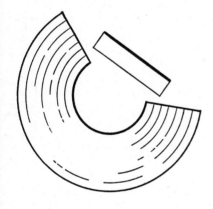

BARRON'S EDUCATIONAL SERIES INC.

GREAT NECK, NEW YORK

CONTENTS

PREFACE

This comprehensive survey of the dramatic literature of the Greeks and Romans is intended to serve the needs and interests of a variety of readers: students of classical literature; students of English, world and comparative literature; and the general reader with an interest in the drama.

Of the thousands of plays written in antiquity only eighty-five are extant, most preserved in their entirety, some in extensive enough portions to make possible their reconstruction. Each of these plays has been analyzed and interpreted. It is necessary to point out that the interpretations are not intended to be definitive, but suggestive of the probable intent of the respective authors. To place the plays in their proper frame of reference, essential biographical data have been given for each playwright, and each period has been provided with a summary of the historical and cultural milieu in which they wrote. Special attention has been given to tracing the evolution of the classical drama from its birth in the cult of the Greek god Dionysus to its decline in the Roman Empire and its ultimate extinction with the rise of Christianity.

The bibliographies, containing more recent works in English selected from the vast literature on the subject, are intended to aid those who desire to explore more thoroughly particular authors or topics. A special bibliography on the influences of the classical drama on later literatures is included.

Meyer Reinhold

CHAPTER ONE

ATHENS IN THE FIFTH CENTURY

HISTORICAL EVOLUTION OF GREECE

1. Early Kingdoms (1400-750 B.C.)

   a. Numerous small kingdoms.

   b. Rulers originally clan kings, possessing military, judicial and religious powers.

   c. Power of kings limited by council of aristocratic elders and assembly of soldiers.

   d. This is the period in which the myths developed that constituted the pool of story material employed by the Greek tragic writers.

2. Aristocracy (750-500 B.C.)

   a. Kings supplanted by hereditary nobility.

   b. Supremacy of aristocrats; elected officials.

3. *Polis* (City-State)

   a. Emerged in 8th Century B.C.

   b. The most characteristic feature of Greek society.

   c. Hundreds of small autonomous cities; the two most famous were Athens and Sparta.

4. Tyranny (600-500 B.C.)

   a. In numerous Greek cities tyrants (unconstitutional rulers) seized power.

1

b. Many of these tyrants advanced their cities culturally and economically.

SOCIAL AND CULTURAL EVOLUTION OF GREECE (1400-600 B.C.)

1. Early tribal institutions: strong kinship ties; collective ownership of clan property; justice based on clan responsibility.

2. Women of the higher classes possessed more respected position and greater freedom than those of similar status in classical times.

3. Disintegration of tribal system: small family units; private property.

4. Growing individualism—limited by strong sense of allegiance to city-state.

EVOLUTION OF ATHENS

1. Ionians; by 700 B.C. the entire peninsula of Attica was organized as a city-state with Athens as its political center.

2. By 7th Century B.C. aristocratic government superseded monarchy, with Council (Areopagus) of nobles supreme; executives (9 archons) elected annually from aristocratic class.

3. Economic, political and social unrest leads to repressive measures by aristocrats and threats of revolution.

4. Solon, moderate aristocrat, sole archon in 594 B.C., introduces broad reform program to mitigate economic, social, and political ferment; extension of vote in Popular Assembly to lowest class of population—first step toward democracy.

5. Tyranny of Peisistratus and his sons, Hippias and Hipparchus (560-510 B.C.).

a. Great cultural progress of Athens.

b. Murder of Hipparchus; tyranny of Hippias, followed by revolution.

6. Cleisthenes' reforms (508 B.C.)—first democratic government in world history.

a. Full political equality of all citizens; Popular Assembly supreme, chief lawmaking body.

    b. Vote by place of residence, not in accordance with wealth or tribal association; election of civil executives (archons) and board of ten generals by all citizens.

ATHENS IN THE FIFTH CENTURY

1. Persian Wars

    a. Annexation of Greek cities in Asia Minor by Persians; harsh treatment of Greek subjects of Persian King Darius (521-486 B.C.); Ionian revolt, supported by Athens and Eretria; suppression of revolt (494 B.C.) by Persians.

    b. Persian invasion of Greece in 490 B.C.; defeat at Marathon by small army of Athenians, led by Miltiades.

    c. Development of Athens as sea power under influence of Themistocles; many Greek cities agree on united opposition to Persia.

    d. Persian invasion in 480 B.C., under leadership of King Xerxes; heroic, but futile, stand of Greek army, led by Leonidas and 300 Spartans, at Pass of Thermopylae; evacuation of Athenians to Salamis; brilliant naval victory of Greeks, led by Themistocles, in Bay of Salamis; smashing defeat of Persians by combined Greek forces at Plataea in Boeotia (479 B.C.); retreat of Persians; liberation of Asia Minor.

2. Athenian Empire (454-404 B.C.)

3. Golden Age of Pericles (461-429 B.C.)

    a. Pericles, elected chief general numerous times, leader of Popular Assembly, unofficial ruler of democratic Athens.

    b. Athenian imperialism based on naval power.

    c. Wealth of Athenian government from tribute exacted from cities of Empire, and from heavy taxation of rich; money used to beautify the city and to extend Athenian democracy.

    d. Athens a great commercial center.

ATHENIAN DEMOCRACY

1. Limited to citizens, who comprised small number (about 10% of population, ca. 40,000); women, foreigners (called metics), slaves excluded.

2. Direct democracy; all important measures passed by majority vote in mass meetings of entire citizen body; executive, legislative, judicial functions directly controlled by all citizens.

3. Only generals elected; all other officials chosen by lot; principle of rotation in office.

4. Citizens paid for all services to community: office holding, jury service, attendance in Assembly, later even for attendance at theater.

5. Importance of citizenship: leisure for performance of civic duty the ideal.

6. Popular jury courts (dicasteries), formed from pool of 6,000 citizens.

WOMEN

1. Principal occupation—housework.

2. Upper class women segregated and secluded.

3. Marriages arranged by parents, with dowry as basic consideration.

4. Marriage with non-Athenians not considered legal.

5. Divorce easy for men with return of dowry; almost impossible for women.

RELIGION AND MORALITY

1. Worship of many gods with human attributes (polytheistic anthropomorphism): principal gods of Athenian state religion—Olympian gods, especially Zeus and Athena (patron divinity of Athens); numerous minor divinities.

2. Belief in Fate as a divine force superior to the gods was widespread.

3. Ritual primary: prayer and sacrifice.

4. Priests not a separate caste; no dogma.

5. Importance of divination to ascertain the will of the gods; prediction of future through omens, dreams, oracles, soothsayers; most famous oracles—of Apollo at Delphi, and Zeus at Dodona.

6. Mystery religions: secret rites for initiated, e.g. Mysteries at Eleusis near Athens; Orphic cult.

7. Numerous religious festivals, e.g. Panathenaea, Dionysia, Anthesteria, etc.

8. Belief in immortality of soul in Hades; but principal emphasis on man in this life. Burial of dead relatives an important religious duty.

9. The gods were believed to be jealous of humans. Excess of any kind (power, wealth, intelligence, beauty, etc.) was believed to arouse divine ire. Possession of anything to excess was thought to expose a person to the sin of *hybris* (pride, arrogance). A person guilty of *hybris* was sure to be assailed by the goddess Atë (Infatuation) and punished by Nemesis sent by the gods. Hence moderation (*sophrosyne*) in everything was the ideal.

INTELLECTUAL FERMENT

1. Pre-Socratic Philosophers (ca. 625-420 B.C.)

a. Effort at rational-philosophical-scientific explanation of the world.

b. Materialistic thinkers: search for material explanation of the universe by Thales, Anaximander, Anaximenes, Heraclitus.

c. Idealistic thinkers: search for eternal, abstract, non-material truth by Pythagoras, Xenophanes, Parmenides, Zeno.

d. Efforts at reconciliation of materialistic and idealistic philosophies by Empedocles, Anaxagoras, Leucippus and Democritus.

2. Sophists (5th Century B.C.)

a. Extreme skepticism was produced by the conflicting and irreconcilable views of the Pre-Socratic philosophers.

b. The Sophists, such as Protagoras, Gorgias, Evenus, Prodicus, Hippias, Thrasymachus, were teachers whose principal interest was man's place in the universe and society.

c. The main emphasis of their teaching was training for success (political and financial) in social life through public speaking. They taught clever methods of argumentation, without regard for truth, on both sides of a question.

d. The Sophists were opposed to traditional morality and religion; they taught skepticism, agnosticism, rationalism.

e. They were opposed to absolute standards of conduct and taught relativity in ethics.

f. Their theory of the state and society was that all individuals and classes are in constant opposition; life is a constant struggle for superiority and power by all. Justice is not absolute but the imposed will of the stronger ("Might makes right").

g. Individual self-interest is the dominant drive of all (Law of Nature).

h. Laws and customs are man-made, subject to constant change.

3. Socrates (469-399 B.C.)

a. Principal opponent of the Sophists.

b. He is the "Father of Ethics;" Socrates transformed philosophy from the study of the external universe to the study of the inner life of man and his relations to other human beings.

c. He sought to establish absolute, universal, unchangeable standards of conduct.

d. Happiness, he taught, consists not in material rewards but perfection of the soul—virtue, which is self-directed, based on reason and understanding.

e. Virtue is teachable: objective standards of conduct, valid for all, can be established and transmitted to others through reason.

LITERARY EVOLUTION

1. Epic Poetry (1000-750 B.C.)

a. Homer (900-800 B.C.): *Iliad* and *Odyssey*—heroic epics.

b. Hesiod (800-750 B.C.): *Works and Days; Theogony*—didactic epics.

2. Lyric Poetry (750-450 B.C.)

a. Elegiac Poetry: written to accompaniment of flute; metrical form—elegiac couplet; used for military themes, banquet songs, political thought, dedications on monuments, epitaphs on tombstones, love songs.

b. Iambic Poetry: rhythms of everyday speech; metrical form —usually iambic trimeter; used for satire and lampoons.

c. Leading elegiac and iambic poets: Archilochus; Tyrtaeus; Solon.

d. Melic Poetry: pure lyric, odes sung to the accompaniment of the lyre; great variety of metrical schemes; monodic lyric—sung by poet to friends; choral lyric—sung and danced by chorus on religious and social occasions; many types of choral lyrics, e.g., hymn, dirge, marriage-song (*epithalamion*), victory song (*epinicion*), hymn to Dionysus (dithyramb).

e. Leading lyric poets: Pindar, Bacchylides, Sappho, Anacreon, Stesichorus, Simonides, Ibycus, Alcaeus, Alcman.

PELOPONNESIAN WAR (431-404 B.C.)

1. Basic cause: rival imperialisms of Athens and Sparta.
2. Plague at Athens (430-429 B.C.); death of Pericles.
3. Peace of Nicias (421 B.C.), soon broken.
4. Melos brutally forced into Athenian Empire in 416 B.C.
5. Disaster of Athenian naval expedition sent to conquer Sicily (415-413 B.C.); failure of siege of Syracuse and loss of all Athenian forces in Sicily.
6. Chaotic political conditions in Athens; final loss of entire Athenian navy.
7. Surrender of Athens (404 B.C.); loss of Athenian Empire and military power.

CHAPTER TWO

THE DRAMA: TRAGEDY

ORIGIN AND EVOLUTION OF TRAGEDY

1. Worship of the god Dionysus, youngest of the gods of the Greek pantheon, whose cult began to spread in Greece about 700 B.C. Especially favored by the common people, he was the god of wine and, in general, of the reproductive forces in life. He was thought to liberate believers from personal trouble, and to be himself a suffering god, undergoing death and resurrection. Hence the cycle of lament and rejoicing in the worship of Dionysus, combining sorrow and despair with exaltation, enthusiasm, ecstasy.

2. Dithyramb, choral lyric in honor of Dionysus, sung and danced around the altar of Dionysus in a circular dancing-place (*orchestra*). It was performed by a chorus of 50 men dressed in skins of goats (the sacred animal of the god)—hence the term *tragoedia* ("goat-song"). They represented satyrs, companions of Dionysus. A story about Dionysus was improvised by the leader of the chorus, who sometimes dressed as a character from mythology, though still remaining the leader of the chorus.

3. Thespis of Attica (ca. 550-500 B.C.—"Father of the Drama"). He created the first actor (*hypokrites*—literally "answerer"), who performed between the dances of the chorus, taking

several roles and conversing at times with the leader of the chorus. Thus was drama (literally "action") introduced.

Several titles of Thespis' plays are known: *Phorbas; The Priests; The Youths; Pentheus.*

4. Gradually myths not connected with Dionysus were employed. Hence the chorus of satyrs became inappropriate, and was replaced by one suitable to the events portrayed in each play.

5. Official recognition of tragedy in the state cult in 534 B.C.

6. Second actor added by Aeschylus; chorus reduced to twelve.

7. Third actor added by Sophocles; number in chorus stabilized at fifteen.

8. The part assigned to the chorus, always an integral part of a classical Greek play, gradually diminished, while the dialogue became increasingly more important. Tragedy thus contained a myth from epic sources and choral odes alternating with dialogue. A Greek tragedy was, like a Wagnerian opera, a musical tragedy.

PRODUCTION OF PLAYS

1. Produced by the state as an annual ritual of the state religion, in a public theater. Classical Greek drama was community art in democratic Athens, with a citizen audience and citizen performers, the dramatist serving as a sort of teacher offering plays for the ethical and moral improvement of his fellow-citizens, to ensure the spiritual survival of the community.

2. Festivals of Dionysus in Athens:

a. Great (or City) Dionysia—five days in March/April. On the first day a procession in honor of Dionysus, in which the entire citizenry participated, took place. On the second day ten dithyrambs were performed. On each of the last three days three tragedies, followed by one satyr play and finally one comedy, were given.

b. Lenaea—January/February. Only comedies were performed.

c. Rural Dionysia—December/January.

3. State official (*archon*) selected three poets to compete for prizes in tragedy.

4. *Choregus* selected to pay for cost of the training and of the

costumes of the chorus. He was a wealthy citizen required by law to perform this duty as a public service (liturgy).

5. Each playwright offered tetralogy, a group of four plays:

a. Trilogy—three plays, at first on one unified theme, later on separate subjects.

b. Satyr play—a mock-heroic tragicomedy, which became part of the official ritual about 500 B.C. The satyr play often dealt with Dionysus, so that the association with the origin of the drama as part of the worship of the god of wine would not be forgotten; also served as relief from the tension of the severe tragedies. (The only complete extant satyr play is the *Cyclops* of Euripides; see pp. 94-96. For the *Trackers* of Sophocles see pp. 49-51.)

6. Prizes, consisting of wreaths, were awarded to the winning poet, the star actor, and the *choregus*. A jury of ten Athenian citizens chosen by lot selected the winners. The prizes were among the highest honors that could be bestowed upon an Athenian by his fellow-citizens.

7. Admission was free at first, later at a nominal fee. In the case of the needy citizens, this fee was paid by the government out of the Theoric Fund (Theater Fund).

ACTORS IN TRAGEDY

1. Originally the playwright took the leading roles; Aeschylus is known to have performed in his own plays.

2. The leading roles were taken by the protagonist, supporting roles by the deuteragonist, others by the tritagonist.

3. Actors were all male. Each played several roles when necessary.

4. Costume: masks (hence the term *dramatis personae*—"masks of the drama"), wigs, and *cothurnus* (buskin), the high-soled boot worn by tragic actors to give them added dignity.

5. Mutes and extras were also used. There was also a flute player who provided musical accompaniment. He was associated with the chorus, and his services were paid for by the *choregus*.

6. Speech of actors usually in iambic trimeter, though actors were expected to sing occasional lyric arias.

7. Acting was conventionalized, consisting mainly of tableaux.

FUNCTIONS OF THE CHORUS

1. Beauty of poetry and dancing.

2. Mood and central themes of the drama. Chorus interprets events, generalizes meaning of the action.

3. The "ideal spectator"—bridge between players and audience.

4. Relieves tension.

5. Often converses with and gives advice to the actors.

6. Gives background, informing audience of preceding events.

7. Choral passages divided into strophe ("movement"), antistrophe ("countermovement") and epode ("afterpiece"). These were originally choreographic notations.

8. *Kommos*—responsive lyric exchange between chorus and actor.

9. The leader of the chorus has a special importance, often acting as spokesman for the group.

STRUCTURE OF TRAGEDY

1. Prologue: action before entrance of chorus.

2. Parodos: entering dance of the chorus.

3. Episodes: action between choral odes.

4. Stasima: choral odes.

5. Exodos: action after last stasimon.

TYPICAL GREEK THEATER

1. *Theatron*—where audience sat, on hollowed-out hillside, in open air; seats of honor for public officials and priests, especially priest of Dionysus. (Seating capacity of Theater of Dionysus at Athens ca. 17,000).

2. *Orchestra*—dancing place of chorus; actors performed in orchestra in front of *proscenium;* there was apparently no raised stage in the Greek theater of classical times.

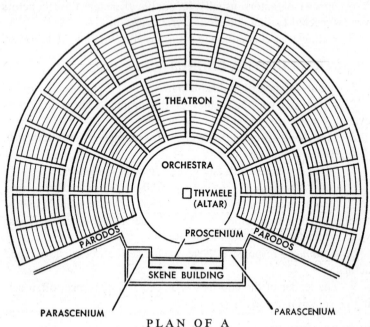

PLAN OF A
TYPICAL GREEK THEATER

3. *Thymele*—altar of Dionysus in orchestra. Sacrifices were performed here before plays were given.

4. *Skene*—dressing rooms for actors. The *proscenium* was the façade of the skene building, and carried the scenery of the play—usually the front of a palace or temple, showing three doorways. There was no curtain. The skene was flanked on either side by *parascenia* ("wings"). On top of the skene was the *theologeion,* a platform from which gods and heroes spoke from on high.

5. *Parodos*—point of entry and exit of the chorus.

6. Mechanical devices used:

a. The "Machine"—a crane suspended from the top of the skene building to raise and lower flying figures and to introduce and remove gods. The *deus ex machina* ("god from the machine") was employed, especially by Euripides, to give a formal miraculous conclusion to the tragedy. The god appeared to come from on high, in the form of a dummy suspended from the "Machine," to unravel all the unsolved problems of the play.

b. *Eccyclema*—movable platform rolled out from behind the scenes to depict, in tableau form, events which take place inside the building before which the action occurs.

CONVENTIONS OF CLASSICAL GREEK TRAGEDY

1. Ceremony of state religion—plays produced only at religious festivals.

2. Scene of drama is always an outdoor one—interior scenes or events taking place away from the scene of the action cannot be shown. They are revealed to the audience through the *eccyclema,* or reported by the ubiquitous messenger of Greek tragedy.

3. Use of the "Machine."

4. Conventionalized acting.

5. No violence portrayed before audience, because of the religious associations of the theater. (There are, however, some exceptions).

6. Continuous presence of the chorus after entry; therefore tendency to concentrate the action in a short period of time.

7. Of the so-called "three unities" only one—unity of action—was adhered to by the Greek tragedians. This involved concentration on the single action, with no irrelevancies or subplots employed.

Unity of time (i.e., limitation of the action to a time period not exceeding 24 hours), and unity of place (one unchanged scene throughout the play), though frequently found in Greek plays, were not formal conventions.

8. Poetic form always employed.

9. No curtain; no intermissions.

10. *Stichomythia*—use of rapid conversation in which characters speak alternating lines.

11. Outlines of plots were known in advance by the audience, because subjects were almost exclusively taken from well-known mythic cycles. There was, therefore, little suspense for the audience.

The main interest was in the religious and ethical instruction, in the spectacle as a whole, and in dramatic irony. Dramatic irony involves double meanings in what is done and said, because the audience, which has foreknowledge of the situation, understands them in a different way from the characters.

12. Economy of roles: since Sophocles' time there was a maximum of three actors used, each of whom might take several roles.

13. No lighting effects—all scenes (even night) acted in broad daylight.

LEADING FIFTH CENTURY WRITERS OF TRAGEDY

1. Phrynichus of Athens (first dramatic victory in 511 B.C.)

   a. Earliest writer of tragedy whose works survived into later classical times.

   b. First to use female masks, or to introduce female characters.

   c. Wrote: *Sack of Miletus; Phoenician Women; Egyptians; Alcestis; Actaeon; Antaeus; Daughters of Danaüs; Women of Pleuron; Tantalus; Troilus.*

2. Choerilus of Athens (wrote 523-468 B.C.)

   a. Said to have invented masks.

   b. Wrote *Alope* and about 160 other plays.

3. Aeschylus of Athens (See Chapter Three).

4. Pratinus of Phlius (wrote from 500 B.C.). Said to have invented satyr plays. Wrote *Palaestae.*

5. Sophocles of Athens (See Chapter Four).

6. Euripides of Athens (See Chapter Five).

7. Agathon of Athens (born ca. 446 B.C.)

   a. His choruses often were incidental, transferable lyrics between episodes.

   b. Invented purely fictional plots, not based on myths.

   c. His plays were highly rhetorical.

   d. Wrote *The Flower; Fall of Troy.*

8. Ion of Chios (ca. 490-420 B.C.)

Wrote about 40 plays, including *The Sentinels; Argives; Alcmene; Omphale; Agamemnon; Laertes; Teucer.*

9. Neophron of Sicyon (dates unknown)
   a. First to use *paedagogus* in tragedy.
   b. Wrote about 120 tragedies.
10. Aristarchus of Tegea (contemporary of Euripides)
    Wrote about 70 tragedies, including *Asclepius; Achilles.*
11. Achaeus of Eretria (born ca. 484 B.C.)
    Wrote about 40 plays, including *Philoctetes.*

CHAPTER THREE

AESCHYLUS

AESCHYLUS OF ATHENS (525-455 B.C.)

1. Aristocratic family from Eleusis, near Athens.
2. Wrote about 90 plays.
3. The real creator of tragedy: first to associate tragedy with moral and religious problems; creator of the tragic style.
4. Added second actor; increased dialogue; reduced importance of chorus.
5. Soldier at battles of Marathon, Salamis, and Plataea.
6. Died at Gela, Sicily.

EXTANT PLAYS

The Suppliant Women (traditionally dated ca. 490 B.C.; recently discovered evidence may justify dating its production after 470 B.C.)

The Persians (472 B.C.)

The Seven Against Thebes (467 B.C.)

Prometheus Bound (date unknown)

Oresteia [*Orestes Trilogy*] (458 B.C.)
  Agamemnon
  Choëphoroe (Libation Bearers)
  Eumenides

THE SUPPLIANT WOMEN

BACKGROUND

Io, daughter of Inachus, King of Argos, was beloved ot Zeus. After much suffering and wandering, she came to Egypt, where she bore Zeus' son Epaphus. His great-grandchildren were the twins Aegyptus and Danaüs. Aegyptus, King of Egypt, had fifty sons, who were betrothed to the fifty daughters of Danaüs. To avoid marriage with Aegyptus' sons, Danaüs fled from Egypt with his daughters.

Prologue and Parados (lines 1-175)

The scene is a sacred grove near the coast of Argos. The Chorus of fifty Danaïds (daughters of Danaüs) prays to Zeus for help. They have just arrived at Argos in flight from Egypt to avoid marriage with their lustful, violent cousins, the sons of Aegyptus. Their father brought them to Argos, a kind and pious land from which their ancestors came. They invoke Zeus because of their descent from his beloved Io. Their sorrow is great; they hope for protection as exiles. The will of almighty Zeus is hidden in darkness. He punishes violence and pride. They sing of their suffering and fears in a foreign land, and pray to the goddess Artemis for protection. If they are not saved from the hateful marriage, they will hang themselves and seek the protection of Hades.

First Episode (176-523)

Danaüs cautions prudence and humbleness to his daughters. He sees armed men approaching and counsels them to behave like suppliants, taking refuge at the altars of the gods. They pray to Zeus, Apollo, Poseidon, Hermes.

King Pelasgus of Argos and his retinue enter. He addresses them as foreign intruders in his land, and tells them of his power and lineage. They claim descent from Argos, through Io, tell him why they left Egypt, and appeal for aid. Pelasgus is in a dilemma. By Egyptian law the Danaïds cannot refuse marriage with their cousins;

on the other hand, he respects the religious rights of suppliants. If he grants them asylum, he has to reckon with military reprisals from the Egyptians. But he will accede to their pleas if the assembly of the people vote to grant them asylum in Argos. The Danaïds declare their intent to hang themselves from the altars if they are not protected, and thus bring pollution to the land. Reverently and kindly, Pelasgus sends Danaüs to the city with instructions to appeal his case to the people of Argos.

First Stasimon (524-599)

The Chorus pray to their ancestor Zeus, and recount the wanderings of his beloved Io and her final peace in Egypt, where she bore Epaphus.

Second Episode (600-624)

Danaüs enters and announces that the Argive people have voted unanimously to grant them asylum.

Second Stasimon (625-709)

The Danaïds offer prayers for peace and prosperity for the Argive land. They testify to the piety of the people, who respect suppliants.

Third Episode (710-776)

Danaüs spies an Egyptian ship approaching. He counsels his daughters to take refuge at the altars while he hastens to summon the aid of the Argives.

Third Stasimon (777-823)

The Chorus of Danaïds voice their fright, dreading the violence and lust of their cousins. They pray to Zeus.

Fourth Episode (824-1019)

An Egyptian herald enters and attempts to hurry them off to the ship, threatening force. As he tries to drag them away, they shriek

their fears. King Pelasgus enters with his troops to carry out the
will of the people, and orders the herald out of his land. Threatening war, the herald leaves. Pelasgus then invites the Danaïds into
the city. They and Danaüs express their gratitude to Pelasgus.
Danaüs cautions his daughters that their maidenly honor is to be
guarded more than their very lives.

Fourth Stasimon and Exodos (1020-1074)

The Chorus blesses the city and prays that they will never be
forced to marry, though they acknowledge the power of Aphrodite,
goddess of love. They are cognizant, too, of inscrutable Fate, of
the need for moderation, of faith in Zeus and justice, and of the
inevitability of suffering.

INTERPRETATION

1. This play, a kind of religious oratorio, in which character
delineation and plot are rudimentary, and in which the Chorus is
actually the protagonist, is difficult to interpret because the other
two plays of the trilogy are lost. In the *Egyptians* Danaüs, finally
forced to acquiesce in the marriage, instructed his daughters to slay
their husbands on the marriage night. All obeyed him but Hyperm-
nestra, who loved her husband Lyncaeus. In the *Danaïds* Hy-
permnestra was brought to trial for parental disobedience, but was
defended and saved by Aphrodite.

2. Primitive modes of thought and behavior are not worthy of
a civilized people. They bring violence, disunity, suffering.

3. There are many conflicts due to the survivals of outmoded
patterns of culture in civilized society: endogamy vs. exogamy;
hostility of male and female vs. male-female harmony; the religious
right of sanctuary vs. secular law; violence vs. reason; tribal law
vs. civic law; obedience to higher authority vs. individual freedom.

4. Love and harmony conquer all.

5. The ways of Zeus are mysterious; he is the source of suffering
as well as happiness. One must have faith in the ultimate goodness
of the gods, above all in the benevolence of the supreme god Zeus.

THE PERSIANS

BACKGROUND

After the defeat of the Persians at Marathon in 490 B.C., during the reign of Darius, his son Xerxes led a huge Persian expedition against Greece in 480 B.C. The time depicted in *The Persians* is shortly after the Battle of Salamis. This play, the only extant Greek play on a historical subject, was not part of an organic trilogy.

Prologue and Parados (lines 1-154)

The scene is the palace of Xerxes at Susa in Persia; nearby is the tomb of Darius. The Chorus of Persian Elders, left by Xerxes to care for his realm while he is engaged in his effort to conquer Greece, has forebodings of disaster. The Persian host left in great splendor and with high hopes. Many famed captains and peoples comprised the enormous army that marched away to subjugate freedom-loving Hellas. The mighty army, led by valiant King Xerxes, is irresistible. They have crossed lands and seas. Yet man is often lured into disaster by the gods. Will woe come to the Persian host? All the men are away, and the womenfolk pine in loneliness.

First Episode (155-531)

As Queen Atossa, mother of Xerxes, approaches in splendor in her chariot, the Chorus prostrates itself.

Atossa, too, expresses a premonition of disaster. She misses the strength of Xerxes' presence. Since his departure she has had many dreams. One dream she had the preceding night forbodes disaster for Xerxes. She sought to avert evil by sacrifices this morning, but saw a frightening omen.

The Chorus counsels prayers and propitiatory sacrifices, and advises her to entreat the soul of her husband Darius for good fortune. Before she goes, she inquires about Athens, and learns of its people and their democratic way of life.

A messenger enters to report the news of the overwhelming

defeat of the Persians by Athens at the naval battle of Salamis. As the Chorus moans, Atossa, retaining her queenly dignity, requests a detailed report. The messenger tells that Xerxes is alive, but that many famous generals lost their lives in the disaster. The smaller Greek navy has been victorious, with divine aid.

The messenger then describes in detail the Battle of Salamis, of which he was an eyewitness. (Aeschylus himself fought at the Battle of Salamis). The disaster was overwhelming, and the slaughter of the defeated incredible. Xerxes, who observed the battle seated on a golden throne on the shore, ordered the troops on land to flee. The ships that escaped fled in a rout. The armies, retreating northward, suffered horribly from lack of supplies and transportation facilities. Few escaped. "Many terrible woes the wrath of God hurled upon our host."

Atossa mourns over the disaster, and departs to offer prayers to the gods and the dead, in order to learn the future.

First Stasimon (532-597)

The Chorus acknowledges Zeus as the author of the woes of Persia. He has punished their excessive pride. They mourn for the dead, the bereaved wives and mothers, the loss of the flower of Asian manhood. Xerxes in pride led a vast armada to Greece, and now he comes home in ignominious defeat. The navy is at the bottom of the sea, and the power of Persia is shattered. The land of liberty has cast off the shackles of Persia.

Second Episode (598-851)

Atossa returns in humbleness to make offerings to Darius, and asks the Chorus' assistance in evoking the soul of Darius from the tomb.

The Chorus chants a necromantic hymn at the tomb of Darius. Presently the ghost of Darius ascends, and they prostrate themselves in awe. Atossa reveals to him the disaster that has overwhelmed Persia.

Darius confirms the fulfillment of the prophecy that the anger of

Zeus would strike his son. Proud men, he declares, are led to their doom by the gods. Xerxes was blind and arrogant, driven to mad deeds by Infatuation. The great empire of Persia slowly grew through many vicissitudes. Now his son Xerxes, in immature abuse of power, has caused it to topple. Darius urges Persia to abandon all war against Hellas. Few of the vast host are destined to return. This is the punishment for the pride and impiety of the Persian army in Greece. Yet another woe awaits them—the disastrous defeat at Plataea (which took place the next year). Pride is not for insignificant man. Excess must be shunned, for Zeus chastens those guilty of the sin of *hybris*.

The ghost of Darius then descends into the tomb. Atossa leaves to comfort her son.

Second Stasimon (852-908)

The Chorus sings that Darius' power was mighty and that his rule brought glory, increase in empire and prosperity to Persia. Now it is humbled.

Exodos (909-1076)

Xerxes enters in stunned grief, his clothes in tatters. Together with the Chorus he bewails the sad lot of Persia. He tells of the disaster at Salamis and the deaths of the great Persian captains. The entire Persian armament is lost. The Chorus rends its garments in grief, as it escorts the mourning Xerxes to his palace.

INTERPRETATION

1. Thanksgiving for the triumph of Greece over Persia, of liberty over despotism, of righteousness over evil—all through the aid and benevolence of the gods.

2. Athens was the instrument through which the gods humbled Persia for its excesses and impiety.

3. The excessive pride and arrogance (*hybris*) of Xerxes resulted in moral blindness, and was finally punished by the vengeance of the gods (*Nemesis*).

THE SEVEN AGAINST THEBES

BACKGROUND

Laïus, King of Thebes, was warned by the Delphic oracle not to have a child. He did not heed the oracle and was duly punished. The curse of the house of Laïus begins with the birth of his son Oedipus (for whose tragic story see pp. 51-55). After an initial period of wandering, Oedipus returned to Thebes, but was soon expelled by his two sons Eteocles and Polynices. Thereupon he uttered the curse that they would divide their inheritance with the sword. Eteocles and Polynices held the royal power alternately. Eventually Eteocles refused to relinquish his power, and kept Polynices in exile. The latter appealed for aid to Adrastus, King of Argos, who supplied Polynices with forces to attack his native Thebes. He has laid siege to the city. (This play was the last part of a trilogy, the first two plays being the lost *Laïus* and *Oedipus*. It was followed by a satyr play, *The Sphinx*).

Prologue (lines 1-77)

The scene is before the citadel of Thebes. Eteocles exhorts the Thebans to defend their city, their gods and soil from the invaders. The most powerful attack of the siege is anticipated. He orders them to man the battlements and gates. A messenger arrives and announces that seven mighty champions of the enemy have sworn an oath to raze the walls of Thebes or die. They have drawn lots for the gate each will assault, and are now approaching. Eteocles prays to Zeus and all the gods for aid in keeping Thebes free.

Parodos (78-180)

The Chorus of Theban Women chants its panicky fears of the invaders, mingling prayers to the gods and goddesses with exhortations to the bloody battle which impends. "O gods, protect Thebes!" they wail as they contemplate the uncertain outcome.

First Episode (181-287)

Eteocles rebukes the Chorus for their timid fears, blind faith in the gods, and unrestrained wailing, which is unnerving the populace. He demands absolute obedience from all, and threatens death to any who disobey, ordering the women not to meddle in the affairs of men. The hour, says Eteocles, demands valor and strength, not prayers to the gods. Women's place is at home. Let them not, in their religious panic, unman the army; rather should they trust the skill and wisdom of their king. As their frenzy subsides, he urges them to pray that the gods join them in making war on the enemies of Thebes. He vows that if Thebes is victorious he will perform huge sacrifices and bedeck the sanctuaries with spoils of war. Then he goes off to pick six other champions to join him in guarding the seven gates of Thebes.

First Stasimon (288-368)

Left alone, the Chorus returns to its utterances of wild fears. They pray again to the gods to protect the city from the enemy. They envision the fall of the city and the ensuing horrors for men, women and children.

Second Episode (369-719)

Eteocles enters with the messenger, who brings more precise information about the disposition of the enemy's forces.

The messenger relates that the sixth of the invading captains, the majestic seer Amphiaraüs, rebuked Polynices for attacking his own native land and Adrastus for siding with him. Though duty forces him to participate, Amphiaraüs is the only one of the seven who showed reverence for the gods. At the seventh gate stands Polynices.

In a fury of hatred Eteocles declares that he will face his brother. In proud resignation he recalls the curse of Oedipus that he and Polynices will divide their inheritance with the sword. As the Chorus expresses its horror of the coming fratricidal combat, Eteocles takes refuge in Oedipus' curse as an inevitable doom. He no longer has any concern for family ties or the gods. They beseech him not to go out to meet Polynices. It is inevitable and divinely ordained, declares Eteocles, as he departs.

Second Stasimon (720-791)

The Chorus broods in fear on the curse of Oedipus that the brothers shall slay each other in guilt and sin. It is an hereditary curse, passing from generation to generation. Laïus, despite the warning of the oracle, begat Oedipus, who slew him, married his own mother, begat incestuous offspring, and blinded himself. Wave follows wave of woe, and now the ancient curse descends on Oedipus' sons.

Third Episode (792-821)

The messenger enters to announce that Thebes is safe, but that the sons of Oedipus slew each other at the seventh gate, thus fulfilling Oedipus' curse.

Third Stasimon (822-956)

The Chorus rejoices over the liberation of Thebes, and bewails the dead sons of Oedipus, destroyed by his curse. Nay, the curse is older, beginning with the blindness of Laïus. As the bodies of Eteocles and Polynices are borne in, they sing a dirge for the fallen brothers. Antigone and Ismene, their unhappy sisters, enter. The Chorus laments for them and their brothers, and enlarges on the curse and woes of the family of Laïus.

Exodos (957-1084)

As Antigone and Ismene join in the dirge, a herald enters to announce that the governing council of Thebes has ordained that Eteocles is to be buried with honors as a patriotic, pious defender of his city. Polynices, however, is to be denied decent burial because of his traitorous attack on his native land.

Antigone declares she will bury Polynices, no matter what the consequences. The herald warns her to desist, but she will not be deterred. The Chorus laments the ruin of Oedipus' line. New woes impend because of Antigone's decision to bury Polynices. The Chorus is divided in its sympathies, half of them siding with Antigone's decision, half upholding the will of the people.

INTERPRETATION

1. It is difficult to interpret this play because it is part of an organic trilogy, of which the first two plays are lost.

2. The play gives a picture of the atmosphere of war.

3. Punishment for sin can be enormous, for sin is often hereditary, and there is a sort of inevitable doom through divine retribution, as the sins of the fathers are visited on the sons.

4. Excess (the fierce hatred of the brothers and the treason of Polynices) causes *hybris,* moral blindness, infatuation—leading to the doom of Nemesis.

PROMETHEUS BOUND

BACKGROUND

The Titans had long ruled the universe. Their king, Cronus (Saturn), had six children, the oldest of the later Olympian gods. Led by Zeus, the youngest, the gods revolted against Cronus' tyranny, and overthrew him. In the ensuing war with the gods the Titans were deserted by the opportunist Oceanus, and by Prometheus (Forethought), who aided Zeus because he embodied intelligence warring against primitive brute force. All the defeated Titans were consigned to Tartarus, except Cronus, who was banished to the West, and Atlas, who was compelled to support the heavens on his shoulders.

Zeus, the new ruler of the universe, now himself became despotic. Prometheus, who had created man, stood forth as the benefactor and champion of mankind, defending and aiding it in its advance toward civilization. When Zeus decided to destroy mankind, Prometheus persisted in defending human beings and championing their cause. Finally, defying the decrees of Zeus, he stole for men forbidden fire in order to better their life.

Prologue (lines 1-127)

Power and Force, servants of Zeus, drag in Prometheus. Zeus has ordered Hephaestus, the smith of the gods, to bind Prometheus to a rock in a desolate gorge in Scythia for giving fire to mankind.

Hephaestus is reluctant to bind his relative and friend Prometheus. He pities him, but fears to disobey Zeus. As Power ruthlessly directs him, Hephaestus shackles the silent Prometheus to the rock. Left alone, Prometheus bewails his lot, with mingled pain, apprehension, and defiance.

Parodos (128-192)

The Chorus of sweet and compassionate Oceanids (daughters of Oceanus) enters, expresses sympathy for his sufferings and distress at Zeus' tyranny. Prometheus hints at a secret he alone knows which endangers Zeus' rule. He defiantly asserts that he will not reveal the secret until Zeus softens, and until he removes his bonds. (The secret: If Zeus consummates his love for the sea-divinity Thetis, a son born of the union will overthrow him.)

First Episode (193-396)

At the bidding of the Chorus, Prometheus tells how he aided Zeus against the Titans, how the new, young ruler became tyrannical once he assumed power, how Prometheus prevented him from destroying mankind and gave them fire, and how Zeus punished him.

Oceanus, a fellow-Titan, enters on a winged horse. He asserts his friendship for Prometheus, counsels him to submit to the new tyrant, to cease his defiance, and to take thought for his own welfare. He offers to intercede with Zeus to secure his release. Prometheus, ever altruistic, cautions him of the danger to himself. Zeus has caused others to suffer, too. Oceanus, feeling rebuked, loses his temper and leaves.

First Stasimon (397-435)

The Chorus bewails the sufferings of Prometheus in the East and of his brother Atlas in the West.

Second Episode (436-525)

Prometheus recounts the advance of human civilization and the varied inventions and discoveries he has bestowed upon mankind.

He declares that Fate has ordained that he will ultimately be released, and again hints at his secret.

Second Stasimon (526-560)

The Chorus pities Prometheus, but expresses reverence for Zeus, emphasizes the limitations of man, and counsels moderation.

Third Episode (561-886)

Io, transformed into a heifer, enters pursued by the ghost of Argus in a stinging insect. She is the symbol of the innocent sufferer. She raves over her sufferings because of Zeus' love for her. When she hears of Prometheus' sufferings at Zeus' hands, she relates the story of her sorrows: how Zeus fell in love with her, how she was driven out by her father to wander; how she was turned into a heifer pursued first by the 100-eyed Argus, the creation of jealous Hera, and, after the slaying of Argus by Hermes, by a stinging fly urged on by Argus' ghost. Prometheus then prophesies her future wanderings over Europe, Asia, and Africa. He tells her, too, that she will finally find rest and be turned again into a woman in Egypt, and that a descendant of Io (Hercules is meant) will release him. He hints a third time at his secret. She leaves in frenzy to continue her wanderings.

Third Stasimon (887-907)

The Chorus prays that they may never be wooed by superior gods, as was Io. Marriage between equals is best.

Exodos (908-1093)

As Prometheus utters renewed defiance against Zeus and predicts his overthrow, Hermes arrives and demands to know precise details of the secret affecting Zeus. Prometheus insults Hermes as Zeus' lackey, and defiantly refuses to tell. Hermes warns him of new punishments to come, especially that the eagle of Zeus will come down to devour his liver daily. As Prometheus hurls defiance against Zeus, a furious storm breaks, the rock is struck by lightning, earth opens up and Prometheus sinks out of sight.

INTERPRETATION

(Interpretation of this play is difficult because it was part of the *Prometheus Trilogy,* of which the other two plays are lost: *Prometheus Unbound; Prometheus the Fire-Bringer*).

1. Conflict of wills between the two leading characters, Prometheus and Zeus, both guilty of lack of moderation (*hybris*).

2. Conflict between divine jealousy of man, stern, arbitrary justice, on the one hand, and the desirability of progress and enlightenment of humanity, on the other; between rebellious efforts at reform and harsh tyranny striving to perpetuate its rule with absolute power; between reason and brute force.

3. After endless ages of suffering, for both Zeus and Prometheus, they are reconciled: Zeus learns mercy, Prometheus respect for authority; compromise between brute force and wisdom.

4. Purification of popular religion, from crude anthropomorphism toward ethical monotheism: Zeus evolves into a humane god combining stern justice with mercy, omnipotence with omniscience.

5. There is a tragic pattern in life: suffering is inevitable; sometimes it comes because of personal sins or defects; sometimes it is the result of the guilt of ancestors; and sometimes even the innocent suffer. But suffering must be endured, and there is personal responsibility for sin. The remedy is moderation. Wisdom comes from suffering.

6. There are good and evil in divinities, but faith in Zeus must be maintained, despite the sufferings of life.

7. Authority must be humane and wise to be respected; reformers must be patient and slow, and respect benevolent authority. Man must subordinate himself to the good state and to benevolent divinities.

ORESTEIA

ORESTES TRILOGY

This is the only extant Greek trilogy. It consists of:
1. *Agamemnon*
2. *Choëphoroe* (*Libation Bearers*)
3. *Eumenides*

BACKGROUND

King Atreus (son of Pelops, grandson of Tantalus) quarreled with his brother Thyestes regarding Thyestes' adultery with Atreus' wife, Merope. In revenge, Atreus slew two of Thyestes' children and fed their flesh to him. Upon discovering what had happened, Thyestes killed Atreus, and he in turn was murdered by Atreus' son Agamemnon. Agamemnon and his wife Clytemnestra had four children: Orestes, Electra, Iphigenia, and Chrysothemis. Before sailing for Troy as commander-in-chief of the Greek forces Agamemnon cruelly sacrificed Iphigenia at the behest of the soothsayer Calchas. Clytemnestra never forgave him for this. During the ten-year absence of her husband at Troy she secretly became the mistress of Aegisthus, a son of Thyestes. In order to facilitate her amours and plans for revenge, she sent her son Orestes away to live with a king in Phocis. Together with Aegisthus she plotted the murder of Agamemnon.

(It is important for an understanding of this trilogy to know that the "house divided" theme of the myth had its historical counterpart in contemporary Athens. At the time the play was written political turmoil, involving a struggle for power between the democrats and aristocrats, had been accompanied by bloodshed.)

AGAMEMNON

Prologue (lines 1-39)

It is night. A watchman is seen on the roof of the palace of Agamemnon. He has been posted there by Clytemnestra, and has been watching many months for the signal fire which is to proclaim the fall of Troy. Suddenly he sees the beacon and hails it with joy. But at the same time he expresses a sense of fear and foreboding.

Parodos and First Stasimon (40-269)

The Chorus of Elders enters. Ten years have passed since Menelaüs and Agamemnon set sail with a thousand ships to avenge the abduction of Helen by the Trojan prince Paris. The men of the Chorus were too old to join the expedition to Troy. Clytemnestra has come out of the palace, and they see her praying and sacrificing at the altar. The Chorus relates the omen seen before the war, two eagles killing a hare and her unborn young. The soothsayer Calchas predicted the destruction of Troy by the two sons of Atreus. Calchas prayed to Artemis and Apollo, and gloomily predicted future woe. The Chorus prays to almighty and benevolent Zeus, who punishes men for their sins.

The Chorus here becomes the vehicle for Aeschylus' tragic philosophy. He expounds the religious law, founded on belief in Zeus as god of justice, that there is inevitable retribution for sin and crime. "The doer must suffer." Once a crime has been committed, it breeds others. Suffering is inevitable for man, partly from conflicting loyalties (religion, state, clan, family) and unresolved religious conflicts, and partly from inner faults of human beings, such as excessive pride and ambition, and moral blindness. There is, however, a divine purpose in suffering, for there exists a higher unifying principle: Zeus, who teaches wisdom through suffering.

Proudly and confidently Agamemnon gathered his forces at Aulis. But Artemis caused the winds to cease blowing because Agamemnon slew a sacred animal. When Calchas ordered him to sacrifice Iphigenia in order to appease Artemis, he hesitated to slay his own child. But his ambition to be a great conqueror overmastered his fatherly love, and he consented. Iphigenia was sacrificed, despite her heart-rending pleas. Justice is inevitable.

First Episode (270-366)

Clytemnestra confidently proclaims the fall of Troy, and relates in detail how the signal was speedily flashed by beacon fires from mountain-top to mountain-top. She depicts the probable sufferings of the Trojans, and meaningfully suggests that the homecoming of the victorious heroes is fraught with peril.

Second Stasimon (367-480)

Zeus has punished Troy for the sin of Paris. Pride leads to inevitable downfall. Great prosperity is harmful. Sin is always punished, and often involves whole cities. So Paris sinned, and was punished for stealing Helen. Predictions of woe for Troy were made at the time. Prophetic dreams of death and destruction came to Agamemnon, visions of funeral urns of dead Greeks, and of the anger of their relatives. The gods note all who commit bloodshed and punish them. Too much fame is dangerous.

Second Episode (481-685)

Several days have elapsed. The Chorus cautiously doubts Clytemnestra's story of the beacon fire proclaiming the fall of Troy. A herald arrives, overjoyed at being home after ten years overseas, and announces the imminent arrival of Agamemnon, glorifying him with excessive praise. The Chorus intimates that there have been difficulties at home during the army's absence, and the herald details the sufferings of the army. Clytemnestra appears and deceitfully proclaims her fidelity to and love for Agamemnon. The herald relates how Menelaüs was diverted by a storm and that he will not arrive with Agamemnon.

Third Stasimon (686-773)

Helen brought misery to the Greeks and the Trojans. The Trojans welcomed her with joyous song, but later their tune was changed. An oxherd reared a lion's cub, but the grown lion became a beast of prey. So Helen brought woe to Troy. Good fortune is said to bring disaster to men; but this happens only when it comes from evil deeds. Pride and arrogance bring retribution and justice. Humility is safest.

Third Episode (774-965)

The conquering hero Agamemnon arrives in a chariot, followed by the captive maid Cassandra, prophetess daughter of King Priam of Troy. The Chorus greets him with tempered joy. Agamemnon gives thanks to the gods for his victory and safe return, and declares he will reorganize the state. But he is haughty and proud, blinded by his great victory, and consequently underestimates the dangers facing him. Clytemnestra unashamedly declares her love to Agamemnon. Of her own accord she informs him that Orestes was sent away for safekeeping. Then she urges him, prompting his pride, to walk into the palace on a purple carpet she has had spread out for him. Agamemnon greets his wife coldly, expresses fear of tempting the gods with a show of pride. When she insists, he is easily swayed, and, removing his shoes, he enters the palace on the purple carpet, thus committing an overt act of pride (*hybris*). Before entering, he arrogantly commits his concubine Cassandra to Clytemnestra's care.

Fourth Stasimon (966-1018)

The Chorus has gloomy forebodings despite the joyful home-coming of the army.

Fourth Episode (1019-1410)

Clytemnestra reappears from the palace, and orders Cassandra within. Cassandra does not answer or move until Clytemnestra re-enters the palace. Then, in a frenzied mood, inspired by Apollo, she raves prophetically of her own sad fate, paints the past horrible crimes of the House of Atreus, predicts the coming murders of Agamemnon and herself, and tells how Agamemnon is to be murdered. The Chorus does not believe her predictions of Agamemnon's death. She continues to rave, mingling the past crimes with predictions of the future, including the coming vengeance by Orestes for the murders of Agamemnon and herself. She recoils as she is about to enter the palace, but finally, submitting to her fate, she goes in stoically and with resignation, symbolizing the innocent sufferer.

Agamemnon's death cry is heard. There is consternation in the Chorus. Clytemnestra now appears in her true colors, holding a bloody axe in her hands, standing over the bodies of her husband and Cassandra. She triumphantly announces how she murdered them.

Exodos (1411-1673)

Clytemnestra vehemently states her reasons for killing Agamemnon: the sacrifice of Iphigenia at Aulis, her love for Aegisthus, Agamemnon's infidelity with Cassandra and other women, and the family curse which involved her in its mesh. The Chorus predicts that murder will be punished. Clytemnestra is momentarily alarmed at this. Her lover Aegisthus enters with his bodyguard and gloats over the death of Agamemnon, admitting his share in plotting the murder, and his association with Clytemnestra. He declares he will become joint ruler with Clytemnestra. The Chorus hopes for vengeance by Orestes, and ineffectively seeks to resort to arms. Clytemnestra and Aegisthus assert that they will establish a stern rule over the kingdom.

CHOËPHOROE

BACKGROUND

Several years have elapsed. Orestes returns with his best friend Pylades. He has been ordered by the god Apollo to avenge his father's death.

Prologue (lines 1-21)

Orestes, in disguise, enters with Pylades. The scene is the palace of the kings of Mycenae. Agamemnon's grave is nearby. He lays a lock of his hair on Agamemnon's tomb. Orestes and Pylades hear a cry of woe from the palace. As they retire to one side, the Chorus enters sorrowfully, accompanied by Electra. They have been ordered to make offerings at Agamemnon's tomb by Clytemnestra, who has had bad dreams.

Parodos (22-82)

The Chorus of war captives wails. Agamemnon's soul is angry. Clytemnestra cannot sleep. They have been sent to placate his soul. But murder must be avenged; justice is inescapable. Such a sin cannot be purged away. They castigate the crimes and despotism of Clytemnestra and Aegisthus.

First Episode (83-304)

Confused and sad, the young, innocent, weak Electra does not want to pray to help her mother. Urged by the Chorus, she prays for the return of her brother Orestes, and reluctantly asks for vengeance. She is unwed, poor, and mistreated. As the Chorus laments over Agamemnon, Electra discovers the lock of hair on the tomb. She recognizes it as like her own hair, and immediately surmises that Orestes had returned. Then her surmise is confirmed by his footprints which she is convinced resemble her own. Orestes comes forward, reveals that he is still wearing the cloak she wove for him years before. The long-parted pair embrace. After praying to Zeus for protection, Orestes relates how he was ordered by the oracle of Apollo to take unfailing vengeance upon his mother and Aegisthus. He is faced with a tragic dilemma: if he does not take vengeance he will be pursued by the Furies of his father; if he does, his mother's Furies will haunt him.

First Stasimon (305-476)

Kneeling at the grave of Agamemnon, the Chorus, Orestes, and Electra chant in a *kommos,* lamenting Agamemnon, exchanging thoughts on his greatness and his murder, and swearing vengeance. At the end Orestes' resolution is fixed, and Electra has become a changed person, savage for revenge.

Second Episode (477-582)

Strengthened in their determination by this mystic communion at the grave of Agamemnon, they pray for guidance and help. The Chorus tells Orestes of Clytemnestra's terrifying dreams, particularly that she dreamed she bore a serpent which bit her as she was nursing it. Orestes' determination is reinforced by the dream. Then he tells his plans for the murder of Clytemnestra and Aegisthus. The Chorus is sworn to secrecy.

Second Stasimon (583-648)

The monsters of the earth are many, but woman's passion causes her to commit horrible crimes, as witness Clytemnestra's sins. Justice will triumph.

Third Episode (649-778)

Orestes and Pylades, disguised, knock on the palace door, asking for hospitality. Clytemnestra appears, accompanied by Electra, and welcomes them. Orestes asserts that he has come as a messenger from Phocis to announce Orestes' death, and that he bears Orestes' ashes in an urn. Clytemnestra is elated, but strives to conceal her emotions. She immediately sends Orestes' sorrowing old Nurse to summon Aegisthus to hear the news. The Chorus suggests to the Nurse that she tell Clytemnestra's husband Aegisthus to come without his bodyguard.

Third Stasimon (779-836)

The Chorus prays for the success of Orestes' plans, and that he may slay them as Perseus slew the Gorgon. No mercy for Clytemnestra and Aegisthus!

Fourth Episode (837-933)

Aegisthus arrives, expressing doubt concerning Orestes' death, and enters the palace. His death-cry is soon heard. A servant informs Clytemnestra of his death. She steels herself, and is prepared to defend herself with weapons, if possible. When Orestes and Pylades appear, she begs her son for mercy. Orestes falters, but Pylades reminds him of Apollo's stern command. She seeks to defend herself, declaring that her deeds were due to Fate and her need to have a man by her side. Orestes becomes pitiless, and drags his mother into the palace to slay her by Aegisthus' side.

Fourth Stasimon (934-970)

Justice has triumphed. There will be deliverance from evil with time.

Exodos (971-1074)

The doors of the palace open, and the bodies of Aegisthus and Clytemnestra are seen on a couch covered with the robe Agamemnon wore at the time of his death. Orestes displays the corpses, and justifies the murders. Disillusioned and bitter at being caught up in a world he never made, he slowly begins to lose his mind. He declares it was Apollo who compelled him to this act. At the onset of his madness he sees the Furies as they begin to haunt and pursue him.

EUMENIDES

BACKGROUND

The mad Orestes flees for protection to the Temple of Apollo at Delphi, pursued relentlessly by the Furies which have been stirred up by the murder of his mother.

Prologue (lines 1-63)

The priestess of Apollo, standing before his temple at Delphi prays to the various divinities associated with the shrine, particularly Apollo (god of light), Athena (goddess of wisdom), and Zeus (god of justice). She enters the temple, but quickly recoils in horror, for she has seen within the bloodstained Orestes at the altar and the Furies sleeping around him.

First Episode (64-142)

The interior of the temple is disclosed. Apollo promises never to desert Orestes. He reviles the Furies as evil forces of darkness, and instructs Orestes to go to Athens to seek the assistance of Athena for deliverance. As Hermes guides Orestes away, the ghost of Clytemnestra appears and rebukes the Furies for their inaction. They slowly awake.

First Stasimon (143-178)

The Chorus of Furies bewails Orestes' escape. They rebuke Apollo scornfully, and promise that Orestes will not elude them.

Second Episode (179-306)

Apollo drives out the Furies from his temple. They defend their pursuit of Orestes, cautioning Apollo that he is defending a guilty matricide. Apollo replies that Clytemnestra deserved death because she slew her husband. The Chorus pledges unrelenting pursuit, asserting that the killing of a blood-relative is more serious than the slaying of a husband by his wife. Apollo maintains that the relationship of man and wife is more sacred, and pledges aid for Orestes.

The scene changes to Athens. Orestes is seen clinging to the statue of Athena in front of her temple. He prays for deliverance.

The Chorus of Furies enters hunting Orestes. They catch sight of him and swear vengeance. Orestes again prays to Athena for divine assistance. He claims that he has atoned for his crime and has been purified. The Chorus proclaims that there is no help.

Second Stasimon (307-395)

The Furies relate their function to avenge unpunished murders. They complain about Apollo's interference in their duties, which have been assigned to them by Fate. They are powers of darkness, and punish the guilty, even after death. They are implacable, bring the proud low, and are feared by all men. They are necessary, for only fear will keep men in check and maintain law and order.

Third Episode (396-489)

Athena enters, coming from afar. She questions the Chorus and learns that Orestes slew his mother. Orestes pleads that he has been purified, and that he murdered Clytemnestra at Apollo's command. Athena declares she will hear both sides, and have the case tried before a jury.

Third Stasimon (490-565)

Orestes must not be acquitted, for this will give license to new crimes. Justice will come to an end, and crime will triumph. There must be some authority in society which men fear. Lack of moderation and insolence are evils. Those who do evil shall perish and be utterly lost.

Fourth Episode (566-776)

Athena enters accompanied by twelve Athenian citizens who are to serve as the jury. [At the time this play was produced in Athens the Areopagus, a council composed of aristocrats, tried murder cases.] Apollo is attorney for the defense, the Furies the prosecutors, and Athena the judge.

Orestes confesses the murder of his mother under orders from Apollo. The latter speaks in Orestes' defense, urging that his command to Orestes had the sanction of Zeus. They argue as to which is the more serious crime—murder of husband by wife or of mother by son. Athena as judge charges the jury. The vote is a tie. Athena then casts the deciding vote for acquittal. Orestes thanks Athena and leaves joyfully, proclaiming undying friendship between his people and the Athenians.

Fourth Stasimon (777-792)

The Chorus of Furies bemoans the rising power of the younger gods, and how they themselves are being dishonored. They threaten dire consequences to Athens.

Exodos (793-1047)

Athena tries to soothe their wrath, arguing that Zeus and his justice have prevailed, and pledging them a new home and high honors in Athens. She pleads with them, persisting until they finally relent and accept the new honors offered them.

The Chorus, softened, prays for varied blessings for Athens and her people, while Athena recounts the new benevolent functions of the Chorus. A procession of Athenians, led by Athena, with joyous chants escorts the Furies, renamed Eumenides (Kindly Ones), to their new home in a cave in Athens. Thus finally have all the problems been solved, and unity and justice achieved under the sovereignty of Zeus.

INTERPRETATION OF THE ORESTEIA

1. Reversion to older, more primitive concepts of justice, religion and individual codes of behavior is not worthy of civilized Athens, and subverts the unity and strength of the city.

2. There is a supreme law of justice: "The doer must suffer"— punishment must be visited on those who commit crimes. But the primitive, inflexible tribal law of justice, the *lex talionis* ("an eye for an eye, a tooth for a tooth") must not replace the established rational legal processes of city-state law and trial by jury.

3. Otherwise, one crime will lead to another in a kind of chain reaction, involving the innocent with the guilty.

4. Justice must be tempered by reason and mercy.

5. Emotion, violence, hate, fear should be replaced by reason, mercy, harmony, cooperation.

6. Clan loyalties and tribal customs and religion, survivals of the past, must be curbed and subordinated to the welfare of the entire city-state and to the civic gods.

7. The old tribal gods must be subordinated to the civic gods of light (Apollo), wisdom (Athena) and justice (Zeus).

8. The female must be subordinated to the male.

9. In these ways, through reconciliation of opposing forces, Athens will be a harmonious, just, happy and strong city.

10. Excess leads to the sin of *hybris*. Retribution through Nemesis is then inevitable. Moderation is best.

11. Human suffering is inevitable, but there is a divine purpose —wisdom is acquired through suffering.

12. On the individual level, there must be recognition of inner faults; Fate is not absolute—there is personal responsibility for sins.

13. There is ultimate forgiveness for sins through beneficent divinities under the omnipotent god of justice, Zeus.

LOST PLAYS OF AESCHYLUS

Alcmena; Argives; Argo; Atalanta; Athamas; Bacchae; Cabiri; Callisto; Carians; Cercyon; Chantriae; Children of Heracles; Circe; Daughters of Danaüs; Daughters of Phorcys; Daughters of the Sun; Dictyolloi; Edonians; Egyptians; Epigonoi; Europa; Female Archers; Glaucus; Glaucus of the Sea; Glaucus of Potniae; Heralds; Hypsipyle; Iphigenia; Ixion; Judgment of the Armor; Laïus; Lemnians; Lion; Lycurgus; Memnon; Men of Eleusis; Myrmidons; Mysians; Necromancers; Nemea; Nereids; Net-Drawers; Niobe; Nurses of Dionysus; Oedipus; Ostologoi; Oreithyia; Palamedes; Pentheus; Perrhaebians; Penelope; Perseus; Phineus; Philoctetes; Phrygians; Polydectes; Prometheus; Propompoi; Proteus; Priestesses; Ransom of Hector; Salaminiae; Semele; Sisyphus; Sphinx; Telephus; Thracian Women; Theoroi; Women of Aetna; Women of Crete; Women of the Fawn-Skin; Weighing of Souls; The Youth.

DRAMATIC TECHNIQUES AND STYLE OF AESCHYLUS

1. Trilogies on unified themes.
2. Integral unity of chorus and actors.
3. Simplicity of plots; relatively static action.
4. Spectacular effects; rugged and archaic grandeur.
5. Stark grandeur of characters, who undergo little or no development. Their tragic suffering is due to forces beyond their control as well as to character defects.
6. Majestic grandeur and exalted sublimity of imagination and style; epic quality; sometimes obscure and bombastic.
7. Aeschylus is a dramatist of ideas, often employing symbolism.
8. In style and vigor he resembles the Hebrew prophets.

BASIC IDEAS OF AESCHYLUS

1. Bold, independent religious thinker; deals with profound moral, religious and political problems.
2. Purification of primitive religion and customs; evolution of gods and law from primitive concepts of force and vengeance toward ethical monotheism and the rational, civilized order of the city-state.
3. Reconciliation of conflicting forces is necessary for the achievement of man's development toward higher forms of civilization, and for greatness of Athens.
4. There is retribution and personal responsibility for sin.
5. Excessive pride and self-will are punished; the cure is moderation.
6. The pattern of life is basically tragic, but wisdom comes from suffering. There is, however, ultimate goodness in divinities.
7. Man has limitations, and must subordinate himself to wise higher authorities, both in the state and among the gods.

CHAPTER FOUR

SOPHOCLES

SOPHOCLES OF ATHENS (497-405 B.C.)

1. Birthplace: Colonus, in Athens.
2. Most successful of the Greek dramatists.
3. Active in Athenian social and political life: held several priesthoods; imperial treasurer, 443 B.C.; general, 440 B.C.
4. Dramatic innovations: added third actor; increased dialogue; decreased importance of chorus; fixed number in the chorus at 15; invented painted scenery; made each play of the trilogy an organic unit—plays in trilogy no longer deal with one unified theme.
5. Wrote about 125 plays; won 24 prizes.

EXTANT PLAYS

Ajax (ca. 447 B.C.)
Antigone (ca. 441 B.C.)
The Trackers (ca. 440 B.C.; a satyr play)
Oedipus the King (ca. 430/29 B.C.)
Electra (ca. 418-414 B.C.)
Maidens of Trachis (perhaps ca. 413 B.C.)
Philoctetes (409 B.C.)
Oedipus at Colonus (written before his death; produced posthumously in 401 B.C.)

AJAX

BACKGROUND

After the death of Achilles at Troy, two of the Greek heroes competed for his famed armor—Ajax of Salamis, the mighty bulwark of the Greek forces, and the wily Odysseus. When the coveted arms were awarded to Odysseus, Ajax, brooding over the decision, became deranged and planned to kill Agamemnon, Menelaüs and other leaders of the Greek forces in their sleep. The goddess Athena intervened, causing him to slaughter instead the cattle of the army in the belief that he was killing the Greek chieftains.

Prologue (lines 1-133)

The scene is the Greek camp at Troy, before the tent of Ajax. Odysseus enters. He has been tracking down the slayer of the army's cattle. Athena appears to him, and informs him that the culprit is the deranged Ajax, who thought he was slaying Agamemnon and Menelaüs. She summons Ajax from his tent. Odysseus pities him. Athena stresses the need for piety and moderation.

Parodos (134-200)

The Chorus of sailors from Salamis, followers of Ajax, proclaim their fidelity to him.

First Episode (201-595)

Tecmessa, the captive concubine of Ajax, joining the Chorus in a lyric exchange (*kommos*), tells of Ajax's madness and the slaughter of the cattle. She relates to the Chorus the details of his recent abnormal behavior. Ajax's voice is heard within. He is revealed in his tent, having just come to his senses, overwhelmed with shame and remorse. He is conscious of having compromised his nobility and the honor of his family, and longs to redeem himself. He believes he is being persecuted by the Greeks and the gods, and feels completely alone. Tecmessa pleads with him to do nothing rash, and the Chorus consoles him. He asks to see his little son by Tecmessa, Eurysaces, and delivers a sort of farewell to him.

First Stasimon (596-645)

The Chorus comments on its long absence from Salamis, bewails Ajax's mental state, and bemoans the sorrow that the news of his condition will cause to his father and mother.

Second Episode (646-865)

Ajax pretends he has decided to submit to the will of the gods and the sons of Atreus, and leaves. The Chorus is overjoyed at his declared reconciliation. A messenger arrives to announce the return of Teucer, Ajax's brother, and declares that he has come to warn that, in accordance with the prophecy of the seer Calchas, Ajax would die as a result of his overweening pride, unless he remained within his tent. Tecmessa and the Chorus, alarmed, rush away in search of Ajax.

Ajax is now seen at the seashore. He prays that Teucer will care for his dead body, and that destruction may befall the Greeks. He then falls on a sword.

Second Parodos (866-890)

The Chorus enters, searching for Ajax.

Third Episode (891-1184)

Tecmessa and the Chorus find the body of Ajax, and mourn his loss, grief-stricken. Teucer arrives, laments his brother's death, and bids Tecmessa bring Ajax's son to him for protection.

Menelaüs enters and arrogantly forbids removal of the body, ordering that it be left unburied. Teucer defies him. Tecmessa brings the child of Ajax, and Teucer bids him cling to the body of his father for protection.

Second Stasimon (1185-1222)

The Chorus recalls the hardships of the war and bewails the tragic loss of Ajax.

Exodos (1222-1420)

Teucer returns; Agamemnon arrives and berates him for his stand. Teucer defies him too. Odysseus appears and counsels respect for the great Ajax's valor and nobility. He advises Agamemnon to permit the burial in the name of justice and religion.

The body is carried out by Teucer and his attendants, followed by Tecmessa, Eurysaces and the Chorus.

INTERPRETATION

1. Ajax is the symbol of the aristocratic ideal of nobility, but he was destroyed by excesses of pride, ambition, and self-importance. His ideal of living nobly and dying nobly allowed of no compromise.

2. Rejection of the gods' aid leads to ruin and divine punishment.

3. Moderation and rationality should triumph over emotion and hate.

4. The disgrace of Ajax is followed by his rehabilitation, in the name of humanity and out of respect for his essential nobility.

5. There are certain inalienable religious rights; one of these is the right of decent burial for the dead.

ANTIGONE

BACKGROUND

Polynices, son of Oedipus, led the expedition known as "The Seven Against Thebes" to seize the throne from his brother Eteocles. After a long siege, it was decided to settle the issue by a duel between the brothers. In the encounter they slew each other. After the invaders fled, Creon, the new king of Thebes, buried Eteocles with honors, but issued an edict forbidding anyone to bury Polynices as a traitor, on pain of death by stoning.

Prologue (lines 1-99)

Antigone and Ismene, the two daughters of Oedipus, stand before the palace of Creon. Resolute and determined, Antigone tells Ismene that she intends to flout the decree of Creon and bury Polynices, even if it costs her life. Ismene tries to dissuade Antigone from her purpose, urging the weakness of women and the necessity of obedience to the state. Antigone, in a burst of furious anger, contemptuously scorns her advice.

Parodos (100-162)

The Chorus of Theban Elders hails the defeat of the Argive army and the lifting of the siege of Thebes. Pride goeth before a fall; Polynices was guilty of treason to his country. He and Eteocles slew each other in a duel.

First Episode (163-331)

Creon enters and declares to the loyal Theban Elders his philosophy that the state is supreme and that devotion to country outranks all other loyalties. To rule well, he asserts, he desires the advice of all. Then he repeats his edict that Polynices is not to be buried, on pain of execution. The body is being guarded to prevent burial. One of the guards, a simple soldier, arrives and hesitatingly announces that someone has given ceremonial burial to the corpse by strewing dust on it. Creon, revealing his tyrannical and proud temperament, flies into a rage, and threatens the guard with death unless the culprit is apprehended.

First Stasimon (332-383)

The greatest wonder in the world is man—with his daring, genius, and inventiveness. But his shrewdness can bring ruin to all, if he uses it in ways that are not righteous and just, particularly when he thereby undermines the state.

Second Episode (384-581)

Antigone is led in under arrest by the guard, having been apprehended repeating the burial rites. She is openly defiant and brutally outspoken, admitting her act freely to Creon, and asserting that it was premeditated. She glories, martyr-like, in the deed, and defends it as being in accord with eternal unwritten divine laws. She is prepared to die. Creon condemns her to death; but suspecting complicity on Ismene's part, he summons Antigone's sister. When she appears, she claims a part in the deed, and asks to share

Antigone's fate. Antigone harshly rejects her offer because of her refusal to aid her in burying Polynices. Despite Ismene's pleading reminder that Antigone is betrothed to his own son, Haemon, Creon orders her execution.

Second Stasimon (582-630)

A family curse dooms great houses, moving from generation to generation, as in the house of Oedipus and his ancestors. Pride, arrogance and blindness lead to ruin. Zeus is all-powerful. When the curse comes, the will of man is impotent.

Third Episode (631-780)

Haemon arrives, and with calm self-control and deference to Creon, tells him in a calculated speech that he is interested in his father's welfare, but that public opinion is against the death of Antigone. As he pleads for her, Creon's anger and pride mount, while Haemon's demeanor is outwardly calm. As Creon assails him for seeking to give advice to his elders, he demands the right to his own opinion and the right to be heard. Finally, losing control, Haemon rushes out determined to die with Antigone when he realizes his father's obdurate decision. Creon again orders Antigone's execution, but, in a sudden reversal, changes the method of punishment to entombment alive.

Third Stasimon (781-882)

The Chorus sings of the power of love. As Antigone is being led to her death she and the Chorus exchange sad feelings on what is going to happen to her. In a moment of regret, she bewails the fact that she has not enjoyed marriage and children. She recalls the past tragedies of her family, and declares that she would gladly sacrifice her life for her father, mother or brothers, but not for husband or child. The Chorus commiserates with her, but reminds her that her downfall came from stubbornness, pride and temper.

Fourth Episode (883-943)

Creon enters to hasten her departure. He orders her entombed. Antigone again defends her act, and bids the people and city farewell.

Fourth Stasimon (944-987)

The Chorus reminisces on others who suffered cruel imprisonment.

Fifth Episode (988-1114)

Teiresias, the blind soothsayer of Thebes, is brought in, led by a boy. He tells Creon that the gods are angry because Polynices is unburied. The city is being polluted. He warns Creon against stubbornness and self-will. In anger Creon accuses Teiresias of having accepted bribes from the people to bring about Antigone's release. Teiresias then predicts that Creon will atone for what he has done to Polynices' body and to Antigone by the death of a member of his immediate family.

Finally realizing the skill of Teiresias in foretelling the future, Creon suddenly decides to reverse his decision, hard as it is for him to admit error. He hastens to bury Polynices first, then to release Antigone.

Fifth Stasimon (1115-1152)

The Chorus joyfully sings of Dionysus, protector of Thebes.

Exodos (1153-1353)

A messenger arrives, and in the presence of Creon's wife, Eurydice, relates how first Creon gave decent burial to Polynices. Then he entered Antigone's tomb, to find Antigone dead by hanging and Haemon lamenting his bride-to-be. Haemon tried to kill Creon with a sword and then committed suicide by plunging it into himself, clinging to Antigone's body.

Creon enters, a broken remorseful man, with the body of Haemon. He finally admits his folly. But soon a second messenger enters to tell him that his queen has killed herself in grief over her son Haemon's death. Creon's cup of woe is full. He prays for death in his utter misery.

The Chorus cautions reverence to the gods, proper use of wisdom, and the dangers of pride.

INTERPRETATION

1. Humans are faced with basic conflicts of loyalties—to state, religion, family. Personal happiness is another powerful and legitimate pull. But perfect balance among these compelling factors is impossible; hence suffering is inevitable.

2. Excess of a virtue, such as fanatical devotion to the state or to religion, is a fault, and leads to disaster.

3. Pride, stubbornness, tyranny lead to blindness, and are grave defects which cause suffering; moderation is necessary.

4. When there is conflict between man-made laws and eternal unwritten divine laws, divine law takes precedence.

5. Both Creon and Antigone are guilty of the same character flaws. Antigone is admirable, but not a true tragic heroine; she suffers from a martyr-complex. The real tragic hero is Creon, who suffers deeply and learns from his errors.

6. Man is limited; reverence for the gods is needed.

7. There is personal responsibility for suffering; wisdom comes from suffering.

THE TRACKERS

About one half of this satyr play, first published in 1912, is preserved, in fragmentary form. The following summary is based on the reconstruction of the entire play by Roger L. Green.

Prologue (lines 1-70)

The scene is before the cave of the nymph Cyllene on Mt. Cyllene in Arcadia. The god Apollo announces, in rage and grief, that his beloved cows have been stolen, and offers a rich reward for their recovery. He has been scouring the world in search of them.

The aged satyr Silenus enters, and offers his assistance, for a price—the reward plus freedom from toil for himself and his sons, the Satyrs. The god agrees, and departs.

Parodos (71-84)

Summoned by Silenus, the Chorus of Satyrs enters. Together with Silenus they begin the search for the cows of Apollo.

First Episode (85-223)

They soon discover the tracks of animals on the ground nearby. Suddenly the sound of a lyre is heard playing softly. At first the Satyrs do not hear this strange new sound. They discover that the tracks are reversed. Then the lyre sounds louder. The Satyrs are frightened, but are soon caught up by the strange sounds and begin a wild dance, giving up the search. Silenus, who has not heard the music, rebukes them for cowardly behavior and urges them to resume the search. Suddenly Silenus hears the lyre and seeks to run away in fear.

First Stasimon (224-235)

The Chorus of Satyrs call into the cave, believing the thief to be inside.

Second Episode (236-461)

The nymph Cyllene enters from the cave, angered at the shouting and the wild dancing of the Satyrs. They inquire about the lovely music they have heard.

Cyllene confides in them that Zeus brought the nymph Maia to this cave, and that of his union with her Hermes was born six days ago. Cyllene was chosen to be his nurse. The wondrous child has been secreted in the cave at Zeus' behest, to protect him from Hera's jealousy. The new god has grown marvelously in a few days. Only today Hermes invented a new instrument, the lyre, from the hollow shell of a tortoise over which he stretched a piece of ox-hide.

The Chorus waxes lyrical over the sweetness of the music, but declare their suspicion that the thief they have been tracking is Hermes. Cyllene, seeking to protect her nursling, rebukes them for their accusation against a god, one, moreover, who is only six days old. The Satyrs demand that she produce the child for questioning. [The rest of the play is lost. Roger L. Green has reconstructed the remainder of the play on the basis of the Homeric *Hymn to Hermes*.]

Second Stasimon (462-491)

The Chorus of Satyrs, anticipating a battle between Apollo and Hermes, sing of the joys they have known in the Dionysiac revels.

Third Episode and Exodos (492-750)

The young god Hermes, grown to manhood in six days, enters. Silenus accuses him of being the thief of Apollo's cows. Hermes steadfastly denies it, swearing a mighty oath. Silenus cites as evidence the piece of newly-flayed skin stretched over the tortoise shell. Hermes plays on the lyre. The Chorus begins to dance wildly to the divine music.

Apollo enters. He has learned from an informer that the thief, a comely youth, covered his feet to conceal his footprints and led the cows backward to deceive the searchers. He has also discovered that two of his cows have been slain. He swears vengeance. The Chorus declares Hermes to be the thief.

Apollo is amused, recognizing Hermes as a son of Zeus and thus his own half-brother. As Hermes begins to play on his lyre, Apollo is entranced by the lovely music. He demands recompense for the stealing of his cows. Hermes swears never again to play tricks on Apollo, and bestows the lyre on him. Apollo frees Silenus and the Satyrs, and departs playing on the lyre, as the Chorus dances after him.

INTERPRETATION

This satyr play is a light and humorous retelling in dramatic form of a well-known myth.

OEDIPUS THE KING

BACKGROUND

Laïus and Jocasta, king and queen of Thebes, were warned by the Delphic oracle that a son to be born would kill his father, Laïus, and marry his mother, Jocasta. When the child was born, it was given to a shepherd to be killed. The shepherd first pierced the child's feet, but, pitying the baby, gave it to another shepherd from

Corinth. The child was then adopted by Polybus and Merope, king and queen of Corinth, who named him Oedipus ("Swollen-foot"). When Oedipus reached manhood, he learned from the oracle that he was fated to kill his father and marry his mother. He left Delphi, determined never to return to Corinth, in order to avoid his horrible fate. On his journey his chariot was blocked by another chariot at a spot where three roads met. In an argument over the right of way, the hotheaded Oedipus lost his temper and killed the rider. It was his father, Laïus. Soon after, he reached Thebes, which was plagued by the Sphinx. She asked all as they entered and left the city a riddle, and killed all who could not answer it. When Oedipus quickly answered the riddle, the Sphinx destroyed herself, and Oedipus was hailed as the savior of the city. Shortly after the news of Laïus' death was received, Oedipus was proclaimed king of Thebes and married Laïus' widow, his own mother Jocasta. They had four children, Antigone, Ismene, Eteocles, and Polynices. After he has ruled for many years, admired for his wisdom and ability, a plague suddenly strikes the city.

Prologue (lines 1-150)

Oedipus enters from his palace and hears from the priest details about the plague which is devastating Thebes. In the name of the people the priest begs Oedipus to aid them now as he did when he rid the city of the Sphinx. Oedipus consoles them, and declares that he has sent his brother-in-law Creon to consult the oracle of Apollo at Delphi. Creon arrives happy, for the cause of the plague has been revealed by the oracle: the undiscovered murderer of the former king, Laïus, is in the city; he must be killed or banished. Oedipus is informed that there was a witness to the murder who reported that it was committed by a group of thieves. Oedipus dedicates himself energetically to discovering the murderer.

Parodos (151-215)

The Chorus of Theban Elders prays to many gods to avert the pestilence which is harrowing the city.

First Episode (216-462)

Oedipus issues the following proclamation: the murderer is enjoined to confess; anyone who knows his identity must denounce him; and no one is to shield or harbor him, under threat of dire penalties. He curses the murderer, and ordains that if the criminal is an alien, he will be put to death; if he is native born, he will be exiled. Finally, he expresses his determination to track him down relentlessly.

The blind prophet Teiresias is brought in, and Oedipus asks him to reveal the identity of the murderer. Teiresias professes ignorance, but when Oedipus loses his temper, taunting him with his blindness and accusing him of complicity in Laïus' murder, he reveals that Oedipus is the criminal. His anger mounting, Oedipus accuses Teiresias of plotting with Creon to overthrow him, and scorns his wisdom since he did not solve the riddle of the Sphinx. Teiresias then reveals Oedipus' past and future, though the irate Oedipus, consumed with anger, pays little attention.

First Stasimon (463-511)

Who is the murderer indicated by the oracle? Retribution is inevitable. But the Chorus cannot bring itself to believe in the guilt of their beloved king Oedipus, who aided them by ridding Thebes of the Sphinx.

Second Episode (512-862)

Creon enters to defend himself against the charge of conspiracy against Oedipus. While Oedipus towers in rage over him, Creon calmly urges him to be rational. He argues that it is well known that he is not ambitious for power, and that he should be judged not on impulse and in anger but by the evidence. As Oedipus rants against Creon, Jocasta enters to intervene between her brother and her husband. She urges Oedipus to have no confidence in the oracle, because it had predicted that Laïus would be slain by her son. But it had been reported that Laïus was killed by a group of thieves at a spot where three roads met, and, moreover, her child was killed soon after its birth.

When Oedipus hears that Laïus was murdered at a crossroads, he recalls that he had killed a man at such a spot. In terror, he fears that he is the murderer revealed by the oracle. He orders the witness to the murder summoned. Oedipus then relates his past at Corinth, and how he had heard from the oracle at Delphi that he would slay his father and marry his mother. He therefore resolved never to return to his "parents." In his wanderings he killed a man at a spot where three roads met. As he bemoans his fate, Jocasta convinces him that the oracle is not to be trusted.

Second Stasimon (863-910)

Reverence for the gods is best. Prosperity leads to hybris, which is punished by inevitable Nemesis. But the Chorus, too, is shaken in its confidence in the oracle.

Third Episode (911-1185)

As Jocasta prays to Apollo, a messenger arrives from Corinth to announce that Polybus of Corinth is dead. Jocasta jubilantly summons Oedipus to show him new evidence of the untrustworthiness of the oracle, which had declared he would murder his father. As Oedipus expresses his concurrence, the messenger reveals that Polybus was not his father. Oedipus questions him and discovers that he was given as a baby to the messenger by a certain shepherd of the household of Laïus, the same who was the witness to the murder. Jocasta, now realizing the truth, tries to dissuade Oedipus from continuing his search. Knowing his determination to learn the entire truth, she rushes into the palace aghast.

The Chorus is overjoyed that Oedipus is a native of Thebes.

The reluctant shepherd is brought in. In the presence of the Corinthian messenger, Oedipus relentlessly forces the shepherd to reveal his origin. In horror he rushes into the palace.

Third Stasimon (1186-1222)

All life is sorrow. See how the great Oedipus has fallen! Time reveals all.

Exodos (1223-1530)

A messenger comes out of the palace and tells how Jocasta has committed suicide by hanging, and how Oedipus, rushing in to kill her, discovered her body and blinded himself with her golden brooches.

Oedipus comes out and bemoans his fate—the murder of his father, his incestuous marriage with his mother, and his incest-bred children. Creon, the new king, enters and addresses him with pity and kindness. Oedipus asks Creon to banish him. Before he goes he requests that he be permitted to touch his two daughters, a request which Creon has anticipated. They come in sobbing, and Oedipus bewails their future unhappiness, because of the nature of their birth. Asking Creon to care for them, he reluctantly parts from his beloved daughters. The Chorus moralizes from Oedipus' experience that no man should be counted happy until he is dead.

INTERPRETATION

1. Intellectual pride leads to blindness.

2. "Murder will out;" breaches of the unwritten laws—incest, parricide—cannot go unpunished by the gods.

3. The power of fate is irresistible; yet human beings are not perfect, and so there is also personal responsibility for suffering.

4. The power of the gods is supreme; man is limited; the Delphic oracle is infallible; human self-confidence and wisdom are illusion before divine truth.

5. Life is basically tragic and full of suffering; even the innocent suffer.

6. Resignation and dignity are essential; there is wisdom through suffering.

7. Happiness is best sought through moderation and piety.

ELECTRA

BACKGROUND

See above, pp. 34-36. In this play it is Electra who took the precaution of sending Orestes away to Phocis. She has never concealed her grief over Agamemnon's death and her hatred for his murderers. Insulted and degraded, she has begun to give up hope that Orestes will ever return to avenge their father's death.

Prologue (1-120)

Orestes, son of Agamemnon and Clytemnestra, accompanied by his best friend Pylades and an old attendant, enters. The old man points out the scenes. They stand before the royal palace of Mycenae. Orestes instructs the old man to obtain knowledge of the situation inside the palace by entering and announcing that he has come from Phocis to report the accidental death of Orestes. He and Pylades meanwhile will honor Agamemnon's grave and then return bearing an urn supposedly containing Orestes' ashes. They leave as Orestes' sister Electra emerges from the palace bewailing Agamemnon's murder, her own hard lot, and Orestes' long absence. She is beginning to lose heart in her loneliness.

Parados (121-250)

The Chorus of Mycenaean women and Electra sing in responsive lyrics. They sympathize with her, condemn murder, urge her to cease her grief and rebelliousness, yet hope for Orestes' return. Zeus guides all. Electra cannot subdue her anguish and hatred of the murderers; she despairs over Orestes' return, and lives in meanness and squalor, unmarried. There must be punishment for murder.

First Episode (251-471)

Electra tells of her unhappy surroundings—the murderer and adulterer Aegisthus on the throne; her mother, Clytemnestra, his partner in crime; their insults and mistreatment of her. She is a girl of unwavering principles, implacable in refusing to compromise with evil. The Chorus assures her Orestes will come.

Her sister Chrysothemis enters, professes agreement with Electra's attitude to Aegisthus and Clytemnestra, but recommends submission to the rulers. Chrysothemis is an opportunist, having chosen the safe, easy path of self-preservation. Electra fiercely rebukes her timidity and cowardice. Chrysothemis tells her that Aegisthus is planning to imprison her in a dungeon if she does not cease her lamenting and insults. Electra is unperturbed. Then Chrysothemis tells her that she has been instructed by Clytemnestra to pour libations on Agamemnon's grave, for she has had a frightening, prophetic dream. Urged by Electra and the Chorus, she agrees hesitatingly to substitute a lock of hair from Electra's head and one from her own as offerings to the soul of Agamemnon.

First Stasimon (472-515)

Justice will triumph, the dream indicates. Adultery will be punished. The house of Atreus has had many woes.

Second Episode (516-1057)

Clytemnestra enters to find Electra in front of the palace. (Clytemnestra's character has been completely blackened by Sophocles in this play.) She tries to defend her murder of Agamemnon on the ground that he sacrificed Iphigenia. Electra counters that the real cause was her love for Aegisthus; and she defends Agamemnon's action on religious grounds. Electra insults Clytemnestra, who threatens punishment. Clytemnestra prays to Apollo for continued prosperity for herself and Aegisthus.

Orestes' old retainer enters and announces the death of Orestes. As Electra is desolated, Clytemnestra eagerly asks for details, which the old man invents at length. His story is believed. Clytemnestra, overjoyed, pretends to be distressed, but finally expresses relief at Orestes' death, as she mocks Electra, and goes into the palace. Electra bewails her new unhappiness, bereft of her last hope for revenge, and prays for death. The Chorus consoles her.

Chrysothemis rushes in joyfully with news. She believes that Orestes has returned, for when she came to Agamemnon's tomb she found it newly decorated and on it a lock of hair, which she believes to be Orestes'. Then Electra tells her of Orestes' reported death, and asks Chrysothemis to join her in accomplishing the murder of Aegisthus. Frightened, Chrysothemis cautions prudence, and is savagely reproached by Electra for cowardice. Electra asserts she will do the deed alone.

Second Stasimon (1058-1097)

Filial devotion is admirable. Sin brings sorrow. The Chorus prays to Agamemnon's soul, telling him of the sisters' quarrel, praising Electra and hoping for her success.

Third Episode (1098-1383)

Orestes and Pylades enter with an urn supposedly holding Orestes' ashes. Electra sadly asks to hold the urn, and then delivers a lament over his death and her own futile life. Orestes, deeply moved, questions her, expresses sympathy for her appearance and suffering, and finally reveals that he is Orestes. When he proves his identity by showing her Agamemnon's signet ring, her grief suddenly changes to wild joy. They embrace, but he cautions her to be careful not to betray his identity by her actions.

The old retainer of Orestes comes out and firmly cautions prudence. As Electra greets him with joy, he urges Orestes and Pylades to act at once. They enter the palace.

Third Stasimon (1384-1397)

Vengeance is about to be consummated.

Exodos (1398-1510)

Electra comes out to watch for Aegisthus. Clytemnestra's death cries are heard, mingled with pleas for pity. Orestes and Pylades come out to report her death. As Aegisthus approaches with joy at the news of Orestes' reported death, Electra eagerly pushes them back into the palace. Aegisthus orders the gates opened. Orestes and Pylades are revealed standing over a covered corpse. Believing it to be Orestes' body, Aegisthus rejoices. He lifts the shroud and in horror sees the corpse of Clytemnestra. As he is taken inside by Orestes to be slain at the spot where Agamemnon was murdered, Orestes declares that the will of heaven has been accomplished and that the woes of the House of Atreus are over.

INTERPRETATION

1. This play, influenced by Sophocles' *Antigone,* and perhaps written as an answer to Euripides' *Electra,* presents the murder of

Clytemnestra and Aegisthus as an admirable deed and as justifiable homicide.

2. Since Aegisthus and Clytemnestra are delineated as completely evil, being adulterers and murderers, the vengeance is presented as accomplished with great dispatch by Orestes acting in the name of justice and religion.

3. All conflicts are reconciled by the triumph of righteousness over evil with the aid of divine justice.

4. But primarily this play is a character study of a principled girl living in a hostile environment but fiercely maintaining her sense of right and her integrity until justice finally triumphs.

MAIDENS OF TRACHIS

BACKGROUND

Heracles, son of Zeus and Alcmena, was a national hero and benefactor of the Greeks, famous for his strength, his "Twelve Labors," and his joviality. Once when he and his wife Deianira desired to cross a river, the centaur Nessus was engaged to carry Deianira across. When he tried to molest her, Heracles shot him with an arrow. The dying Nessus counseled Deianira to preserve some of his blood as a charm to regain the love of Heracles some day, for he was a notorious philanderer.

Prologue (lines 1-93)

The scene is the house of Heracles at Trachis. Deianira tells her Nurse of her unhappy life. When she was a beautiful young maiden, she was wooed by the horrible river god Acheloüs. She lived in terror until Heracles fought Acheloüs and delivered her. After they were married, her woes continued, for Heracles was ever away from home on some exploit. Moreover, since Heracles' wanton slaying of Iphitus they have been living in exile in Trachis. She sits lonely and worried, waiting for him to return. This time he has been away for fifteen months, without a word of his whereabouts.

The Nurse counsels her to send her eldest son Hyllus to seek tidings of Heracles. Hyllus enters and reveals that he has heard about Heracles. For a year of his absence, rumor has it, he served as a slave to a Lydian woman (Queen Omphale); at this very moment he is preparing war against King Eurytus of Euboea. Deianira, troubled, informs Hyllus that before he left Heracles told her of an oracle that the exploit against Euboea was to be his final one, and that he would find death in it, or thereafter lead a peaceful life. Hyllus hastens off in quest of his father.

Parodos (94-140)

The Chorus of Trachinian Maidens enters. They speculate on Heracles' whereabouts and console Deianira. Heracles is ever on some dangerous exploit. Life is full of sorrow, but joy comes too, and, moreover, Zeus guards his children.

First Episode (141-496)

Deianira tells the Chorus of her sorrows. Her fears for Heracles are now desperate, for when he left fifteen months before, he made his will. He revealed to her that an oracle had predicted that in exactly fifteen months he would die or, if he survived, forever after lead an untroubled life. That day is here, and she is fearful of the death of her husband, "the noblest of all men."

A messenger enters with the news that Heracles is alive, has been victorious in battle, is returning with spoils, and will be home soon. Deianira and the Chorus give way to unrestrained joy.

Lichas, the herald of Heracles, arrives accompanied by the captive women of Heracles. He tells her that Heracles is now in Euboea offering sacrifices to Zeus. He had served a year as a slave to Queen Omphale of Lydia, sold into slavery by Eurytus of Oechalia in Euboea. Zeus thus punished Heracles for his violent deeds, but Heracles swore vengeance against Eurytus. Now Eurytus is dead. The captive women, symbols of Heracles' victory, are delivered into Deianira's hands.

Deianira rejoices over the happy tidings, but is overwhelmed with pity for the captives, particularly Iole She speaks to her, inquiring who she is, but Iole remains mute. Lichas conceals from Deianira her identity as King Eurytus' daughter, for Heracles is enamored of her. Lichas and the captive women enter the house.

The messenger accosts Deianira and reveals that Heracles' real purpose in destroying the land of Eurytus was his love for Iole, whom her father had refused to give him as a concubine. Deianira is prostrated. When Lichas enters, she demands the truth about Iole, as the messenger prods him with facts. Deianira pretends understanding of Heracles' frequent inconstancies, but must have the truth. Moreover, she genuinely pities innocent Iole's suffering. Lichas admits Heracles' love for Iole, but declares that Lichas himself concealed the truth from her in order to spare her feelings. He begs her to be kind to Iole for Heracles' sake. She is overtly calm, and asks Lichas to bear a gift from her to Heracles.

First Stasimon (497-530)

The Chorus sings of the universal power of love, even over the great gods. The river god Acheloüs and Zeus' son Heracles fought in mighty combat for the hand of Deianira.

Second Episode (531-632)

Deianira enters from the palace to confide her thoughts to the Chorus. She cannot bear to share Heracles with Iole, who is very young, while she is on in years. She tells how Nessus was shot by Heracles, and that before his death he advised her to take some of his blood as a love philtre to win back Heracles' love. Now she has smeared the blood on a robe which she is sending to Heracles as a gift. She entrusts the robe to Lichas as he departs to rejoin Heracles.

Second Stasimon (633-662)

The Chorus hails with joy the imminent arrival of Heracles, the conquering hero, and prays that the magic robe may fire him with renewed love for Deianira.

Third Episode (663-820)

Deianira rushes out in alarm. She now regrets her haste in sending the robe, fearing that the blood may harm Heracles. The wool she used to smear the blood on the robe has disintegrated. She fears that Nessus deceived her to avenge himself on Heracles. "Too late, too late, when knowledge naught avails, my eyes are opened." If she causes Heracles' death, she will kill herself.

Hyllus enters and assails his mother for destroying his father. He relates in detail how, while Heracles was sacrificing to celebrate his victory, Lichas brought him the robe. He put it on at once, but, while he was sacrificing, the poison in the robe began to consume him. He seized the innocent Lichas and dashed him to death. In excruciating agony he cursed Deianira, and begged Hyllus to carry him home to Trachis. Hyllus curses his mother, blaming her for slaying "the noblest man who ever lived." Deianira silently re-enters the house.

Third Stasimon (821-876)

The Chorus declares that ancient prophecies foretold the end of Heracles in twelve years. Deianira, through an error of judgment, unwittingly caused his death, seeking to keep his love.

Fourth Episode (877-946)

The Nurse rushes out to announce the suicide of Deianira. She describes her last tortured moments in the house before she drove a sword through her heart. Hyllus, learning the truth, is overwhelmed with remorse.

Fourth Stasimon (947-970)

The Chorus bewails the double disaster.

Exodos (971-1278)

Hyllus and an Old Man enter, followed by attendants carrying Heracles on a litter. Hyllus bewails his father, as the Old Man advises restraint. Heracles raves in agony, begging for release from his pain. He begs Hyllus to kill him at once, describing his pain in detail. Then he asks him to bring out Deianira so that he may kill her. He recalls his mighty exploits (Twelve Labors), comparing them with his present impotence, he the son of Zeus. Hyllus defends his mother from Heracles' rage, telling him that she has committed suicide, did not intend to harm him, but tried to win back his love through Nessus' blood.

Heracles, realizing his death is near, tells Hyllus of oracles that predicted his death. He compels Hyllus to swear an oath that he will have him carried to the shrine of Zeus on top of Mt. Oeta nearby. Then he is to prepare a funeral pyre, lay him on it while still alive, and cremate him. He also enjoins Hyllus to marry his concubine Iole. Hyllus shrinks from this, but reluctantly agrees to obey his father.

The attendants lift the litter and start off to Mt. Oeta, as Hyllus comments on the suffering of man under the very eyes of the gods.

INTERPRETATION

1. This play, influenced by Euripides' *Heracles,* is "Euripidean on the surface," but "Aeschylean to the core."

2. It is primarily a melodrama, presenting the atmosphere of the traditional myth of the hero Heracles, worshipped as a demigod among the Greeks.

3. Excess leads to human blindness and errors of judgment. The love of Deianira, however sincere, and the callous thoughtlessness of Heracles, however heroic he was in tradition, lead to disaster.

4. The fulfillment of destiny, as revealed by oracles, is inevitable. Resignation to the will of the gods is necessary.

PHILOCTETES

BACKGROUND

The Greek hero Philoctetes had been a close friend of Heracles. It was to Philoctetes that he gave his famous bow and arrows as a last legacy. Philoctetes joined the expedition against Troy. En route Philoctetes was bitten in the foot by a snake. The wound was incurable; and the odor from it was so vile, his agonized cries so offensive, that he was carried off to the deserted island of Lemnos by Odysseus and Diomedes and abandoned there. After the death of Achilles at Troy ten years later, a prophecy declared that Troy could not be taken by the Greeks without the aid of Philoctetes and the bow and arrows of Heracles. Odysseus and Neoptolemus, Achilles' son, were dispatched to bring Philoctetes with his bow and arrow back to the Greek army by fair means or foul.

Prologue (lines 1-134)

Odysseus and the young Neoptolemus stealthily approach the cave where Philoctetes has been living on the island of Lemnos. Philoctetes is out. The wily Odysseus, in the name of patriotic duty and religion, instructs Neoptolemus how to win the confidence of Philoctetes by deception, in order to get possession of his bow and arrows. Neoptolemus, hesitating to compromise his honor for the sake of expediency, finally consents, being also ambitious for glory.

Parodos (135-217)

The Chorus of Greek sailors engage in a lyric dialogue (*kommos*) with Neoptolemus. They pity Philoctetes' suffering, but are prepared to assist Neoptolemus.

First Episode (218-678)

Philoctetes enters. Neoptolemus, revealing his identity to Philoctetes, listens to his tale of woe and hatred of the Greek chieftains. Neoptolemus pretends that he too is embittered against Agamemnon and the Greeks because the arms of his father Achilles were awarded to Odysseus, and declares that he is therefore sailing home. Philoctetes appeals to Neoptolemus to take him away from the island to his own home in Greece. Neoptolemus, seconded by the Chorus, agrees.

At this point a sailor disguised as a merchant enters looking for Neoptolemus. Carrying out a prearranged ruse, he states that he has come to warn Neoptolemus that Greeks have been sent to seize both Neoptolemus and Philoctetes. The two prepare to leave the island at once. Neoptolemus requests permission to handle the famous bow.

First Stasimon (679-729)

The Chorus pities the loneliness and suffering of Philoctetes, and trusts he will return to his home.

Second Episode (730-826)

Philoctetes is suddenly seized by agonizing pains. He entrusts his bow to Neoptolemus, exacts a promise from him that he will not desert him, and then falls into a profound sleep.

Second Stasimon (827-865)

The Chorus urges Neoptolemus to abandon Philoctetes and take the bow away.

Third Episode (866-1080)

Philoctetes awakes, and Neoptolemus, overcome with sudden moral revulsion at the deception, declares the truth to Philoctetes— that he intends to take him to Troy as a matter of patriotic duty. Philoctetes demands his bow. As Neoptolemus wavers, Odysseus enters and threatens to seize Philoctetes by force in the name of Zeus. Philoctetes, with unbending stubbornness and pride, and overwhelming hatred, resists and threatens suicide. Odysseus seizes the bow and orders that Philoctetes be guarded. Odysseus and Neoptolemus leave.

Third Stasimon (1081-1216)

Philoctetes, in a lyric exchange with the Chorus, bewails his misery. The Chorus urges him to serve the common cause and come to Troy willingly.

Exodos (1217-1471)

Odysseus and Neoptolemus return. Neoptolemus has by now undergone a complete change of heart about the use of deception or force to achieve their ends. Alarmed, Odysseus hastens away to summon help. Neoptolemus forthwith returns the bow to Philoctetes. When Odysseus reappears, Neoptolemus prevents Philoctetes from killing Odysseus, who promptly flees.

Neoptolemus now seeks to persuade Philoctetes to come to Troy of his own free will, but Philoctetes, in his overwhelming pride, refuses, even when he is informed that it is destined for him to be cured at Troy and win fame there. Failing to persuade him, Neoptolemus promises to take him home.

At this impasse, Heracles appears as the *deus ex machina* to report the will of Zeus—that Philoctetes is to go to Troy, where he will be cured, slay Paris, help to sack Troy, and win fame and wealth. He must reverence the gods. Philoctetes now agrees to go to Troy of his own free will.

INTERPRETATION

1. War engenders unscrupulous and morally objectionable means to achieve the highest goals of country and religion.

2. Idealistic youths, inexperienced in the ways of the world, are faced with the conflict of pursuing justice, humanity and honor, while expediency and compromise with evil seem necessary to achieve personal success and to serve the gods, one's leaders and country.

3. Excessive pride is an evil that is self-defeating.

4. Conflict between individual conscience and patriotism, duty to leaders and gods.

5. The realist uses morally reprehensible methods to achieve admirable ends; the idealist, following conscience and honor, thwarts the achievement of such goals.

6. The most noble human character traits, such as pity, humanity, friendship, integrity, truth can thwart the will of the gods and betray the general welfare.

7. In these dilemmas the will of the gods is finally triumphant, reconciling the ethical greatness of man with divine purposes and the common good of the state.

OEDIPUS AT COLONUS

BACKGROUND

About twenty years have elapsed since Oedipus' discovery of his true identity (see pp. 51-55). In accordance with an oracle revealed after his first exile, Oedipus had been permitted to remain at Thebes. But he was again exiled, this time with the concurrence of Creon, his uncle, and of Eteocles and Polynices, his two sons. He cursed his sons and went into exile, becoming a wandering beggar,

cared for by his devoted daughter Antigone. Meanwhile, Eteocles
became king of Thebes and thrust out his brother Polynices. The
latter fled to Argos where he organized an expeditionary force
against Thebes ("The Seven Against Thebes") to seize the
kingdom.

Prologue (lines 1-116)

Oedipus, blind and humble, but possessed of an imposing pa-
triarchal grandeur, arrives at Colonus, near Athens, guided and
tended by Antigone. He still possesses his temper and pride that
were his bane in the past, but in this play these traits are directed
only against the forces of evil. He learns from a native that he is
in the sacred grove of the Eumenides at Colonus, and that it is
forbidden ground. He prays to the Eumenides for assistance.

Parodos (117-257)

The Chorus of Elders of Colonus enters looking for the stranger
reported trespassing in the sacred grove of the Eumenides. Oedipus
comes forward, shocking the Chorus both by his sacrilege and appearance. He is warned out of the grove and asked to tell who he is.
Reluctantly and under compulsion, he tells them. They express
horror when they learn his identity, and order him to leave the
country at once, though they express pity for Oedipus and Antigone.

First Episode (258-667)

Oedipus in a persuasive speech, in which he declares his innocence of intent to kill his father and marry his mother, begs for
asylum and convinces the Chorus to wait for King Theseus, who
has been summoned. Ismene, Antigone's sister, suddenly arrives on
horseback. Oedipus and Antigone greet Ismene lovingly. He inquires about his neglectful sons, comparing them with his devoted
daughters. Ismene tells how her brothers Polynices and Eteocles
had quarreled over the royal power, deposing Creon, of the expul-
sion of Polynices by Eteocles, and of Polynices' projected attack on

Thebes with an Argive army. She also reports a new oracle that
Thebes will prosper only if Oedipus is brought back. Creon is coming to take control of him, so as to possess for his own ends the
deciding factor in the welfare of Thebes. Oedipus curses his sons
because they did not recall him when they heard the oracle but
thought only of the throne of Thebes. He offers his services to the
Chorus as a future protector of Athens, if they aid him now. Instructed by the Chorus he prays and sacrifices to the Eumenides,
but because of his blindness, Ismene performs the rites. The Chorus
then hears with horror from Oedipus of his murder of his father,
his incestuous relationship with his mother, and his incest-bred
children.

King Theseus of Attica arrives, recognizes Oedipus, and at once
offers his sympathy and help. Oedipus tells Theseus of the coming
attempt to seize him and take him to Thebes. He begs to be permitted to remain in Attica. Theseus grants his wish, and promises
him protection from harm.

First Stasimon (668-719)

The Chorus describes in lyrical terms the beauties of Attica,
particularly Colonus.

Second Episode (720-1043)

Creon arrives, and with deceitful words pleads with Oedipus to
return to Thebes with him, but the latter refuses, revealing that he
knows Creon's purpose. An angry quarrel ensues, and Oedipus
hears from Creon that Ismene has been seized. When Creon orders
his guards to carry off Antigone, the Chorus tries to rescue her but
fails. Oedipus is about to be dragged off by Creon when Theseus
arrives with his bodyguard. Upon hearing what has happened, he
orders Antigone and Ismene to be brought back, holding Creon
as hostage for their safe return and rebuking him for his high-
handed actions. Creon attempts to justify his acts on the grounds of
Oedipus' crimes. Oedipus, with great feeling, proclaims innocence
of wrongdoing, and rebukes Creon. Theseus then forces Creon to
lead the way in rescuing the two girls.

Second Stasimon (1044-1095)

The Chorus, anticipating the combat between Theseus and Creon's guards, prays for sure victory for their king to Zeus, Athena, and Apollo.

Third Episode (1096-1210)

Antigone and Ismene return with Theseus to Oedipus. There is mutual joy, and Oedipus thanks Theseus. Oedipus learns from Theseus that a relative wishes to talk with him. Knowing that it is Polynices, he refuses to see his hated son. But Antigone persuades him to consent.

Third Stasimon (1211-1250)

Desire for long life is folly, for age brings much grief and suffering, as witness Oedipus.

Fourth Episode (1251-1555)

Polynices enters, professing to be distressed by the sad lot of Oedipus and Antigone. He tells of his quarrel with Eteocles, his plan to attack Thebes, and asks for Oedipus' aid, knowing the recent oracles. He promises to take Oedipus back to Thebes. Oedipus in a crushing speech reminds Polynices of his past treatment of him, when he helped exile his father; then he curses both brothers and predicts their deaths. Oedipus orders him to begone. Before departing, Polynices begs his sisters to give him decent burial if he perishes in the assault of Thebes, which he cannot be dissuaded from undertaking.

As the Chorus comments on the woes of Oedipus and the cyclical pattern of life, thunder is heard. Oedipus intuitively surmises his imminent death and summons Theseus. When Theseus arrives, he tells him that his end is near and that he will reveal to him in secret where he is to die. The spot is to remain the guarded secret of the kings of Athens; it will protect Athens against Theban aggression. Then a divine summons urges him on, and he moves slowly and confidently away toward the fated place where he is to die.

Fourth Stasimon (1556-1578)

The Chorus prays to the gods of the underworld that Oedipus may have a painless death.

Exodos (1579-1779)

A messenger enters to announce the death of Oedipus. He relates how Oedipus prepared himself when he reached the fated spot, and bade farewell to his daughters. Thunder was heard and a divine voice called Oedipus not to delay. Before going he asked Theseus to aid his daughters. Only Theseus was permitted to be present as Oedipus mysteriously disappeared—a perfect end for Oedipus.

Antigone and Ismene enter lamenting together with the Chorus. They are apprehensive about the future but are reassured. When Theseus returns they beg to see Oedipus' tomb, but he relates that Oedipus enjoined him to keep the place secret. He agrees to send them back to Thebes.

INTERPRETATION

1. This play was written when Sophocles was about ninety years of age, at a time when the power of Athens had been shattered by Sparta near the end of the Peloponnesian War.

2. On the personal level, it is a testimonial of the aged Sophocles' faith in divine goodness.

3. On the political level, it is a patriotic reaffirmation of his belief in Athens; it idealizes his native city and entrusts its fate to divine guidance.

4. On the mythical level, it stresses the heroic dignity of an essentially great and good man who, despite faults and sins, is transfigured by death into a hero.

5. The righteous help each other, are harmonious, and possess true piety; the evil are self-interested and cause disunity.

6. Reconciliation of Oedipus and the gods is intended to teach trust in divine justice, that man is limited, and must endure adversity, for there is a divine purpose in suffering.

LOST PLAYS OF SOPHOCLES

Acrisius; Aegeus; Aegisthus; Ajax the Locrian; Alcmaeon; Aleadae; Aletes; Alexander; Amycus; Amphiaraüs; Amphitryon; Andromeda; Athamas; Atreus; Banqueters; Camicus; Captive Women; Cedalion; Chryses; Clytemnestra; Creusa; Daedalus; Danaë; Dumb Men; Dolopians; Epigoni; Erigone; Eriphyle; Eris; Ethiopians; Eumelus; Euryalus; Eurypylus; Eurysaces; Hermione; Hipponoüs; Hybris; Heracles at Taenarum; Inachus; Infant Dionysus; Infant Heracles; Iobates; Ion; Iphigenia; Ixion; Judgment of Paris; Laconian Women; Laocoön; Lemnian Women; Lovers of Achilles; Marriage of Helen; Meleager; Men of Larisa; Minos; Muses; Momus; Muster of the Achaeans; Mysians; Nauplius; Nausicaä; Niobe; Odysseus, Oeneus; Oecles; Oenomaüs; Palamedes; Pandora; Peleus; Phaeacians; Phaedra; Philoctetes; Phineus; Phoenix; Phrixus; Polyidus; Polyxena; Priam; Procris; Reclaiming of Helen; Salmoneus; Scyrians; Scythians; Shepherds; Sinon; Sisyphus; Sons of Antenor; Sorceress; Tambourine Players; Tantalus; Teucer; Telephus; Tereus; Thamyras; Theseus; Thyestes at Sicyon; Triptolemus; Tyndareus; Troilus; Tyro; Water-Carriers; Women of Colchis; Women of Phthia.

DRAMATIC TECHNIQUES AND STYLE OF SOPHOCLES

1. Skillfully constructed, more complex plots; single play as the dramatic unit.

2. Three actors; more dialogue; decreased importance of chorus.

3. Master of the use of dramatic irony.

4. Character drawing:

a. "The Homer of tragedy;" varied personalities, complex characters subtly delineated.

b. Idealism ("Men as they should be"): generally finer traits of character with fewer faults. Sophocles also employs some characters who are completely perfect or completely evil.

c. Character drawing through the use of "dramatic foil"— characters used as sharp contrasts with other characters to highlight personality.

d. Development: principal characters usually undergo sudden change of outlook through sharp reversals of fortune.

5. Style: charm, grace, lucid simplicity, together with vigor, strength, dignity; Attic refinement and reserve.

BASIC IDEAS OF SOPHOCLES

1. Orthodox religious views: when divine and human purposes conflict, the gods are supreme. "No deed is shameful which the gods direct."

2. Fall of great people through character flaws; heroic dignity of man despite imperfections.

3. Arrogance, pride, sin lead to disaster; retribution is inevitable; moderation is the best guide; reverence towards the gods is necessary.

4. Human suffering is inevitable because of man's imperfection; even the innocent suffer; one must endure suffering with dignity.

5. Central theme: wisdom through suffering—which teaches humility and the limitations of man.

CHAPTER FIVE

EURIPIDES

EURIPIDES OF ATHENS (480-406 B.C.)

1. Born at Salamis, perhaps on the day of the Battle of Salamis.

2. Deeply influenced by the Sophistic movement; rationalist; philosophic interests; scholarly recluse.

3. Most modern of the three great Athenian tragedians ("the Ibsen of the Greeks"); called in antiquity "the philosopher of the theater."

4. Least popular among his contemporaries, as compared with Aeschylus and Sophocles, but most appreciated by later generations.

5. Spent last years of his life in Macedonia, north of Greece, where he died and was buried. A cenotaph was erected for him in Athens.

6. Wrote ca. 90 plays; won few victories in dramatic contests.

EXTANT PLAYS

Alcestis (438 B.C.)

Medea (431 B.C.)

Hippolytus (428 B.C.)

Children of Heracles (ca. 427 B.C.)

Andromache (ca. 426 B.C.?)

Hecuba (ca. 425 B.C.)

Cyclops (ca. 423 B.C.?)

Mad Heracles (ca. 422 B.C.)

Suppliants (421 B.C.?)

Ion (ca. 417 B.C.)

Trojan Women (415 B.C.)

73

ALCESTIS

BACKGROUND

In retaliation for Zeus' slaying of his son Asclepius, Apollo killed the Cyclopes. As punishment he was assigned as a slave to Admetus, King of Pherae in Thessaly. Admetus treated him with all deference, and in recompense the god granted him the privilege of not dying when his time came, provided someone else would volunteer to take his place. The day has arrived. Only Admetus' wife, Alcestis, has offered to sacrifice herself.

Prologue (lines 1-76)

Apollo stands before the palace of Admetus. He tells how he became Admetus' slave, and that he has made it possible for Admetus to avoid death provided another took his place. Only his wife Alcestis was willing. She is already dying.

Thanatos (Death), dressed in black, appears to claim Alcestis. Apollo predicts that he will be thwarted.

Parodos (77-140)

The Chorus of old men laments Alcestis' imminent death, and praises her virtues.

First Episode (141-434)

A handmaiden tells the Chorus of Alcestis' devotion to Admetus and her children, and of her final preparations for leaving them. The Chorus laments.

Admetus enters with Alcestis. She is carried on a litter, followed by her two children. Alcestis is wasting away, delirious. Admetus consoles her. She asks him to promise never to marry again, so that their children will never have a stepmother to plague them. He readily agrees, swearing eternal fidelity to her memory. She bids farewell to her children, and dies. They mourn and prepare for her funeral.

First Stasimon (435-476)

The Chorus proclaims Alcestis' glory and undying fame.

Second Episode (477-577)

Heracles, engaged in one of his celebrated "Twelve Labors," comes to visit Admetus, who welcomes him. Out of courtesy to a guest, Admetus conceals from Heracles the fact that his wife has died. Despite Heracles' protestations, for he has been told of a death in Admetus' family, he offers him unrestricted hospitality.

Second Stasimon (578-605)

The Chorus sings the praises of Admetus as an exemplary host.

Third Episode (606-861)

Admetus enters at the head of Alcestis' funeral procession. His father, Pheres, comes uninvited to join the ceremonies. He praises Alcestis, but Admetus rejects his offerings, berates his father as selfish and cowardly for not offering to die in his place. Since he is no longer young, and has lived a full life, he should have died instead of Alcestis. Admetus then disowns his father and mother for their refusal to die for him. Pheres indignantly recounts all he has done for his son Admetus. He reminds Admetus that life is sweet for him too, declaring "I won't ask you to die for me, and I won't die for you." Pheres blames Alcestis' death on Admetus' selfishness and cowardice. The funeral procession then moves on.

A servant enters and relates how Heracles, entertained in the palace, became drunk and indulged in revelry. Heracles enters, somewhat tipsy, and is informed by the servant that it is Alcestis who has died. Sobered by this sorrowful news, he vows he will do all in his power to restore Alcestis to life. The hero then goes off to do battle with Death.

Kommos (862-1007)

Admetus returns from the funeral in utter desolation. The Chorus and Admetus in responsive lyrics exchange thoughts on his sad loss and on the inevitability of death.

Exodos (1008-1164)

Heracles enters leading a veiled woman by the hand. He offers her to Admetus, telling him he won her as a prize. Admetus begs Heracles to take her away; she reminds him of his wife. Heracles, however, encourages him to remarry, and presses him to accept the woman. Admetus finally accepts out of politeness to a guest. Then Heracles lifts the veil, and Alcestis is revealed alive, though she may not talk for three days. As Heracles departs on his appointed labor, Admetus proclaims a celebration throughout his realm.

INTERPRETATION

1. This play was presented as the fourth play of a trilogy, in place of a satyr play. Hence the fusion of comic and tragic elements.

2. Psychological study of a weak, dull, essentially selfish man, who permitted his devoted wife to die for him. Admetus in the end emerges humbled and ennobled by Alcestis' sacrifice.

3. Excess of a virtue (in this case, hospitality) proves Admetus' salvation.

MEDEA

BACKGROUND

When Jason came to Colchis in quest of the Golden Fleece, Medea, the king's daughter, who had the powers of a sorceress, fell madly in love with him and aided him in his dangerous mission. She fled her country with him, and, because of her overwhelming love for Jason, slew her own brother to aid them in their flight, and later caused the death of Jason's traitorous uncle. Banished from his own land, Iolcus, Jason with Medea received sanctuary in Corinth. Here they lived peacefully for ten years and had two sons. When Creon,

King of Corinth, offered Jason his daughter in marriage, he consented, for he was an ambitious man. Creon designated him suc-
cessor to the throne of Corinth.

Prologue (lines 1-130)

The Nurse of Medea's children prays that Jason had never come
to Colchis. For then began the passionate love of Medea for Jason,
on which account she committed murders. But now Medea hates
Jason because he abandoned her to marry the princess of Corinth.
Medea is ill and emotionally unstable. She is remorseful over her
crimes, and may yet commit other horrible deeds in revenge.

The children's male guardian enters with Medea's two sons, and
tells the Nurse of more bad news—that King Creon is about to
banish Medea and her children. The Nurse is shocked, and fearing
Medea's reaction plans to keep the children away from her.
Medea's voice is heard within bewailing her lot. The Nurse discourses on the wisdom of moderation.

Parodos (131-213)

The Chorus of Corinthian Women inquires from the Nurse about
Medea's troubles. As Medea's voice is heard lamenting, praying for
death, and threatening vengeance or suicide, the Chorus with
understanding consoles her and advises caution. The Nurse describes her fierce, emotional personality, and comments on the
sadness of life and the soothing comfort afforded by music.

First Episode (214-409)

Medea enters, self-possessed, and recounts in a formal, highly
rhetorical speech not only her own troubles, emphasizing that she is
an alien, but also the sorrows of married women in general. She will
find some way to avenge herself.

Creon enters and orders her out of Corinth with her children at
once. He has heard of her threats of vengeance, and fears her
powers. She deceitfully belittles her own cunning, vows that she will
hold her peace, and begs to be permitted to remain. When he is
adamant, she prevails upon him, as a father, to allow her one day

to prepare her departure and make provisions for her children. After he leaves, Medea reveals to the Chorus that her purpose in gaining a day was to accomplish some grim vengeance through sorcery, whatever the consequences.

First Stasimon (410-445)

The world is changing rapidly. Old standards are being shattered. Woman's place in society is gaining in importance. Medea is a woman of vitality and independence of mind.

Second Episode (446-626)

Jason enters, and tells Medea she has brought banishment upon herself by her threats. He offers her money to meet her needs, and advises her to hold her tongue. Medea then assails him bitterly in a passionate speech, pointing out many reasons why his divorcing her was unjust, and describing her future troubles as a homeless woman with children in an alien land. She insists she was completely altruistic in all she did for him. Jason, in an unconvincing rhetorical speech, attempts to refute her arguments one by one, insisting that he married the princess to better the fortunes of his sons and family. He rebukes the selfishness of married women, accusing her of egoism, jealousy and self-interest in desiring him all to herself. He claims selfless altruism in all his actions toward her and the children. Medea in turn throws up to him the fact that he married the princess secretly, and that his new bride is younger than herself, and that his purpose in marrying her was ambition. When she spurns his renewed offers of material assistance in her exile, he leaves her to settle her own problems.

Second Stasimon (627-662)

Unrestrained love is harmful. Moderation is best, especially in love. Exile from one's fatherland is a pitiful thing.

Third Episode (663-823)

Aegeus, King of Athens, passing through Corinth, greets Medea. She tells him of her troubles and begs for asylum in Athens. When she hears that he has been to the Delphic oracle because he has been childless, she promises to provide him with children through her magic skill. Unaware of the crimes she is planning, he swears an oath to give her sanctuary in Athens. After his departure Medea's plans for revenge are crystallized. She now realizes more than ever how much children may mean to a man, and she has decided to destroy all of Jason's hopes of issue. She will pretend to be reconciled to Jason's wishes, and will send her sons with poisoned gifts for the princess, which will cause her death and the death of all who touch her. Then she will kill her own children to prevent their falling into anyone's hands, and to deal a cruel blow to Jason.

Third Stasimon (824-865)

Athens is a blessed land. How will it receive a murderess who has killed her own children? How can a mother coldly do such a horrible deed?

Fourth Episode (866-975)

Jason enters, and Medea deceitfully begs forgiveness for her recent words of hate, claiming now to understand his action. He happily commends her change of heart. She asks him to intercede with Creon for permission that her sons remain in Corinth. She sends gifts with her children to Jason's wife—a robe and a diadem, both poisoned.

Fourth Stasimon (976-1001)

The Chorus pities the children, who will be accomplices in Medea's crime. Poor Medea, who is about to murder them too!

Fifth Episode (1002-1250)

The children's guardian enters and announces to Medea that the decree of exile has been rescinded for her children. Medea is now a "divided soul," torn between her love for her children and her desire to take even greater vengeance on Jason by slaying them. In this clash of her emotions, she first weakens in her purpose, as her mother love becomes dominant, but finally her grim hatred overwhelms all reason, and she is resolved to kill them.

Fifth Stasimon (1251-1292)

Rare is the woman of wisdom. Childless people do not suffer the endless cares of those who have children. Children do not always fulfill one's expectations.

Exodos (1293-1419)

A messenger arrives and describes in detail, as Medea gloats, the death of the princess and King Creon, who clasped his daughter as she was being consumed by the poisoned robe and diadem. With grim determination she rushes inside to kill her children. As the Chorus condemns Medea's action, the children's death cries are heard. Jason comes hurriedly to rescue his children from the fury of the people of Corinth. As he hears of the death of his sons, Medea miraculously appears above the house, acting as a kind of *deus ex machina,* in a chariot drawn by dragons. Jason regrets ever having known such a barbaric woman, bemoans the loss of all he held dear, and begs for the bodies of his sons, so that he may give them decent burial. Denying his request, and predicting his future unseemly death, she leaves him a completely broken man. She flies off in her chariot, bearing off the bodies of her slain children, to seek sanctuary with Aegeus in Athens.

INTERPRETATION

1. Euripides humanizes Medea and thus creates sympathy for all women, who suffer as inferiors in Greek society.

2. Uncontrolled emotions of hate and jealousy overcome reason and bring disaster to all.

3. Fear of insecurity can lead people to commit horrible crimes.

4. Internal conflict in Medea between emotions of mother love and desire for revenge.

5. Character study of an emotional oriental woman, an alien among the Greeks, whose love turns into hate and fierce desire for revenge.

6. "Hell hath no fury like a woman scorned."

HIPPOLYTUS

BACKGROUND

Hippolytus is the illegitimate son of Theseus, King of Athens, by the Amazon queen Hippolyte (in some versions, Antiope). He shuns women, and spends his time hunting. Theseus married the young princess of Crete, Phaedra, by whom he had several children. When Phaedra first saw Hippolytus she fell madly in love with her stepson, for he was handsome and about her own age. But being a virtuous married woman, though emotionally weak, she is determined to conceal her love for Hippolytus, no matter how much she suffers from unrequited love.

Prologue (lines 1-120)

Appearing before Theseus' palace at Troezen, Aphrodite, goddess of love, resents that Hippolytus, the son of Theseus and Hippolyte, ignores her worship and is a fervent devotee of Artemis, goddess of hunting. (Hippolytus is a smug, self-righteous, proud, tactless and unconventional person). Aphrodite announces that she will punish him for the slight to her. On this day she will bring it about that Theseus will hear of Phaedra's concealed passion for her stepson Hippolytus. In this way she will cause the deaths of both Hippolytus and Phaedra.

Hippolytus enters with his fellow-hunters. They praise Artemis exclusively, and Hippolytus places a wreath at her altar, boasting of his purity. An old hunter, symbolizing the experience of age, warns him against pride and his shunning of women. The hunter is shocked at his irreverence toward Aphrodite.

Parodos (121-175)

The Chorus of Women of Troezen has heard of Phaedra's illness. They speculate on the cause, suggesting insanity, or Theseus' love for another woman, or some trouble in Phaedra's own family in Crete, or that she is going to have a baby.

First Episode (176-524)

The Nurse brings Phaedra out and comments on her restlessness. She is deeply distressed at her illness. Phaedra is revealed as possessed by vanity in the midst of her fevered suffering. She raves, wishing she were in some woodland or mountainous region. Suddenly realizing that she has been talking of places associated with Hippolytus, she is consumed with shame, and hopes for swift death. She is a "divided soul," rent by her uncontrolled passion for Hippolytus and her concern for honor, family and society's opinions. The Nurse expresses her overwhelming love for her mistress, but praises moderation in all things. She then questions Phaedra about the cause of her illness, but Phaedra maintains silence. The Nurse warns her that if she allows herself to die, her children will be harmed, for Hippolytus will succeed to the throne. At the mention of his name, Phaedra starts up. Questioning her relentlessly, the Nurse discovers that she is in love with Hippolytus.

Phaedra, having unburdened herself, is now calm. She talks of the difficulties of following the path of righteousness. She is ashamed and resolved to die because of her uncontrolled passion for Hippolytus. She reviles unfaithful wives, who besmirch the family honor. Phaedra places honor before personal happiness. The Nurse in a clever speech full of sophistic argumentation gives her many reasons against her decision, and urges her to give in to her love, and thus save her life. Phaedra weakens somewhat, torn by the conflict between her passion and her honor.

First Stasimon (525-564)

The power of Eros (passion) is mighty. Even Heracles and Zeus were overpowered by Eros and loved outside their marriage ties.

Second Episode (565-731)

Quarreling voices are heard within. The Nurse, taking matters into her own hands, has approached Hippolytus. First asking him to swear an oath never to reveal what she has to say to him, she tells him that Phaedra desires him. Hippolytus is profoundly shocked. He rushes out in a towering rage, threatening to tell Theseus. He is reminded of his oath by the Nurse, but, he says, he does not feel bound by it under the circumstances. He thrusts the Nurse aside, and in Phaedra's presence bursts forth into a furious tirade against all women as the root of evil. After he leaves, Phaedra fumes against the Nurse for approaching Hippolytus, but the Nurse tries to defend herself, arguing that she did it out of love for Phaedra, and that, if she had succeeded, Phaedra would not be thus assailing her.

Her love now turned to hate, through the injury to her vanity and pride, Phaedra knows only one way to save the honor of her family and punish Hippolytus—to kill herself and drag down Hippolytus with her in death.

Second Stasimon (732-775)

The Chorus wishes there were some escape from this mess by running far away. Poor unhappy Phaedra!

Third Episode (776-1101)

Phaedra has committed suicide by hanging herself. At this moment Theseus arrives happily from a journey, only to discover his wife's death. As he bewails this new misfortune in his sea of troubles, he observes a note tied to Phaedra's wrist. Phaedra's suicide note accuses Hippolytus of having violated her. In uncontrolled fury, he impulsively prays to Poseidon to grant him one of three promised wishes by killing Hippolytus that very day. He then orders him banished.

Hippolytus enters to greet his father and discovers Phaedra's body. At first his inquiries as to the cause of her death meet with stony silence. But then Theseus assails him as a corrupt man who conceals his evil intention under an outward cloak of purity, and orders him into banishment. Hippolytus defends his innocence, emphasizing his purity and his universally known character. He is about to reveal what he knows, but his sense of honor compels him to uphold his oath to the Nurse. When he mentions the manner of his own birth from the ravished Hippolyte, Theseus in a rage orders him out at once. Hippolytus bids a sad farewell.

Third Stasimon (1102-1150)

Life is full of chance and unexpected suffering. O, for some happiness in this life! Poor unhappy Hippolytus!

Exodos (1151-1466)

One of Hippolytus' friends enters in haste and reports in detail how, as Hippolytus was leaving Troezen in his chariot, great tidal waves and a sea-monster sent by Poseidon frightened Hippolytus' horses. Hippolytus has been mortally wounded. Theseus is moved, and asks to see Hippolytus. As the Chorus comments on Aphrodite's success in punishing Hippolytus' pride, Artemis suddenly appears above the palace on a cloud. She tells the stricken Theseus the entire truth, and berates him for his haste in condemning the pure Hippolytus. The dying Hippolytus is brought in, suffering from great pain. He converses reverently with his beloved Artemis. She consoles him with the promise that one day she will take vengeance on Aphrodite by killing one of her devotees (Adonis is meant). Forgiving his remorseful father, and embracing him, Hippolytus dies in his arms.

INTERPRETATION

1. Conflicts between conventional standards set up by society and individual needs to achieve personal happiness; between the power of sex and ascetic chastity; between uncontrolled passion and excessively controlled emotion.

2. Moderation and harmony between these conflicting forces are desirable to avoid suffering.

3. Criticism of jealous, vindictive gods of popular religion who remain in conflict at the end, while human beings humanely reconcile their differences when the truth is known. The three divinities who affect the action of the play, Aphrodite, Artemis, and Poseidon, are not dramatically necessary. They are employed as conceived in Greek popular religion, for the sake of satirizing them. "Gods who do shameful things are no gods at all," reads a fragment

from one of Euripides' lost plays. For Sophocles' view see p. 72.

4. Psychological study of unrequited love, involving the "eternal triangle;" of uncontrolled emotions and human weaknesses causing tragedy; of pride, vanity, fear, jealousy, insecurity, and anger overcoming reason.

THE CHILDREN OF HERACLES

BACKGROUND

Eurystheus, King of Argos, persecuted Heracles, imposing upon him the Twelve Labors. After Heracles' death and deification, Eurystheus transferred his hatred to Heracles' family. Attended by Iolaüs, Heracles' old friend and war-comrade, they have wandered far and wide seeking asylum, pursued by Eurystheus' malice.

Prologue (lines 1-72)

The scene is set before the temple of Zeus at Marathon near Athens. Iolaüs enters, accompanied by Heracles' small sons. They are suppliants at Zeus' altar. Iolaüs tells of Eurystheus' continual persecution of Heracles' family and of their exile and wandering. Wherever they go, Eurystheus, through his political power and agents, causes them to be expelled. Now they have come to Marathon. Alcmene, Heracles' aged mother, is guarding the small daughters of Heracles inside the temple.

Copreus, the herald of Eurystheus, arrives and attempts to seize the boys. In the struggle, he casts Iolaüs to the ground.

Parodos and First Episode (73-352)

The Chorus of old men of Marathon, shocked at the brutality of Copreus, learns of the identity of the refugees. Demophon, son of Theseus and king of Athens, enters with his brother Acamas. Copreus declares he has come to recover escaped Argive natives, who have been condemned to death. He offers Athens the friendship of Eurystheus if the refugees are released to him; the alternative is war.

Iolaüs declares that they are voluntary exiles, and that they place their trust in the repute of Athens as an asylum for the oppressed.

Besides, there are blood ties between Heracles and the royal family
of Athens; moreover, Heracles once saved the life of Theseus,
Demophon's father; finally, they are suppliants at the holy altar.
Demophon forthrightly decides in favor of Heracles' family, in the
name of piety and honor. Copreus tries again to seize the children.
He is repulsed, and departs threatening war against Athens.

Iolaüs expresses his gratitude to Demophon, who departs to
mobilize his army.

First Stasimon (353-380)

The Chorus sings of Athenian valor and the traditions of Athens
as an asylum for refugees.

Second Episode (381-607)

Demophon declares to Iolaüs that Athens is prepared for defense.
He is distraught because it has been prophesied that Athens must
sacrifice a young woman of noble birth to the goddess Persephone.
Thereupon Iolaüs offers to surrender himself to Eurystheus to prevent further suffering. At this point Macaria, Heracles' young
daughter, enters and bravely offers herself as the sacrificial victim.
She bids farewell and departs to her death.

Second Stasimon (608-628)

The Chorus sings of the ups and downs of life. Noble Macaria!

Third Episode (629-747)

The attendant of Heracles' eldest son, Hyllus, arrives. Alcmene
comes out to hear the news—that Hyllus has come with troops and
has united his forces with Demophon's. Iolaüs, though aged, arms
himself and leaves to join the troops.

Third Stasimon (748-783)

The Chorus praises Athens and her piety to the gods, and prays
to Athena, patron goddess of the city.

Fourth Episode (784-890)

An attendant reports to Alcmene that the enemy has been conquered. Hyllus and Iolaüs are both safe. In battle Iolaüs was re-

juvenated and covered himself with glory. He describes the battle in detail. Hyllus offered single combat to Eurystheus, but he would not accept. Eurystheus has, in fact, been taken prisoner, and will soon be brought in.

Fourth Stasimon (891-927)

The Chorus dances an ode of joy, honoring Zeus, Heracles and Athens.

Exodos (928-1055)

Eurystheus is brought in, bound in chains, before Alcmene. She heaps violent abuse on him for his treatment of Heracles and his family. When she declares he deserves to be killed at once, the Chorus expresses its horror at mistreatment of a prisoner of war, who enjoys protection under Athenian law.

Eurystheus proudly defends himself, asking for no mercy. He tells of an old oracle that his body, buried in Athens, will protect the city some day against descendants of Heracles. Alcmene and the Chorus, now cognizant of the advantage for Athens in having the body of Eurystheus buried on their soil, agree to his death, and he is taken away to be slain.

INTERPRETATION

1. This play is not a tragedy, but melodrama.
2. It is a wartime play, containing patriotic elements, glorifying Athens as a refuge for the oppressed, as a devout and law-abiding city.
3. It exposes the brutalizing effect of war on all.

ANDROMACHE

BACKGROUND

After the capture of Troy Andromache, widow of Hector, was given as war booty to Achilles' son Neoptolemus, and she became his slave-concubine. Menelaüs brought Helen back to Sparta. Their daughter Hermione, long betrothed to her cousin Orestes, son of

Agamemnon, was given in marriage to Neoptolemus for political reasons. Their marriage has been childless.

Prologue (lines 1-116)

The scene is before the house of Neoptolemus in Thessaly; nearby is the shrine of Thetis. Andromache sadly recalls her tragic life since the death of Hector and the fall of Troy. She bore Neoptolemus a son, Molossus. Later Neoptolemus married Hermione, who, because of her childlessness, has been persecuting her, accusing her of alienating her husband and making her childless by secret spells. Now Menelaüs, in the absence of Neoptolemus, has come to aid Hermione in bringing about Andromache's death. Therefore she has taken refuge in the shrine of Thetis, and has hidden her son because she fears for his life. Neoptolemus has gone to Delphi to expiate his previous impiety in demanding of Apollo why Achilles was slain.

Her handmaiden brings her news that Menelaüs and Hermione are plotting the death of her son. She sends the handmaiden to summon King Peleus, Neoptolemus' grandfather. Andromache mourns her sad lot, the death of Hector, and her enslavement.

Parodos (117-146)

The Chorus of Phthian Women sympathizes with and pities Andromache's hard lot.

First Episode (147-463)

Hermione, resplendent in her royal attire, enters. She attacks Andromache as the cause of her estrangement from Neoptolemus and her barrenness. She threatens her with death or a lowly position as a scrubwoman in her own household. She rebukes her for her moral insensibility in having slept with the son of the man who killed her husband.

Andromache reminds the younger Hermione of her present lowly status. Hermione's incompatibility with her husband is due to her own faults: her Spartan arrogance and provincialism, her jealousy and insecurity. Andromache, as a good wife should, indulged Hec-

tor in his occasional marital infidelities. She counsels her not to
rival her sex-ridden mother Helen. As they abuse each other,
Hermione threatens to burn her out of the shrine if she does not
leave voluntarily.

After she departs, Andromache comments that women are the
worst evil in the world. The Chorus recounts the Judgment of
Paris and the ensuing Trojan War with all its suffering.

Menelaüs enters leading Andromache's son Molossus. He threatens to kill him if she does not leave the shrine. She heaps scorn on
his reputation as a warrior-king at Troy. She warns him of the
consequences of his violent deeds and puts her trust in Neoptolemus. Menelaüs defends his acts as necessary expedients in the interest of his daughter. To every woman her husband is the most
important person in the world. Either Andromache or Molossus
must die. Andromache defends herself as an innocent victim of
war's evils. She offers her life for her son's. She is promptly seized,
and informed that Menelaüs' ruse has succeeded. The fate of
Molossus is to be put into Hermione's hands. At this Andromache
lets forth a tirade against the Spartan people, accusing them of
treachery, lying, hypocrisy, injustice, murder and greed. She departs hurling defiance at him.

First Stasimon (464-500)

The Chorus comments on the evil consequences of disunity in
the home, in the government of cities, and on shipboard. They condemn Hermione and pity Andromache and her innocent son.

Second Episode (501-765)

Menelaüs ushers in Andromache and Molossus, who are both
in chains. They are informed that they are both to be slain. As they
mourn their sorrows, Menelaüs is cruelly insensitive to their
suffering.

The aged King Peleus arrives, and learns of Menelaüs' intentions
from Andromache. He orders their release. When Menelaüs defies
him, he heaps scorn on Menelaüs, Helen and Spartan women,
blaming the sufferings of the Trojan War on him. He had warned

his grandson Neoptolemus not to marry Hermione, the daughter of adulterous, worthless Helen. He defends Andromache and Molossus.

Menelaüs replies that Andromache was the sister-in-law of Paris, who slew Peleus' son Achilles, and seeks to defend his acts in an unconvincing, rhetorical speech. Peleus defends the character of humble folk as against the arrogance and ambition of aristocrats, and removes the bonds from the hands of Andromache and her son.

Menelaüs retires, alleging the urgency of a military expedition against a city near Sparta. He intends to return later and confront his son-in-law Neoptolemus, to see if he will aid him in disposing of Andromache. Peleus promises protection of her and her son.

Second Stasimon (766-801)

The Chorus respects noble birth and riches, but the use of power to gain unjust victories through violence is to be shunned. Praise to the noble hero Peleus!

Third Episode (802-1008)

The Nurse tells that Hermione, now fearful of what Neoptolemus may do when he hears of her plot against Andromache, and filled with remorse, tried to kill herself. Hermione rushes in, raving hysterically and talking of suicide. Menelaüs has gone off without her, and she fears Neoptolemus and loneliness.

At this moment Orestes, Menelaüs' nephew, depicted in this play as a brutal, callous ruffian, enters. Hermione rushes to him for protection and consolation. She tells of her jealousy of Andromache. Orestes declares he has come to take Hermione away with him, for she was originally betrothed to him. Then he informs her that he has set a trap for Neoptolemus and arranged for friends at Delphi to kill him there at the oracular shrine with the aid of the god Apollo, whom Neoptolemus once offended. The cousins go off together—the wife of Neoptolemus with his murderer.

Third Stasimon (1009-1046)

The Chorus recounts the suffering of Troy and of the House of Atreus, blaming Apollo. "O Phoebus, how am I to believe?"

Exodos (1047-1288)

Peleus has heard of Hermione's departure with Orestes. The Chorus tells him of Orestes' plot against Neoptolemus.

A messenger enters, and announces the murder of Neoptolemus, telling in detail how it happened—that he was slain, while praying in the temple of Apollo, by Orestes himself and his agents in a ghastly battle. This, says the messenger, is how Apollo metes out justice to those who seek to make amends.

The body of Neoptolemus is brought in. Peleus bewails his dead grandson, and blames his death on the marriage with Hermione and on the god Apollo.

Suddenly the sea-goddess Thetis, wife of Peleus, appears as the *deus ex machina*. Neoptolemus is to be buried in Delphi. Andromache is to be married to Hector's brother Helenus, now in the Molossian country, and she will through Molossus become the founder of a new royal line. Peleus she will soon transform into a god and take to live with her in the palace of her father, the sea-god Nereus.

INTERPRETATION

1. Political attack on the arrogance, treachery, ruthlessness, stupidity, and unprincipled behavior of Sparta.

2. Attack on the oracle of Apollo at Delphi (which was pro-Spartan during the Peloponnesian War).

3. Study of female psychology: how jealousy, fear, insecurity drove Hermione to brutality and degradation.

HECUBA

BACKGROUND

During the Trojan War Priam and Hecuba, king and queen of Troy, had entrusted their youngest son Polydorus to Polymestor, King of Thrace. They also gave him a large quantity of gold to hold in safekeeping. When the war ended, Polymestor killed the youth to obtain the fortune. Hecuba is now the slave of Agamemnon,

whose army has stopped at the Thracian Chersonese on the way
home to Greece.

Prologue (lines 1-97)

The scene is set before Agamemnon's tent. The ghost of Polydorus, youngest son of Hecuba and Priam, appears. He tells how
he had been entrusted to Polymestor, friend of Priam, and, after
news of the Trojan defeat reached the Thracian Chersonese, was
treacherously slain for the fortune in gold placed in his trust. He
also tells that his sister Polyxena is to be sacrificed by the Greeks
to appease Achilles' spirit.

Aged Hecuba comes from Agamemnon's tent. She is terrified by
visions she had during the night that make her apprehensive about
the fate of Polydorus and Polyxena.

Parodos (98-153)

The Chorus of captive Trojan Women tells Hecuba that the
Greeks have decided to sacrifice Polyxena at Achilles' tomb.

First Episode (154-443)

Hecuba shrieks lamentations to the skies. She tells the sorrowful
news to Polyxena, who accepts it with resignation. Odysseus enters
to take Polyxena away. Hecuba pleads for her daughter's life, begging him to convince the Greeks to rescind the decision. She reminds Odysseus that she once spared his life, and that he promised
her eternal gratitude. If anyone is to be sacrificed, it should be
Helen. Odysseus asserts he promised to spare Hecuba's life only.
The soul of Achilles merits an unusual sacrifice, to honor properly
the brave deeds he wrought for his countrymen.

Polyxena refuses to humble herself by begging for her life. She
proudly prefers death to a life of slavery, for she is the daughter of
a king. Hecuba asks to be killed with her daughter. Polyxena counsels resignation, bids a tearful farewell, and departs with Odysseus.

First Stasimon (444-483)

The Chorus laments its enslavement and its sorrows, wondering
to what part of Greece they will be taken.

Second Episode (484-628)

The herald Talthybius enters to take Hecuba to bury Polyxena. He tells Hecuba how, in full view of the Greek host, Polyxena was sacrificed at the tomb of Achilles by his son Neoptolemus. She prepares to leave to give Polyxena proper burial.

Second Stasimon (629-656)

The Chorus laments the woes unleashed for Greeks and Trojans by Paris' love for Helen.

Third Episode (657-904)

A servant enters with attendants bearing a corpse. It is the body of Polydorus, just discovered washed up from the sea onto the shore. Hecuba laments anew, surmising that Polymester slew him for the gold.

Agamemnon enters to enquire about Hecuba's delay in caring for Polyxena's body. Hecuba tells him about Polydorus, and entreats him to help her take vengeance on Polymestor. She plays on his emotions, asking his aid in the name of the love he bears for her daughter Cassandra. Agamemnon at first will not become involved in the death of their host, the Thracian king, for fear of the Greek army. However, Hecuba succeeds in winning from him the promise to keep secret her plan to avenge herself on Polymestor. She sends someone to summon Polymestor and his children.

Third Stasimon (905-952)

The Chorus laments the fall of Troy, its destruction, and their own enslavement. Accursed Helen and Paris!

Exodos (953-1295)

Polymestor and his children arrive. He weeps crocodile tears for Hecuba. When she tells him she must speak to him and his children in private, he dismisses his guards. He lyingly tells her that Polydorus is still alive and that the gold is secure. She pretends she knows of certain hidden vaults of gold belonging to Priam, and that she has additional treasure in her tent. They all enter the tent.

The anguished cries of Polymestor are soon heard. His two children have been slain and he has been blinded. Polymestor rushes out, blood streaming from his eyes. As he bellows for aid, Agamemnon appears and learns what has happened. Polymestor declares he killed Polydorus out of friendship for the Greeks, to prevent his becoming some day an avenger for the destruction of Troy. He tells how, when they entered the tent, they found many Trojan women there, who stabbed his children; then some of them held him while others stabbed out his eyes.

Hecuba, in a vigorous, rhetorical speech, unmasks Polymestor's deception and his betrayal of a guest-friend relationship for the sake of money. Agamemnon thereupon refuses to aid Polymestor because of his crime. Polymestor now predicts that Hecuba will be transformed into a bitch, and that Cassandra is to die at the hands of Agamemnon's wife Clytemnestra, who will also slay Agamemnon himself. Enraged, Agamemnon orders him dragged away by his guards and cast on a desert island. He then orders Hecuba and the Trojan women to prepare for the voyage to Greece.

INTERPRETATION

1. This play is not a tragedy, but a melodrama.
2. War, greed, superstition, political expediency bring out the worst in humanity and cause suffering for all.
3. War has a brutalizing effect on everyone.

THE CYCLOPS

BACKGROUND

Silenus and the Satyrs, followers of Dionysus, wandering in search of the god, landed in Sicily, near Mt. Aetna, where they were enslaved by the Cyclops Polyphemus. (This play is the only extant complete satyr play.)

Prologue (lines 1-40)

The scene is before the cave of Polyphemus at Aetna. Silenus tells how he and the Satyrs sailed in search of the wandering god

Dionysus, and were driven by bad weather to the land of the one-eyed giants, the Cyclopes. Here they were captured by Polyphemus, and are now his slaves, tending his flocks of sheep and doing other menial tasks.

Parodos (41-81)

The Chorus of Satyrs prays to Bacchus, telling of their present indignities.

First Episode (82-355)

They espy a Greek ship, and soon Odysseus and his men enter, looking for food and water. Odysseus learns of the cannibalistic nature of the Cyclopes. In exchange for cheese and lambs he gives wine to Silenus, which he drinks eagerly.

Suddenly Polyphemus appears, to the consternation of everyone. Silenus betrays Odysseus and his men, and Polyphemus decides to eat the strangers as a change of diet. Odysseus begs Polyphemus to spare him and his men because of their piety to the gods, including Poseidon, Polyphemus' father. Polyphemus scorns the request, and drives them into the cave.

First Stasimon (356-374)

The Chorus tells of the cooking and devouring of some of the Greeks by Polyphemus.

Second Episode (375-482)

Odysseus comes out of the cave and relates in horrible detail how two of his men were roasted and eaten. Odysseus plied Polyphemus with wine and made him drunk. He now tells the Chorus of a clever plan he has conceived to enable them all to escape from the clutches of the Cyclops. When he falls asleep he will burn out his one eye with a sharpened and heated stake.

Second Stasimon (483-518)

The Chorus anticipates the blinding of the Cyclops, and praises the drinking of wine.

Exodos (519-709)

The Cyclops enters, tipsy and asking for more wine. He wants to share it with his brothers, but Odysseus dissuades him. When he asks Odysseus his name, he replies, "Noman." Polyphemus, in gratitude, promises to eat him last of all. He continues to drink, then enters the cave to sleep.

The Chorus aids Odysseus in preparing the stake, but, in fear, they beg off from participating in the burning out of Polyphemus' eye. Odysseus enters the cave, and soon they hear the anguished cries of Polyphemus. The Cyclops blocks the exit from the cave to prevent the escape of the Greeks. As the Chorus taunts him, the Greeks escape by clinging to the undersides of the sheep as they are let out of the cave. Odysseus now reveals his identity. Polyphemus predicts that Odysseus will wander over the seas. As the blind Cyclops threatens them, the Greeks and the Chorus depart for the shore.

INTERPRETATION

This satyr play contains much humor and buffoonery, affording light entertainment through the burlesquing of a myth.

MAD HERACLES

BACKGROUND

Heracles was persecuted by the goddess Hera ever since his birth. Before departing on the last of his Twelve Labors, namely, the descent to Hades to seize the dog Cerberus, he entrusted his aged father Amphitryon, his wife Megara and their three sons to his father-in-law Creon, King of Thebes. In his absence Lycus of Euboea killed Creon and usurped the throne of Thebes with the aid of dissidents in the city. Lycus is determined to wipe out all the relatives of Heracles, whom he believes to be dead, in order to solidify his power.

Prologue (lines 1-106)

The scene is the royal palace of Thebes; nearby an altar of Zeus. Amphitryon tells of Heracles' long absence on his exploit to bring back Cerberus to earth. The tyrant Lycus has decided to kill Amphitryon, Megara and Heracles' sons to prevent the rise of an avenger. Therefore they have taken refuge at the altar of Zeus, friendless and in desperate need. Megara and the children, in tears, yearn for Heracles. Amphitryon comforts them.

Parodos (107-137)

The Chorus of Theban Elders greets the suppliants and praises the hero Heracles and his children.

First Episode (138-347)

Lycus, asserting that Heracles will never return from Hades, advises Amphitryon, Megara and the children to prepare for death. He scorns the exploits of Heracles, calling him a coward. Amphitryon defends his son's valor and fame. He requests permission for his family to leave Thebes unharmed, and upbraids the Thebans for their cowardice and ingratitude to Heracles, and for not coming to the defense of the family of the heroic benefactor of Greece. Lycus, in anger, orders logs to be brought to burn them to death at the altar. The Chorus heaps indignation on Lycus. Megara bravely urges that they submit to the inevitable and die with honor, so as to be worthy of the great Heracles. Amphitryon begs that he and Megara be slain first; Megara requests and receives permission to deck her sons in funeral attire. Amphitryon questions the wisdom and justice of Zeus.

First Stasimon (348-450)

The Chorus sings of the Twelve Labors of the hero Heracles, whereby he exhibited his famed strength and cunning and rid Hellas of many monsters and evils.

Second Episode (451-636)

Megara bewails their unhappy lot, bemoaning the blighted hopes of her children for glory, and her own shattered life. She prays for Heracles' aid. As they are saying their farewells, Heracles suddenly returns. When he hears of the state of affairs, he girds for action against Lycus, rebuking the Thebans for cowardice and ingratitude. He comforts his family affectionately and leads them to their home.

Second Stasimon (637-700)

The Chorus sings of the sweetness of youth and the sadness of old age. They also sing the praises of glorious Heracles.

Third Episode (701-762)

Lycus returns, and finding only Amphitryon hurries off to Heracles' house to seize Megara and her sons. The death cries of Lycus and his bodyguard are heard.

Third Stasimon (763-821)

The Chorus dances a song of rejoicing for the deliverance of Thebes from the tyrant. Hail Heracles!

Exodos (822-1428)

Iris, the messenger of Hera, and Madness suddenly appear above the palace. Now that his Twelve Labors are over, Hera has decided to visit a terrible punishment on Heracles, whom she has always hated because he was reputed to be an illegitimate child of Zeus. She will cause Heracles to become mad and slay his family. Madness pleads with Iris to spare the great, pious hero, but in vain. Madness enters the palace of Heracles, as the Chorus waits with ineffectual trepidation.

A servant enters, and reports in detail the onset of Heracles' sudden madness, and his insane raving. Thinking his children to be the sons of King Eurystheus, who imposed on him the Twelve Labors, he slew his sons and Megara who tried to protect them. Athena saved Amphitryon. Then Heracles fell into a coma, and the slaves bound him to a pillar.

Heracles gradually wakes, having recovered his sanity. When Amphitryon tells him what he has done, Heracles, feeling polluted by his crime, wants to commit suicide. Heracles veils himself in order not to pollute others.

Theseus, King of Athens, out of gratitude to Heracles for rescuing him from Hades, has come with an army to help expel the usurper Lycus. When he learns what has happened, he is profoundly sympathetic and requests Heracles to uncover himself. Theseus is skeptical about the concept of pollution. He declares that suicide is not worthy of the hero Heracles. The latter recalls the sadness in his life, the continual hatred of Hera, his many dangerous exploits. He feels completely unclean and prefers death. Theseus urges him to leave Thebes in exile and come to Athens, where he will be purified, honored and accorded the glories of a demigod at death. Heracles, suddenly ashamed at his cowardice, agrees that it behooves him to endure his lot with dignity. He sadly arranges for the burial of Megara and his sons and bids farewell to his father as he leaves for Athens with Theseus.

INTERPRETATION

1. This play attacks conventional anthropomorphic theology.

2. Much human suffering is undeserved, not due to personal flaws of character. In this case the greatest Hellenic hero, famed for his benefactions to the Greeks and his piety to the gods, is crushed by the ingratitude of men and gods. The universe is irrational, and innocent people often suffer through chance and external forces. The reversal of fortune comes at the height of the hero's greatness, but it is undeserved.

3. The courage to live on, in the face of the most extreme adversity, is the noblest quality of man.

4. The loyalty of loved ones in the family and of true friends relieves human suffering in a brutal world.

5. Athens is the haven of the oppressed.

THE SUPPLIANTS

BACKGROUND

The expedition of the Seven against Thebes, led by Polynices and his father-in-law Adrastus, King of Argos, was defeated by the Thebans. The victorious Thebans refused to allow the burial of the slain Argive chieftains.

Prologue (lines 1-41)

The scene is before the temple of Demeter at Eleusis, near
Athens. Aethra, mother of Theseus, King of Athens, prays that the
aged suppliant mothers of the fallen Argive champions may be able
to bury their dead. Adrastus, King of Argos and father-in-law of
Polynices, lies at the altar overwhelmed with grief. The mothers of
the dead warriors have entreated Aethra to persuade her son
Theseus to help restore their dead to them. She has summoned
Theseus.

Parodos (42-87)

The Chorus of Argive mothers entreats Aethra again to help.
They bewail their unburied dead.

First Episode (88-364)

Theseus enters, and Aethra tells him who the suppliants are. She
points out Adrastus and the sons of the dead chieftains. Adrastus
tells him of his defeat, clasps his knees in entreaty, and begs him
to help restore the dead for decent burial. Only mighty Athens,
which always aids the suffering, can help them.

Theseus states his belief that man is a rational being, but that his
happiness is marred by pride, unrighteous war, ambition and religious confusion. Why should the peace of Athens be disturbed because of Adrastus' errors? The Chorus entreats his aid. Aethra,
pitying them, weeps. She urges Theseus, in the name of piety and
honor, to aid the women in performing the rites of the dead, according to immemorial custom.

Theseus agrees to use his power to this end. He will use persuasion or force, but he must first put the matter to a vote by the
Athenian people.

First Stasimon (365-380)

The Chorus prays that Theseus may succeed.

Second Episode (381-597)

Theseus decides to send a herald to Creon, King of Thebes, to
request the bodies for burial. Failing peaceful settlement, the al-

ternative will be war. The people of Athens have voted their approval of this course of action.

Just then a Theban herald arrives. Theseus proclaims to him that Athens is a democracy and shuns despotism. The Theban herald reports that Thebes forbids Athens to grant asylum to Adrastus. They must expel him this very day; otherwise, he warns, war will be declared. Theseus asserts that Thebes, by this decision, is injuring not only Argos but all of Hellas, by denying the right of burial. He will bury the dead, by force if necessary: piety, justice and custom require it. Theseus orders mobilization of his forces.

Second Stasimon (598-633)

The Chorus is fearful of the outcome and prays for Theseus' success.

Third Episode (634-954)

A messenger arrives, and reports the victory of Theseus over Thebes. He describes the battle in detail. After the victory, Theseus restrained his men from further violence when he had achieved his purpose of obtaining the bodies.

Adrastus, a chastened man, asserts the almighty power of Zeus and the folly of men. Cities that could end their disputes by arbitration resort instead to needless war.

The bodies of the seven chiefs are brought in. Adrastus and the Chorus chant a dirge. Theseus requests to be told the lineage of the fallen men. Adrastus pronounces a eulogy over each of them. The burials are arranged for; the body of Capaneus, who was struck by lightning, is to be buried apart. The bodies are removed, and soon the fire from the funeral pyres is seen.

Third Stasimon (955-989)

The Chorus bewail their dead sons.

Exodos (990-1234)

Evadne, wife of Capaneus, is seen on a rock overhanging the burning funeral pyre of her husband. She chants a song of sorrow for her blighted marriage, and plans to leap into her husband's pyre. Iphis, her father, enters. His son Eteoclus, Evadne's brother, is also one of the dead chiefs. Despite his pleas, she leaps into the pyre to her death. Iphis, bereft of his entire family, bewails his lot.

The Chorus and the children of the slain chieftains chant a lament, carrying the ashes of their husbands and fathers in funeral urns. Theseus admonishes the children to remember the boon of Athens, and to hand down this memory to their descendants. Adrastus promises eternal gratitude to Athens from Argos.

Suddenly Athena appears on high as the *deus ex machina*. She advises Theseus to have Adrastus swear a sacred oath of friendship and peace between Athens and Argos. She promises that some day the sons of the dead Argive chieftains will win vengeance against Thebes. Preparations for the oath are made.

INTERPRETATION

1. This play is not a tragedy, but an episodic drama whose principal purpose is political.

2. It is basically a glorification of Athens, with reservations. It praises Athenian democracy, its traditional aid to the oppressed, and its piety.

3. It condemns war as a means of settling disputes.

4. Lack of reason and folly, especially of political leaders, leads to suffering for all.

ION

Prologue (lines 1-183)

The scene is before the temple of Apollo at Delphi. The god Hermes tells how Apollo raped Creusa, the daughter of King Erechtheus of Athens, in a cave there. She bore a baby boy, and exposed it with a cradle and some tokens in the same cave. The child was saved by the god, taken away to the temple at Delphi, and brought up by the priestess there, without either knowing his true identity. He grew up as a temple attendant. Meanwhile, Creusa was married to Xuthus, an Achaean, who is now king of Athens.

They are childless, and because of this have come to the oracle at Delphi. It is Apollo's purpose now to declare the boy the son of Xuthus, to conceal his amour with Creusa.

Ion, the son of Apollo and Creusa, enters from the temple, and sings of Apollo's glories and powers. He tells of his own service to the temple, and looks on Apollo as his own father. He purifies and cleanses the temple.

Parodos (184-218)

The Chorus of Creusa's maids admires the sculptures on the temple.

First Episode (219-451)

The Chorus learns from Ion some of the rules governing the temple. Creusa enters, and converses with Ion, who inquires of her ancestry. She tells him of the mission of her husband and herself—to inquire of the oracle about their childlessness. She and Ion are attracted to each other. She pretends that she also came on behalf of a friend who had had a child by Apollo and now desires to know where the child is. Ion declares that the oracle will not shame the god by revealing his secret.

Xuthus arrives and promptly enters the temple. Ion is disturbed about what he has heard of Apollo's behavior. The gods, he declares, should be virtuous and not require of men what they themselves do not practice.

First Stasimon (452-508)

The Chorus prays to Athena and Artemis for aid in ending the childlessness of Creusa and Xuthus. Unhappy the union of Apollo and Creusa!

Second Episode (509-675)

Xuthus comes forth from the temple, and at once greets Ion as his son. The oracle of Apollo had revealed to him that the first man he should meet as he left the temple is his son. Xuthus surmises that Ion was born of a youthful affair he had had. Xuthus is overjoyed, but Ion is depressed because of the uncertain future that awaits him as the illegitimate son of an alien in Athens whose wife is childless and likely, therefore, to hate him. Besides, a king's life is full of unhappiness, and he prefers the moderate, peaceful life he has enjoyed at Delphi as attendant of the god. Xuthus prevails upon him to come to Athens, and plans to keep his identity a secret from Creusa. He warns the Chorus, on pain of death, to keep the secret from Creusa. The two leave to celebrate their reunion.

Second Stasimon (676-724)

The Chorus pities Creusa and dreads the oracle's disclosure, regarding it as an underhanded trick. They heap abuse on Xuthus and Ion.

Third Episode (725-1047)

Creusa and an Old Retainer enter. The Chorus tells Creusa she will never bear a child, and that Xuthus has a son. Creusa is crushed. The Old Retainer declares that Xuthus, an alien in Athens, has betrayed her. He believes that Xuthus had a son by a slave girl and invented the story attributed to the god, because all along he planned to have his illegitimate son succeed him. He counsels Creusa to kill both her husband and Ion, and offers assistance. Creusa resolves, at the expense of her good name, to expose Apollo as her seducer. She reviles the god for abandoning her and her baby. The Old Retainer is shocked by her story, and now all the more urges her to kill the boy Ion. She gives the man poison and instructs him how to kill Ion in the temple.

Third Stasimon (1048-1105)

The Chorus prays for the success of Creusa's plan to get rid of Ion. May he never be king of Athens! Men are more sinful than women.

Exodos (1106-1622)

A slave of Creusa rushes in to report that the Delphians are hunting for Creusa to kill her. While Ion was preparing a feast in honor of his reunion with his supposed father, the Old Retainer offered his services in dispensing refreshments. He put the poison in Ion's cup, but the trick was discovered, and he confessed. The rulers of Delphi then voted to put Creusa to death. The Chorus laments the unfortunate turn of events.

Creusa enters in terror, seeking to escape the vengeance of the Delphians. She clings to the altar as a suppliant. Ion and the armed Delphians enter. She defends her acts on the grounds that Ion has no right to the throne of Athens. Ion is deterred from dragging her off by a grudging respect for the sanctity of Apollo's altar.

At this point the prophetess of the temple of Apollo enters carrying the basket in which Ion was brought to Delphi as a baby. It contains tokens of his birth, which will help him discover his mother. She removes the swaddling clothes from the cradle. Creusa recognizes them, and embraces Ion. By describing the other objects in the cradle she convinces Ion that she is his mother. Reluctantly she tells him that Apollo is his father. He is skeptical, finding this difficult to reconcile with Apollo's declaration that he is Xuthus' son. "Is the god true or are his oracles lies?" He insists on the truth, and is about to enter the temple in order to question the oracle.

Suddenly Athena appears as the *deus ex machina*. Apollo sent her because he was unable to face them. Apollo devised the deception that Xuthus was his father in order to protect him from harm until he came to Athens as an accepted member of the royal family. Ion is to be taken to Athens, and he will become king of the city. He is to be the ancestor of the Ionians. Xuthus will have two sons by Creusa, Dorus and Aeolus, the ancestors of the Dorians and the Aeolians. Athena orders them to conceal the identity of Ion's father from Xuthus. Creusa and Ion offer praise to Apollo.

INTERPRETATION

1. This play is basically a thrilling melodrama, an obvious forerunner of the New Comedy with its romantic theme, intrigue, coincidences, and recognition of a foundling through tokens.

2. It is typically Euripidean in its exposure of traditional Olympian theology and the Delphic oracle.

3. It portrays the disillusionment and intellectual revolt of an attendant of the temple of Apollo.

TROJAN WOMEN

BACKGROUND

Troy has just been captured through the stratagem of the Wooden Horse. The captive Trojan women have been herded into huts before the burning city.

Prologue (lines 1-152)

Poseidon, god of the sea, stands before the walls of Troy, which he once had helped build, and laments the fall of the city. As he tells sadly of the captured Trojan women who are about to be apportioned to the Greek leaders as slaves, Athena, goddess of wisdom, comes to assure Poseidon that she will join him in bringing disaster upon the Greeks for their sins. He agrees to cause a storm to punish the homecoming Greeks.

Hecuba, the aged Queen of Troy, awakes. She is staunch, but cannot help bewailing her woes and pain. Because of Helen's acts the Greek ships came and destroyed all that was dear to Hecuba, and now she has become a slave. She summons the Trojan women.

Parodos (153-234)

The Chorus of captive Trojan women and Hecuba together in responsive song tell of their future slavery and separation when they have sailed from Troy to Greece as captives. They speculate fearfully on the chiefs to whom they may be allotted, and on their coming life of work and shame.

First Episode (235-510)

The herald Talthybius enters, and informs them of their future masters to whom they have just been assigned by lot. Cassandra is to be Agamemnon's concubine. Polyxena, another daughter of Hecuba, is to be sacrificed at Achilles' tomb. Andromache, dead Hector's wife, has been given to Achilles' son Neoptolemus; Hecuba to Odysseus. Hecuba bewails her own fate, because of Odysseus' hateful character.

On Talthybius' orders Cassandra, the prophetess daughter of Hecuba and Priam, appears. She is in an insanely joyful mood, holding a torch, and sings of her future relationship with Agamemnon. As Hecuba calms her, she predicts the death of Agamemnon, and bids them hope for this revenge. Though rebuked by Talthybius, Cassandra raves insanely about the future sufferings of Odysseus and Agamemnon. She bids Hecuba farewell and departs for Agamemnon's ships.

Hecuba in anguish tells to what a low station she has fallen in her old age from her former glory. She sorrows over the loss of her husband and sons, and her coming separation from the women of her family.

First Stasimon (511-576)

The Chorus bewails the capture of Troy through the stratagem of the Wooden Horse, telling how the Trojans joyfully celebrated the supposed end of the war, but were soon overwhelmed by the Greeks.

Second Episode (577-798)

Andromache, Hecuba's daughter-in-law, enters with her son Astyanax in her arms. She and Hecuba mourn over their woes. Hecuba laments the newly-reported death of Polyxena. Andromache envies Polyxena, and wishes she herself were dead, rather than suffer the shame of becoming the slave of Achilles' son, not to mention his concubine. Hecuba comforts her and tells her to devote her energies to bringing up Astyanax as a future avenger of Troy.

Talthybius returns and reports with pity that it has been decided to kill Astyanax, in order to prevent the rise of an avenger, by casting him from the walls of Troy. Sadly but bravely Andromache bids a pathetically tender farewell to Astyanax and relinquishes the baby to Talthybius.

Second Stasimon (799-859)

The Chorus tells how Troy was captured once before by Heracles and Telamon of Salamis. The Trojans used to be favorites of the gods, witness Ganymede and Tithonus. They no longer love the Trojans.

Third Episode (860-1059)

Menelaüs, King of Sparta, enters, gloating over the recapture of Helen, who is now held prisoner with the Trojan women. When he orders her summoned, Hecuba urges him to be merciless with her. As he threatens to kill her, Helen begs to be heard. Playing on his sympathies, she tells that she was forcefully stolen by Paris. In turn, Hecuba accuses her of lying, and insists that Helen went willingly with Paris, captivated by his charm and beauty, and that she lived quite happily in Troy. Menelaüs is convinced of Helen's duplicity. She begs for mercy. Swayed by her beauty, Menelaüs orders her taken back to Sparta to await punishment.

Third Stasimon (1060-1122)

Troy is being abandoned by the gods and men. Husbands and children have died in the cruel war. The women are left to suffer.

Exodos (1123-1332)

Talthybius enters with the body of Astyanax. Announcing that Andromache has sailed, he bids Hecuba bury the baby quickly. Hecuba sadly mourns over her grandson and prepares him for burial on Hector's shield. The Chorus mourns with her over the last hope of Troy. Talthybius returns and orders the women to be ready for the sailing of the ships. As Hecuba bids farewell to Troy, she wants to leap into the flames of the city. The Chorus laments for the fallen Troy. Hecuba prays to her dead, bewailing her lot. As the walls topple in smoke, the women turn toward the Greek ships.

INTERPRETATION

Written in the midst of the Peloponnesian War, after the brutal destruction of the Island of Melos by the Athenians (see p. 7), this episodic play seeks to arouse pathos for suffering brought about by war, and condemns the barbarity, folly and futility of war, which ruins victor and vanquished alike.

IPHIGENIA IN TAURIS

BACKGROUND

In one version of the myth of Iphigenia, when Agamemnon was on the point of sacrificing her at Aulis, the goddess Artemis substituted an animal in her place, and wafted Iphigenia away to the land of the savage Taurians. There she became the priestess of the temple of Artemis, to whom all foreigners who entered the land were sacrificed. It was Iphigenia's duty to consecrate the victims before their death. A short time before the play opens, Orestes, still not free of guilt because of his killing of his mother Clytemnestra, had been ordered by the oracle of Apollo to go to Tauris, steal the image of Artemis (Apollo's sister), and bring it to Attica.

Prologue (lines 1-122)

Iphigenia relates how she was to be sacrificed at Aulis, was saved by Artemis, became a half-savage among the Taurians, bound by an oath, out of gratitude to Artemis, to perform human sacrifices to the image of the goddess. Last night she had a dream which she interprets as meaning that her brother Orestes is dead. She enters the temple to perform sacrifices to Orestes.

Orestes, accompanied by his best friend Pylades, enters to accomplish his dangerous mission. He has just landed, and appears frightened. He berates Apollo for imposing so many orders on him. He is under the delusion that he is being pursued by the Furies. The latest orders of Apollo are for him to seize the statue of his sister Artemis and bring it to Attica. Orestes and Pylades retire to a cave near the shore to hide until darkness conceals the deed they plan.

Parodos (123-235)

The Chorus of captive Greek women, handmaidens of Iphigenia, enters, and joins Iphigenia in a *kommos*. They lament the "death" of Orestes, Iphigenia's woes and their own.

First Episode (236-391)

A herdsman enters to report that two Greeks have been captured. He relates in detail how one of them had a seizure, believing himself to be pursued by the Furies. The herdsman declares he saw no Furies, and states that the man is obviously mentally ill. When the man began to attack the cattle with a sword in a mad frenzy, aid was summoned and thus the two Greeks were disarmed and captured.

Iphigenia, desiring to avenge herself on Greeks, declares she is even more resolute because of her dream of Orestes' death. Suddenly she makes an attack on cruelty in the name of religion. She cannot believe that Artemis, or any divinity, could condone such practices. "Evil dwelleth not in heaven." The Taurians have attributed their own savagery to the goddess, making their gods in their own image.

First Stasimon (392-466)

The Chorus comments on the arrival of Greeks in this far-distant land of the Taurians. They yearn for freedom from captivity and for return to their homeland.

Second Episode (467-1088)

The two Greeks are brought before Iphigenia for consecration. She is suddenly softened at the sight of fellow-Greeks, and weeps. She informs them that she too is Greek, and inquires of the heroes who went to Troy. When she hears of Agamemnon's death, though he supposedly sacrificed her at Aulis, she is heartbroken. She learns of Clytemnestra's death at Orestes' hands. He tells her Orestes is still alive, and she realizes her dream was a false one. Orestes, disheartened by his apparent failure to carry out Apollo's order, is completely disillusioned with the gods.

Suddenly, Iphigenia has an idea. She will betray her oath as priestess and release Orestes if he will deliver a letter for her in Greece. Pylades must remain to be sacrificed. Orestes begs her to release Pylades instead, and sacrifice him. She is impressed by his noble character. Then she leaves to write the letter. Pylades prefers to die with his friend Orestes, but Orestes insists he must be saved, for he is to marry Electra and continue the line of Agamemnon. Orestes savagely attacks the oracle of Apollo.

Iphigenia returns with the letter. She requires Pylades to swear he will deliver the message. When Pylades points out that, should the letter be lost en route, he would be guilty of false swearing because of inability to fulfill the oath, she reads the message to him. It is addressed to Orestes, and begs him to rescue her from Tauris. Pylades at once delivers the letter to Orestes. She is skeptical, but, after they reminisce about incidents in their youth, she is convinced it is Orestes, and falls into his arms. Orestes tells her of his past suffering and present mission. He now believes again in the oracle, and asks her to help him seize the image.

She shrinks from the sacrilege and betrayal of her religious duty, but resolves her dilemma in favor of her family and return to her Greek homeland.

Quickly she devises a deception to seize the statue, save Orestes and Pylades, and escape with them from Tauris. If necessary, she will sacrifice her own life, for "women are but little worth." A suggestion that they kill King Thoas is abhorrent to her, for he has always been kind to her. She proposes to assert that the two Greeks, because one of them has killed his mother, have defiled the image of Artemis, and that, therefore, the image and the Greeks must be ceremonially cleansed in the sea. The Chorus is sworn to secrecy.

Second Stasimon (1089-1151)

The Chorus yearns for return to the homeland.

Third Episode (1152-1233)

King Thoas enters to take the strangers to be sacrificed. He is told that they and the image are unclean, and must be cleansed at the seashore. He trusts her implicitly. She orders all the Taurians to veil their eyes to avoid defilement, and thus Orestes, Pylades and Iphigenia (carrying the image of Artemis) move off to the shore.

Third Stasimon (1234-1283)

The Chorus sings a hymn to Apollo and the oracle at Delphi.

Exodos (1284-1496)

A messenger enters to report that the three have escaped with the image, and are on a Greek ship that is leaving the harbor. The Chorus seeks to misdirect him away from Thoas, but in vain. Thoas is informed, and with his guard rushes to the shore to seize the ship. Meanwhile a sudden storm is driving the ship back to shore.

At this critical juncture suddenly Athena (goddess of Reason) appears as the *deus ex machina*. She reveals that Apollo's oracle ordered what has happened. The image is to be removed to Attica, where a temple to Artemis is to be built, and the ancient savage rite is to be commemorated annually by the shedding of a few drops of human blood. Thoas is ordered by Athena to release the Chorus too. King Thoas devoutly agrees to everything. The Chorus departs to the shore to board the ship to Greece.

INTERPRETATION

1. This play is basically a melodrama, in which plot is primary. A good deal of the play is taken up with the recognition scene.

2. It is at the same time a study of human character, revealing how people in crises waver in their views according to circumstances and expediency.

3. It is a criticism of the savage and irrational elements in religion.

4. The barbarian Taurians are depicted as in some ways more admirable than the civilized Greeks.

ELECTRA

BACKGROUND

Electra had been married off by Clytemnestra and Aegisthus to a peasant, partly to humble her, partly to prevent the birth of a child by Electra of high social status who might become the avenger of Agamemnon's murderers. (It is difficult to determine whether Euripides' *Electra* was written before or after Sophocles' *Electra*. One persuasive view, supported by internal evidence, is that Sophocles' play was written as a dramatic reply to Euripides' *Electra*.)

Prologue (lines 1-167)

The peasant husband of Electra stands before their hut in the country and tells of the murder of Agamemnon by Clytemnestra and her lover Aegisthus. Orestes was saved by an old retainer of Agamemnon and secretly sent away to be brought up in safety in Phocis. A price has been set on his head by Aegisthus. Electra was married to himself, but he swears that his respect for her social status is so great that the marriage has not been consummated.

Electra enters, meanly clad, about to fetch water. She is, in this play, not the grandiose, heroic figure of legend. There is mutual respect between her and her husband-in-name-only. She is ambivalent toward him, respecting his nobility of character but rejecting him as a husband because of his inferior rank. As Electra and the peasant go their ways, Orestes and Pylades enter, and Orestes explains that he has been ordered by the oracle of Apollo to avenge his father's death by slaying his murderers. (In this play Aegisthus is depicted as the villain, Clytemnestra as merely an accomplice.) Orestes has come to look for Electra. She returns from the spring with water, full of brooding and self-pity, bewailing her lot, the murder of Agamemnon, and the absence of Orestes.

Parodos (168-212)

The Chorus of peasant women enters to announce to Electra that all the women of the region are to participate in a sacrifice to Hera soon. Electra declines to join the festival, because of her unhappiness and her wretched appearance. They console her, but she is thoroughly disheartened.

First Episode (213-431)

Orestes and his best friend Pylades come out from their place of concealment. Orestes tells Electra that her brother is alive, and she tells the stranger of her humble marriage, and of her husband's respect for her. She hopes for Orestes' return, and is grimly prepared to assist in the murder of Clytemnestra and Aegisthus. Orestes is, however, in this play, a rather weak and uncertain person. Electra tells him of her lowly position, of her mother together with Aegisthus lording it over Agamemnon's realm, of Aegisthus' defilement of Agamemnon's grave, and of his constant mockery of a possible avenger. Above all, it is clear that basically Electra is jealous of her mother's position and material possessions.

The peasant returns and graciously welcomes the strangers into the hut. Orestes comments on the nature of virtue, concluding that personal worth and character, not birth, nor wealth, nor physical strength, are the criteria for judging the truly virtuous man. Electra, irritated at first at her husband's inviting such distinguished individuals into their mean hut, sends her husband for Agamemnon's foster-father to assist in entertaining the strangers.

First Stasimon (432-486)

Achilles, son of the goddess Thetis, accompanied Agamemnon to Troy, accoutred in his resplendent armor and bearing his famous shield. Suchlike were the valiant heroes commanded at Troy by Agamemnon, who was cruelly murdered with the assistance of his wife. Vengeance will come.

Second Episode (487-698)

The old man arrives with food to entertain the guests. He weeps over the miseries of the family, and reports that he has just seen evidence of fresh honorary sacrifices at Agamemnon's tomb. He has found some locks of hair, and surmises that Orestes has returned. Electra rationalistically [This is Euripides' criticism of the recognition scene in the *Choëphoroe* of Aeschylus] rejects the possibility of recognizing Orestes by any similarity between her hair and his, or by the shape of his footprint, or by any garment once made by Electra that he might still be wearing.

Orestes and Pylades come out of the hut. The old man recognizes Orestes by a scar on his forehead. The long-parted brother and sister embrace. As the Chorus rejoices, Orestes enquires how he is to accomplish the murders. The old man advises him. They plot the two murders separately: Aegisthus is to be killed first, at a sacrificial feast. Suddenly Electra gets an idea: she will lure Clytemnestra to her hut by the false announcement that she has given birth to a son. She is certain that this will bring Clytemnestra hastening to visit her. Electra encourages the weak Orestes, planning suicide if the plot fails. He is very unsure of himself.

Second Stasimon (699-746)

Atreus was blessed by Pan with a golden lamb among his flocks. But his wife fell in love with his brother Thyestes, and, through collusion with her, the latter obtained the precious animal and with it the throne of Mycenae. But Atreus, when he discovered the treachery, committed horrible crimes. Because of these happenings Zeus transformed all nature. Yet Clytemnestra blindly slew her husband.

Third Episode (747-1152)

As loud voices are heard from afar, Electra comes out, and a messenger enters to report to her in detail how Aegisthus offered hospitality to Orestes and Pylades, not knowing who they were, and how, while Aegisthus was sacrificing, Orestes slew him with an axe. As Electra and the Chorus rejoice, Orestes and Pylades enter with Aegisthus' body.

Standing over the corpse, Electra is ashamed to vent her fury over the body, fearing public opinion. She recounts all his evil deeds, comments on the adulterous relationship of Aegisthus with her mother, declares that his power was based on wealth not character, and that, moreover, he was effeminate. She spurns his body with her foot, expressing loathing of him, and hoping for a more virile husband. The body is then concealed in the hut.

As Clytemnestra is seen approaching, Orestes' nerve fails at the thought of matricide. He blames the oracle of Apollo for fiendish cruelty. But when Electra nags him and stiffens his weak resolve, he agrees in the name of Apollo.

Clytemnestra arrives. She is no superwoman in this play. Euripides has humanized her, making her a remorseful, conscience-stricken woman, concerned with Electra's attitude toward her and hopeful of a reconciliation. She defends her part in the removal of Agamemnon because he sacrificed Iphigenia and committed adultery with Cassandra. In turn Electra accuses her of adultery with

Aegisthus, and attributes the crime to her desire for Agamemnon's wealth. Clytemnestra is moved to some remorse for her past mistreatment of Electra, now that she has heard she has had a baby. Electra asks her to enter the hut to perform the necessary purification sacrifices after her confinement. Electra is exultant.

Third Stasimon (1153-1182)

Vengeance is at hand; justice is about to overtake the murderous wife.

Exodos (1183-1359)

Clytemnestra's death-cry is heard. After the deed is done, Orestes and Electra are overwhelmed with remorse over what they have done. Electra actually had to help Orestes do the deed. They are both apprehensive about the future, blaming Apollo for the deed.

At this point the Dioscuri (the gods Castor and Pollux) appear above the hut as the *deus ex machina*. They reveal that Clytemnestra deserved to be punished for her part in the murder, but that blood-vengeance ordered by Apollo was not righteous. They declare Electra to be as guilty as Clytemnestra for her part in the murders, but order Orestes to marry Pylades to Electra. Her punishment is to be exile. Orestes himself will be pursued by the Furies, but will be formally acquitted in Athens after due trial. The bodies of Clytemnestra and Aegisthus are to be given proper burial. They also reveal that Helen will soon return. She never was at Troy, but Zeus sent a phantasm in the shape of Helen to start this entire chain of events as a grand joke on man.

The now polluted Orestes regrets his new parting with Electra, and they bid each other a tender farewell. The Dioscuri warn against injustice.

INTERPRETATION

1. There is good and evil in divinities; criticism of Apollo and the oracle of Delphi; condemnation of the blood-feud and matricide. Murder at the command of the oracle is wrong.

2. Clytemnestra is humanized, and her motives and behavior are

Roman

Last 3 centuries B.C. - R. Lit.

Roman plays adaptations of the Gk.
   often c̄ Contaminations - mixing
   two plots.

Plautus

Terence

R. To Thee, O Lord.
Through the mercy of Thine only-begotten
Thine all-holy, all good and life-giving
R. Amen
(The people stand)
Peace be to all.
R. And to thy spirit.
Let us love one another, that with one m
IX R. The Father, the Son, and the Holy Spi

The doors, the doors, Let us attend in w

CREED (by the people) (recite standing)
I believe in one God, the Father almight
visible and invisible. And in one Lord
born of the Father, before all ages: Li
made, consubstantial with the Father, t
for our salvation came down from heaven
Virgin Mary; and was made man. Who was
and was buried, and arose the third day
heaven, and is sitting at the right han
glory to judge the living and the dead,
Holy Spirit, the Lord, the Maker of lif
with the Father and the Son together is
prophets. And in one, holy, catholic,
the remission of sins. I expect the re
to come. Amen

BEGINNING OF THE CANON (stand)
Let us stand well, let us stand with fe

Greek

700 B.C. Worship of Dionysus (God of wine & reproductive forces.

Song & dance around an altar dressed in goat skins. Tragoedia (goat song) representing satyrs (Companions of Dionysus

500 BC Gradually things not connected c̄ Dionysus were added

dramatis personae — masks of the drama wigs & Cothurnus (high soled boot)

Comedy — developed from farces & choral element of tragedy

comic masks, soccus (sandal) heavily padded costumes.

n in peace let us pray to the Lord.

and sanctified, let us pray to the Lord.

these gifts on this holy, heavenly, and
, may send down upon us in return His di-
us pray to the Lord.

wrath, danger, and necessity, let us pray

idence and without blame to call upon Thee,

Name; Thy Kingdom come; Thy will be done
our daily bread, and forgive us our tres-
us, and lead us not into temptation,

e glory of the Father, and the Son, and
ever.

very much like those of Electra. If we sympathize with one, we must understand the other. Their motives are realistic and personal: they both seek happiness, security, luxuries, and high social status.

3. Psychological drama: realistic study of the tortured soul of Electra, her strength and weaknesses, and how circumstances and personal motives drove her to become involved in murders, and the psychological effects of murder.

HELEN

BACKGROUND

The Trojan War was a huge joke the gods played upon humans. It was not Helen herself but a phantom of Helen that fled to Troy with Paris, while the gods whisked the real Helen away to Egypt, where she has been living for many years.

Prologue (lines 1-166)

The scene is set before the palace of Theoklymenus, King of Egypt; nearby is the tomb of his father Proteus. Helen tells of her lineage and the Judgment of Paris. Hera, angry at losing the beauty contest, created a phantom of Helen, which Paris took to Troy, while she herself was taken by Hermes to Egypt to live in Proteus' palace. It is foreordained that she will be reunited, unsullied, some day with her husband Menelaüs. Now that the honorable Proteus is dead, his son Theoklymenus pursues her, seeking her as his wife. Therefore she has sought to protect her honor by becoming a suppliant at Proteus' tomb.

The Greek hero Teucer, in exile from his fatherland, has landed in Egypt. When he sees Helen, he is astounded at the likeness to the loathed woman who caused the Trojan War. She conceals her identity, and inquires about his present troubles. She learns that Troy was destroyed seven years ago. All these years Menelaüs has been lost, wandering somewhere on his way home. She learns of the suicides of her mother Leda and of her brothers Castor and Pollux. Helen counsels Teucer to flee from Egypt, for Theoklymenus slays all Greeks who come to his land. As he departs, she bewails her unhappy lot.

Parodos (167-251)

The Chorus of captive Greek maidens enters, and joins Helen in a *kommos,* bemoaning the sorrows of Helen and her family.

First Episode (252-1106)

Helen regrets that her beauty caused so much unhappiness to the Greeks. Because of this she has earned an evil reputation, lives among barbarians, and her husband Menelaüs, her mother and brothers are dead. There is nothing left for her but suicide. The Chorus counsels her to consult the prophetess Theonoë, sister of Theoklymenus, to verify Teucer's news. After she laments again the suffering she has caused, they all enter the palace.

Menelaüs enters and tells of his lineage, his wanderings after the Trojan War together with his "wife Helen," whom he recaptured at Troy. He has just been shipwrecked nearby, and has left his wife and men in a cave on the shore to search for provisions and aid. He knocks at the door, but is warned by a Greek woman slave to depart because Greeks are not welcome here. He learns to his amazement that Helen is in the palace. He decides to wait for the king to plead for aid, and retires to one side.

The Chorus and Helen reenter. Menelaüs, they have been told by the prophetess Theonoë, is alive and wandering nearby. As Helen takes refuge again at the altar, Menelaüs comes forth. They recognize each other. Helen is overjoyed, but Menelaüs is wary, for he has just left "Helen" in the cave. As he rejects her in fear and confusion, a messenger arrives to tell Menelaüs that his "wife" has vanished from the cave, declaring before she disappeared that she was merely a phantom and that the real Helen was innocent. Helen and Menelaüs fall into each other's arms.

Helen tells Menelaüs of how she came to Egypt through Hera's malice. He orders the messenger to report the good news to his men on the shore and to bid them wait for him. The messenger denounces the seers who gave advice on the Trojan War. Helen warns Menelaüs that King Theoklymenus is bent on marrying her and will kill anyone who tries to thwart him. It would be wise to conceal the fact that Menelaüs has arrived, but Theonoë, the prophetess, will tell her brother Theoklymenus. They decide to plead with her to connive at the secret. If they fail, they will die together after Menelaüs challenges Theoklymenus.

Theonoë enters. She has decided to tell her brother of Menelaüs presence. Helen pleads with her, in the name of justice and humanity, not to do this. Menelaüs joins in her plea, telling of his determination to kill Theoklymenus or die with Helen. Theonoë is won over and leaves.

Their problem is how to escape. Helen proposes a plan—she will declare to Theoklymenus that Menelaüs is dead, and that she requires a ship to perform burial ceremonies at sea, pretending this to be a Greek custom. Then she will profess her readiness to marry him.

First Stasimon (1107-1164)

The Chorus mourns the many Greeks and Trojans who died because of Paris' sin and Hera's malice. They condemn the false reports about Helen, the religious confusion, and the suffering caused by the unnecessary war.

Second Episode (1165-1300)

Theoklymenus enters. He has been informed about the arrival of a Greek, whom he intends to kill to prevent him from taking Helen away. Helen reenters, dressed in mourning. She tells him Menelaüs is dead, drowned in a shipwreck. She is resigned to marriage with Theoklymenus, but must first perform ceremonies at sea, since Menelaüs was drowned. Menelaüs, meanwhile, pretending to be one of his own men, tells what must be done. In particular, a ship is needed, and Helen herself must perform the rites. Theoklymenus is taken in, and grants their every request.

Second Stasimon (1301-1368)

The Chorus chants of Demeter's sad search for her daughter Persephone, abducted by Hades. There is joy in life, too, in the gifts of Aphrodite and the revels of Bacchus.

Third Episode (1369-1450)

Helen reenters. Theonoë has kept the secret, and now Menelaüs has supplies and arms. Theoklymenus and Menelaüs enter with the funeral offerings. The king bids them conduct the ceremonies, and orders preparation for his marriage to Helen.

Third Stasimon (1451-1511)

The Chorus bids bon voyage and a happy return to Greece for Helen and Menelaüs.

Exodos (1512-1692)

A messenger hastens back from the harbor to report to Theoklymenus that the Greek is Menelaüs. As they were preparing the ship, a band of Greeks appeared and were welcomed aboard by Menelaüs. After they were launched, Menelaüs gave a signal to the men, who quickly killed all of Theoklymenus' men, but himself. The ship has sailed off to Greece. Theoklymenus now knows that he has been betrayed by his sister Theonoë too. He decides to kill her in vengeance.

Suddenly Castor and Pollux appear on high as the *deus ex machina*. They declare that their sister Helen is destined to return to Greece with her husband Menelaüs. Moreover, Theoklymenus is ordered not to harm Theonoë, who has acted in accordance with the will of the gods. They, as gods of mariners, will protect the ship. When Helen dies she will become a goddess; Menelaüs on his death will attain the glorious Isles of the Blest. Theoklymenus bows to the will of the gods.

INTERPRETATION

1. This play is not a tragedy but a melodrama, with romantic elements. It resembles *Iphigenia in Tauris,* both in plot and structure, and appears to be an imitation of it.

2. It condemns war, and mocks prophets and the evils in traditional religion.

PHOENICIAN WOMEN

BACKGROUND

In this version of the Oedipus legend, when Oedipus discovered his identity, he blinded himself, but Jocasta, his mother and wife, remained alive. Since his two sons, Polynices and Eteocles, did not treat him with kindness, he cursed them, prophesying that "they would divide their inheritance with the sword." Polynices and Eteocles agreed to rule alternately. But when it came to Polynices' turn, Eteocles refused to relinquish his power, and exiled his brother. Polynices thereupon took refuge with King Adrastus of Argos, whose daughter he married and who helped him to organize the "Seven Against Thebes."

Prologue (lines 1-201)

Jocasta tells of the woes and the curse of the royal family of Thebes from Cadmus on. She relates in detail the life of her son Oedipus, his slaying of Laïus, his marriage to her, the birth of their two sons Eteocles and Polynices and of their two daughters Antigone and Ismene, and Oedipus' discovery of the horrible truth. Treated like an outcast, Oedipus cursed his sons. Now Polynices stands with Argive troops at the seven gates of Thebes. Jocasta has persuaded her sons to meet, in an effort to reconcile their dispute, and she now goes to see Polynices.

An old servant enters with Antigone. They mount to the walls, and he points out to her the seven captains of the Argive host, including her brother Polynices.

Parodos (202-260)

The Chorus of Phoenician women, just arrived in Thebes on their way to Delphi as a gift to Apollo, sing of the wonders of Thebes and of the awful battle impending.

First Episode (261-637)

Polynices enters Thebes cautiously. The Chorus summons Jocasta, who embraces her son, and bemoans the woes and curse of the family. Polynices, deeply moved by the sight of his mother and native city, inquires of his father and sisters. He tells of his unhappy exile, his marriage to King Adrastus' daughter, the marshalling of the host against Thebes. He frankly declares his desire for power and wealth.

Eteocles enters, and Jocasta urges them to talk things over. Polynices demands his heritage and alternate rule with Eteocles as the price of peace. Eteocles frankly covets power and will not yield it, accusing his brother of treason and resort to force to attain his ends. He is willing to let him live as a private citizen in Thebes, and is prepared to fight anyone for his power.

Jocasta rebukes Eteocles for his overweening ambition, counseling harmony, equality, justice. She also admonishes Polynices for leading troops against his native land. Both are adamant. They quarrel vehemently. Eteocles refuses Polynices' request to see his father and sisters. Angry, he returns to his troops.

First Stasimon (638-689)

The Chorus sings of Thebes, where Dionysus was born and Cadmus sowed the dragon's teeth, from which armed men sprang. O gods, help Thebes!

Second Episode (690-783)

Eteocles and Creon, brother of Jocasta, discuss the defense of the city. Eteocles is rash and desires to lead out his troops at once beyond the walls to meet the Argives. Creon counsels him to choose seven captains, each to defend one of the gates of the city against the champions of the Argives. Eteocles personally will face Polynices. If anything happens to him, he wants Antigone to marry Creon's son Haemon. But he will first consult the prophet Teiresias. If Polynices is killed, his body is not to be buried by anyone on pain of death. He departs to arm himself for battle.

Second Stasimon (784-832)

The Chorus sings of terrible Ares, the impending battle, the birth of Oedipus, the Sphinx, and other Theban legends.

Third Episode (833-1018)

The blind prophet Teiresias, summoned by Creon's son Menoecus, is led in by his daughter. Asked to predict the outcome of the strife, he prophesies that there will be horrible slaughter and that Thebes will be destroyed unless the entire family of Oedipus leaves Thebes. To save Thebes Creon must sacrifice his son Menoecus to Ares, in recompense for the slaying of the dragon by Cadmus. Thus, by the consecration of Menoecus, Thebes will be redeemed. Creon has the choice of saving Thebes or his son. Therewith Teiresias departs.

Creon urges Menoecus to flee from the city at once, for Teiresias will undoubtedly tell the Theban chieftains his prophecy, and they will demand his sacrifice. Menoecus agrees and Creon leaves. But Menoecus tells the Chorus he has deceived his father and that he intends to give his life to save Thebes. He leaves to kill himself in the very cave where the dragon of Ares was slain.

Third Stasimon (1019-1066)

The Chorus tells of the Sphinx that troubled Thebes and how Oedipus liberated the city by solving her riddle. Glory to heroic Menoecus, savior of the city!

Fourth Episode (1067-1283)

A messenger summons Jocasta and tells her that, after the initial battle for Thebes, both of her sons are still alive. After Menoecus slew himself for Thebes, a mighty combat ensued, and Thebes repelled the invaders. But, to Jocasta's horror, he tells her that Polynices and Eteocles are intent on meeting in single combat to decide the issue. Jocasta summons Antigone, and they hasten to the battlefield to try to stop the duel.

Fourth Stasimon (1284-1306)

The Chorus expresses horror at the fratricidal strife.

Exodos (1307-1766)

The body of Menoecus is brought in. As Creon bewails the loss of his son, a messenger arrives to announce that Polynices and Eteocles slew each other in combat. Jocasta came too late to intercede. Polynices, before he died, begged to be buried in his native land. Utterly distraught, Jocasta seized a sword and killed herself. Then the battle was renewed by the Thebans and Argives. The Thebans were victorious.

Antigone enters with the bodies of her brothers and mother. She bemoans the woes of her family. She summons Oedipus, who joins in her sorrow. Creon declares that Eteocles granted him the royal power. It is therefore his duty to exile Oedipus in accordance with the prophecies of Teiresias. He also orders Polynices' body to be cast forth, and rules that it is not to be buried—on pain of execution.

Antigone declares she will bury Polynices. Creon is unbending. Thereupon Antigone renounces her betrothal to Creon's son Haemon, and assures Oedipus that she will accompany and tend him in his exile. He begs to touch the bodies of his wife and sons. According to the Delphic oracle, he will find asylum in Athens and die there. Antigone declares she will secretly bury Polynices. Sadly they depart into exile.

INTERPRETATION

1. This play is basically a dramatic pageant of the legends of Thebes.

2. The theme of patriotism and the sufferings of war are in the forefront.

3. Ambition for power and wealth can cause untold suffering.

ORESTES

BACKGROUND

After Orestes avenged Agamemnon's murder by killing his mother Clytemnestra, he was haunted by the Furies and driven insane.

Prologue (lines 1-139)

The scene is before the royal palace at Argos. Electra, Orestes' sister, watching beside Orestes' couch as he sleeps, tells of the woes of the House of Atreus. Orestes, in obedience to the oracle of Apollo, slew Clytemnestra, with the aid of Electra and Pylades, just six days ago. He was immediately driven mad by the Furies, and has not moved from his couch since. The people of Argos have declared Orestes and Electra polluted by matricide, and have forbidden them contact with everyone. It is expected that they will condemn them to death today. The only hope of Orestes and Electra is Menelaüs, whose arrival is anticipated. Meanwhile, Helen, because of her fear of harm at the hands of the people of Mycenae, has been living with Orestes and Electra, together with her beloved daughter Hermione.

Helen enters and consoles Electra, while she mourns the death of her sister Clytemnestra. Since she fears the people of Argos too, she decides to send Hermione, instead of going herself, to place locks of hair and drink-offerings at Clytemnestra's tomb. When they leave, Electra reviles the vain, selfish Helen as the cause of her woes.

Parodos and First Episode (140-315)

The Chorus of Argive Women enters quietly so as not to wake Orestes. Electra attacks the oracle for ordering the matricide and thereby bringing untold suffering upon herself and her brother.

Orestes wakens. Electra lovingly ministers to him, and tells him that Menelaüs will soon come. His madness returns and he fights the Furies. Then in a lucid moment he blames Apollo for his troubles and urges Electra to rest and take care of herself.

First Stasimon (316-347)

The Chorus beseeches the Furies to relent. Unhappy Orestes!

Second Episode (348-806)

Menelaüs arrives and sees the wreck of Orestes. He learns of his present suffering, his ostracism, of the Furies, and the imminent death sentence. He begs Menelaüs to help him in the name of kinship.

Tyndareus of Sparta, Clytemnestra's father and Orestes' grandfather, arrives. He is a blind old man. Tyndareus denounces Orestes' matricide, attacking the vendetta as a primitive concept of justice and upholding civic law. He urges Menelaüs not to aid Orestes, but allow him to be stoned to death by the Argives. Else Menelaüs is never to return to Sparta to become its king.

Orestes, in a clever sophistic speech, seeks to defend himself. He claims his deed is a service to all of Greece, for it will be a warning to women not to commit adultery or kill their husbands. Further, had he not killed his mother, his father's Furies would have haunted him. Is it not so that Tyndareus begat two adulterous daughters— Helen and Clytemnestra? In addition, Apollo is to blame, for his oracle ordered the deed. Tyndareus leaves in anger to urge the Argive council to decree that Orestes and Electra, his grandchildren, be stoned to death. He warns Menelaüs of the consequences of aiding Orestes.

Menelaüs is in a dilemma. Orestes, in the name of gratitude for what Agamemnon did for him, begs him to save his life. Menelaüs concedes the justice of his arguments, but pleads lack of power, in a cautious, equivocal speech. He is one against many, and therefore cannot use force. He can only try to win back the city to temperance. Orestes is bitter at being utterly abandoned.

Just then his best friend Pylades arrives from Phocis. He has been banished from his home by his own father for his part in the slaying of Clytemnestra. They decide that, come what may, the only hope is to appeal directly to the council. First they will go to Agamemnon's tomb to pray for deliverance.

Second Stasimon (807-843)

The Chorus tells of the curse and the woes of the House of Atreus, in particular Orestes' slaying of his mother and the ensuing madness.

Third Episode (844-1352)

Electra enters and learns of Orestes' decision. She is horrified. A messenger announces the decree of the council—Orestes and Electra are to die. At the meeting Orestes and Pylades were present. Various views were set forth on both sides. Tyndareus spoke in favor of the death penalty. Menelaüs did not attend. Orestes, attended by Pylades, spoke in his own defense, to no avail. He won permission, however, for them to commit suicide. Electra bewails her unhappy lot and the sufferings of her family.

Orestes and Pylades return. Electra and Orestes console each other and prepare their farewells. Pylades announces his intent to die with his best friend and his betrothed Electra. Then he urges them to take vengeance on Menelaüs—by killing Helen! Electra advises that they seize Hermione as a hostage, so that they will have a bargaining advantage in forcing Menelaüs to aid them. If not, they will slay her too. They pray for aid to Agamemnon's soul. Orestes and Pylades enter the palace.

As Electra waits for Hermione, Helen's death cry is heard inside. Hermione returns from Clytemnestra's grave, and is enticed into the palace, where she is promptly seized by Orestes.

Third Stasimon (1353-1364)

The Chorus comments on Helen's death.

Fourth Episode (1365-1535)

A loyal slave of Helen, who has escaped death inside, enters and reports in detail how Helen was trapped and brutally slain, despite the efforts of her bodyguard. Orestes appears, completely brutalized by his last act, and eagerly awaits Menelaüs' return.

Fourth Stasimon (1536-1548)

The Chorus comments on the curse of the House of Atreus.

Exodos (1549-1693)

Menelaüs rushes in, having heard what has happened to Helen and Hermione. Orestes and Pylades, holding Hermione as hostage,

appear on the roof of the palace. Orestes declares his intent to kill
Hermione and set fire to the palace, unless Menelaüs succeeds in
saving his life and persuading the Argives to grant him the kingship over Argos.

As they are about to fire the palace and carry out their threat
to Hermione, Apollo appears as the *deus ex machina*. He declares
that Helen was not slain but wafted away by the gods to become a
sea divinity together with her brothers Castor and Pollux. Orestes
is to go into exile, then proceed to Athens, where he will be tried
and acquitted. Hermione is to be wed to Orestes, not Neoptolemus;
and Pylades is to marry Electra. Apollo himself will win over the
Argives.

Orestes now praises Apollo as a true prophet. Menelaüs gives
his blessings to the betrothal of Orestes and Hermione, and all
ends well.

INTERPRETATION

1. This play is a melodrama, not a tragedy.

2. It is considered by some to be a reply to Sophocles' *Electra,*
which is, in turn, believed to be a reply to Euripides' *Electra.*

3. The play condemns the vendetta as a primitive form of justice, denounces matricide as a horrible crime, as well as the oracle
of Apollo for abetting the murder.

4. It is a study of insanity and abnormal psychology, portraying
man's inhumanity to man.

IPHIGENIA AT AULIS

BACKGROUND

While the Greeks were marshalling their forces at Aulis for the
expedition against Troy, Agamemnon killed a deer sacred to Artemis. The winds then stopped blowing and the fleet was becalmed.
In recompense the prophet Calchas instructed Agamemnon to sacrifice his eldest daughter Iphigenia to Artemis.

Prologue (lines 1-163)

The scene is set before the tent of Agamemnon at Aulis. Agamemnon, commander of the Greek forces, tells of the wooing of Helen and her marriage to his brother Menelaüs, of her flight to Troy with Paris, and of the gathering of the Greek host preparing to invade Troy. When the fleet was becalmed, the seer Calchas declared that Iphigenia must be sacrificed. Agamemnon desired to disband the armies rather than kill his daughter, but, persuaded by his brother Menelaüs, he wrote to his wife Clytemnestra instructing her to send Iphigenia to Aulis to become the bride of Achilles.

Agamemnon has now repented, and has written another letter to his wife. He instructs his old servant to deliver it. The letter informs Clytemnestra not to send Iphigenia because the wedding has been postponed indefinitely. Agamemnon is in a deep dilemma, torn by the necessities of the military situation and his affection for his daughter.

Parodos (164-300)

The Chorus of Women of Calchis enters to see the mighty fleet and the famous Greek heroes.

First Episode (301-542)

Menelaüs has intercepted the letter and read it. He quarrels with Agamemnon, rebuking him for his instability, weakness, fear of the army, ambition and incompetence. Agamemnon taunts his brother for his inability to hold his wife Helen and for his desire to win her back. He asserts he will not sacrifice his beloved daughter for such a purpose.

A messenger enters to announce that Iphigenia, Clytemnestra and little Orestes are arriving for the wedding. Agamemnon, deeply troubled, gives way to tears; at this Menelaüs is touched and urges him not to go through with the sacrifice of his daughter for his sake. But Agamemnon now declares he has no choice because the army will demand it and the wily Odysseus will stir them up. He asks Menelaüs to see to it that Clytemnestra learns nothing of his real intent, and they depart.

First Stasimon (543-606)

The Chorus prays for love in moderation, without passion. Paris' unrestrained love for Helen caused the Trojan War.

Second Episode (607-750)

Clytemnestra enters in her chariot, bringing the "bride," her dowry, and the boy Orestes. Iphigenia greets Agamemnon affectionately; he cannot restrain his tears. Clytemnestra inquires about the "bridegroom" Achilles' lineage. Agamemnon tries to persuade her to return at once to Argos, to care for her other daughters.

Second Stasimon (751-800)

The Chorus chants of the coming war against Troy for the sake of Helen.

Third Episode (801-1035)

Achilles, impatient to sail for Troy, is greeted by Clytemnestra. He is dumbfounded to hear that he is going to "marry" Iphigenia. Clytemnestra is amazed at this turn of events, and equally embarrassed. An old servant reveals Agamemnon's intention to sacrifice Iphigenia to Artemis for the sake of the army. Clytemnestra implores the hero Achilles to save Iphigenia's life, and he gallantly vows to prevent the sacrifice. He feels insulted at being used as a dupe in the affair. But he has no interest in unnecessary violence, and counsels Clytemnestra to confront Agamemnon with the facts, and to seek to persuade him not to conduct the sacrifice.

Third Stasimon (1036-1097)

The Chorus sings of the wedding of Peleus and Thetis, from whom sprang the glorious hero Achilles. Poor Iphigenia, who is about to be sacrificed!

Fourth Episode (1098-1474)

Iphigenia has heard the news and is heartbroken. Clytemnestra pleads with Agamemnon, in the name of their successful marriage, not to sacrifice their daughter for unfaithful Helen's sake. Iphigenia makes a tearful plea for her life, as little Orestes weeps too. Agamemnon, however, feels he must perform the sacrifice because the army will insist on it, and it is, moreover, his duty to Hellas. He then leaves to make preparations.

Iphigenia bewails her lot, sorrowing that she must die for evil Helen. All life is sorrow. Achilles returns and declares that, despite the hostile clamor of the soldiers, including his own troops, he will protect her singlehandedly.

But suddenly Iphigenia calmly offers her life for the success of the great Hellenic expedition. Her death will be a noble act; she will die for the sake of all Hellas, and she will be forever famous. She bids farewell, and departs bravely.

Fourth Stasimon (1475-1531)

The Chorus praises Iphigenia, and sings a hymn to Artemis.

Exodos (1532-1629)

(The present conclusion of the play appears not to be genuine. Scholars believe it to be a later addition.) A messenger enters and tells Clytemnestra how, in the presence of the entire army, Iphigenia was sacrificed. She was very brave. As the girl was being sacrificed, suddenly she vanished, and in her place was a dying deer. Clytemnestra is not comforted by this news that her child has been wafted away miraculously to live with the gods.

(A fragment indicates that the play ended with Artemis as the *deus ex machina* consoling Clytemnestra.)

INTERPRETATION

1. This play, unfinished at Euripides' death, was completed by his son and produced posthumously.

2. It is basically a melodrama, not a tragedy.

3. It reveals Greek drama in transition to Middle and New Comedy, for it deals with a domestic and social situation in which ordinary people are portrayed facing up to a crisis in varied ways.

4. Fear, ambition and self-interest cause suffering.

BACCHAE

BACKGROUND

Semele, daughter of Cadmus, former king of Thebes, had been loved by Zeus, who visited her only in disguise. Semele was goaded by her sister to ask her lover to reveal his true self. She accordingly cajoled Zeus into granting her any wish she requested. When he consented, she asked to see him in his true form. Having no choice, he revealed himself, and she was at once destroyed by Zeus' lightning. Since she was to have a child by him, Zeus saved the embryo in his thigh, and thus Dionysus was born.

Prologue (lines 1-63)

Dionysus, god of wine, stands before the palace of Pentheus, King of Thebes. He tells the story of his birth, and how he has been spreading his worship throughout the non-Greek world. Now for the first time the Dionysiac cult has entered a Greek city, the home of his mother Semele. Because of opposition to his cult, he has caused the women of Thebes to be roused to an emotional frenzy and to revel in uncontrolled religious ecstasy celebrating his rites. He will teach the city humility and avenge the wrongs done to his mother. The present ruler of Thebes, Pentheus, Cadmus' grandson, rejects the worship of Dionysus. Therefore, Dionysus plans to show him on this very day that he is indeed a god to be reckoned with. To carry out his plans, he has disguised himself as a human being, impersonating a sort of missionary of Dionysus. The god here symbolically represents elemental forces of life—joyous ecstatic emotion, physical pleasures, especially sex, natural primitive instincts, release from the restrictions of civilized life.

Parodos (64-168)

The Chorus of Bacchants sings a hymn to Dionysus, a sort of dithyramb, filled with lyric beauty, blind faith and fanatical devotion to the god and his revels, which include sexual orgies, wild dances, the rending of a goat and the drinking of its blood.

First Episode (169-369)

Teiresias, the blind prophet of Thebes, enters. He, though the priest of Apollo, god of moderation and sobriety, has succumbed to the worship of Dionysus. He is accompanied by the aged Cadmus, both somewhat tipsy and feeling rejuvenated by the worship of the god. They are so far the only men in Thebes to adopt the new cult.

King Pentheus arrives. He has been absent from the land and has just returned to find the city convulsed by the new cult, which he abhors. Young Pentheus is an intellectual, stubbornly skeptical of the irrational and the emotions. He is almost puritanical in his rejection of the physical, a kind of extreme idealistic bigot, who tyrannically insists on the rightness of his own views. He is aghast at the sexual looseness of the women of Thebes under the influence of Dionysus. He has had a number arrested and imprisoned, and is preparing to hunt the others in their mountainous revel haunts. If he captures the stranger who has been leading them, he will execute him. He rebukes Teiresias and Cadmus for their unseemly behavior.

Teiresias, a kind of theological Sophist in this play, rationalizes his interest in the new god. He sees no reason for taking the chance that Dionysus is not a true god, and cleverly tries to reconcile the Dionysiac cult with the Apollonian. He advises Pentheus not to be proud, but to submit to the god. Cadmus defends himself, urging Pentheus to accept the god pragmatically ("It were a splendid falsehood"). Pentheus orders the capture of the stranger. Teiresias warns of Pentheus' excessive pride and of his folly.

First Stasimon (370-432)

The Chorus praises the physical delights of life, such as wine drinking, sex and food, and glorifies the simple pleasures of the masses.

Second Episode (433-518)

An officer of the guard reports to Pentheus that the stranger has been captured, but that all the imprisoned women have been mysteriously released, and have rejoined the revels in the mountains. Pentheus questions the stranger, who tries to save him with gentle persuasion, urging him not to persecute the new religion. He orders the stranger detained in chains.

Second Stasimon (519-575)

The Chorus sings of the beauties and joys of the emotions and the natural life.

Third Episode (576-861)

Dionysus has released himself and now enters. He has caused the palace of Pentheus to be shaken to its foundations and to go up in flames. Pentheus, enraged, enters. A messenger, a herdsman from the country, arrives and relates that he has seen the frenzied Bacchants reveling in the mountains. He describes in detail their wild Bacchic orgies, and urges acceptance of the god, for he provides the joys that release one from sorrow—soothing wine and love.

As Pentheus summons his army, Dionysus changes into a cruel, destructive force, a ruthless, fiendish god. Pentheus gradually comes under his spell, becomes drunk, and puts on the garb of a Bacchant. He begins to display a subconscious but marked curiosity in sex and the emotions.

Third Stasimon (862-911)

The Chorus counsels humility before all the gods. Unnatural behavior, such as Pentheus', is punished.

Fourth Episode (912-976)

Pentheus, now maddened and under Dionysus' spell, behaves like a female Bacchant. Dionysus plots his fate at the hands of the women of Thebes.

Fourth Stasimon (977-1023)

The Chorus comments on the fearful aspects of the Dionysiac cult.

Exodos (1024-1392)

A messenger arrives from the mountains and describes in detail the death of Pentheus. He had desired to view the Bacchic orgies, and with the help of Dionysus he secretly observed them from a treetop. Then Dionysus betrayed Pentheus' hiding place to the women. The frenzied women, led by Pentheus' mother Agave, rushed to the tree, believing Pentheus to be a wild beast. They seized and tore him to pieces.

Agave, now mad, enters, carrying her son Pentheus' head. Cadmus enters with attendants bearing the remains of Pentheus. Agave asks for her son, to show him her trophy, and to urge him to submit to the cult. She gradually returns to her senses, and realizes what she has done. She and Cadmus lament the death of Pentheus, recounting all his fine qualities.

Dionysus appears as the *deus ex machina*. He reveals that the entire family of Pentheus is to be punished. (This seems unreasonable in view of the acceptance of the cult by Agave and Pentheus.) Agave criticizes Dionysus' extreme cruelty, saying "The gods should not be like men in anger." The two then depart in exile from Thebes.

INTERPRETATION

1. In this play Euripides explores some of the fundamental conflicts in civilized society:

a. Emotion, physical pleasure and other elemental natural forces are not to be scorned.

b. On the other hand, exclusive interest in these activities may lead to disaster.

c. There is beauty and truth, yet danger and cruelty in the natural life.

d. If man submits completely to the physical, he may become degraded and brutish in his behavior.

e. If man resists faith, it conquers in the end.

2. Some mid-point between blind faith and cold reason, between extreme intellectual skepticism and fanatical religion, between the physical and the intellectual must be found to avoid suffering.

LOST PLAYS OF EURIPIDES

Aegeus; Aeolus; Alcmena; Alcmeon at Corinth; Alcmeon at Psophis; Alexander; Alope; Andromeda; Antigone; Antippe; Archelaüs; Auge; Autolycus; Bellerephon; Busiris; Chrysippus; Cresphontes; Danaë; Daughters of Pelias; Dictys; Epeus; Erechtheus; Eurystheus; Hippolytus Veiled; Hypsipyle; Ino; Ixion; Licymnius; Melanippe in Bonds; Melanippe the Wise; Meleager; Men of Crete; Oedipus; Oeneus; Oenomaüs; Palamedes; Peleus; Phaëton; Philoctetes; Phoenix; Phrixus; Pleisthenes; Polyidus; Protesilaüs; Reapers; Sciron; Scyrians; Sthenoboea; Syleus; Telephus; Temenidae; Temenas; Theseus; Thyestes; Women of Crete.

DRAMATIC TECHNIQUES AND STYLE OF EURIPIDES

1. Plots complex; some use of suspense; some plays merely episodic, not organically unified; beginnings of melodrama.

2. Prologues formal, nondramatic, expository, addressed to the audience.

3. Epilogue usually contains the *deus ex machina* (in 12 of his extant plays).

4. Choral odes of great poetic beauty; decreased importance of chorus; choral odes conventionalized, and tend to become irrelevant to action and develop into mere musical interludes.

5. Uncompromising realism: "Men as they are."

6. Use of humorous touches.

7. Use of the sensational.

8. Psychological dramas (problem plays), not plays of fate or divine power:

    a. Conflicts of human emotions the main interest of Euripides, either between characters or within one character ("divided soul").

    b. Tragedy of human situations primary.

    c. Tenderness and pathos principal emotions aroused.

    d. Introduction of love theme in drama.

9. Characters: subtle psychology of human beings; realism— epic heroes debunked to stature of ordinary persons; humble people (peasants, women, slaves) elevated; emphasis on human weak-

nesses; hence, especial importance of female characters (Euripides' greatest creations); interest in abnormal psychology.

10. Style: simple, lucid, everyday speech; lyric beauty; extensive use of rhetorical eloquence, formal debates, and sophistic argumentation; frequent use of sententious statements.

BASIC IDEAS OF EURIPIDES

1. Keen interest in contemporary social, political, religious, and philosophical problems.

2. Rationalism, liberalism, skepticism; criticism of orthodox formalism in religion, and of conventional ethical and social standards.

3. All extant plays are on three basic subjects: war; women; religion.

a. Hatred of aggressive war.

b. Criticism of double standard with regard to women; Euripides seeks to elevate the status of women.

c. He seeks to elevate humble people and expose the degeneracy of aristocrats.

d. Not an atheist, but opposed to traditional anthropomorphic divinities; criticizes the evils of religion, oracles, soothsaying.

4. Though persistently critical of his fellow-Athenians, Euripides glorified Athens with genuine patriotic pride.

5. Presents insoluble conflicts of real life: clash of conflicting emotions, of reason and emotion, of absolute standards and relative standards of conduct.

6. Sympathy for all human suffering, and tolerant understanding of ordinary aspirations and emotions of all human beings.

CHAPTER SIX

OLD COMEDY: ARISTOPHANES

ORIGINS OF COMEDY

1. The choral element probably derives from the phallic choruses and processions at the festivals of Dionysus intended to stimulate fertility, or in the ribald drunken revels in his honor (*komos*); the dramatic element from the Doric farces, semidramatic improvisations in the marketplace. Comedy means, literally, "song of revelry."

2. There was impressed on Greek comedy at the start frank indecency, particularly about sex.

3. Comedy was absorbed into the state cult of Athens in 487/6 B.C.

NATURE OF OLD COMEDY

1. Poetic musical comedy, comparable to the operettas of Gilbert and Sullivan.

2. Subjects: unrestrained fantasy combined with use of characters representing well-known persons of the time.

3. Loose, carelessly constructed plots; broad farce and buffoonery.

4. Frank coarseness and obscenity.

5. Usually a satire on important contemporary issue in Athenian life: political, social, moral.

6. Topical satire of well-known contemporaries.

PRODUCTION OF OLD COMEDY

1. At festivals of Dionysus, following tragedies and satyr plays.

2. Contest among three playwrights, each exhibiting one comedy.

3. Actors wore comic masks, the *soccus* (sandal), and heavily padded costumes with prominent phallus appended in the case of male characters.

4. Chorus—24 in number; often wore fantastic costumes.

STRUCTURE OF OLD COMEDY

1. Prologue: leading character conceives "happy idea."

2. Parodos: entrance of chorus.

3. Agon: dramatized debate between proponent and opponent of "happy idea," ending in defeat of opposition.

4. Parabasis: "coming forward" of the Chorus, which addresses the audience directly, airing the poet's views on a variety of subjects.

5. Episodes: the "happy idea" is put to practical application.

6. Play often ends with feasting and male-female union (*gamos*).

LEADING WRITERS OF OLD COMEDY

1. Magnes of Athens (ca. 500-430 B.C.)
   Wrote: *Birds; Gall-Flies; Frogs; Harp-Players; Lydians.*
2. Cratinus of Athens (ca. 490-420 B.C.)
   a. First great comic poet.
   b. Wrote: *Archilochoi; Busiris; Caught in a Storm; Chirons; Descendants of Euneus; Dionysalexandros; Nemesis; Odysseus and his Comrades; Panoptae; Plutoi; Pylaea; Satyrs; Seasons; Seriphians; Softies; Thracian Women; Those Set on Fire; Trophonius; Wine Flask; Women of Delos.*

3. Crates of Athens (acme 450-424 B.C.)
Wrote: *The Beasts.*

4. Pherecrates of Athens (contemporary of Aristophanes)
Wrote: *Ant-Men; Chiron; Corianno; Crapatali; Deserters; Forgetful Men; Miners; Old Women; Persians; Petale; Pseudo-Heracles; Resident Aliens; Savages; School for Slaves; Tyranny; Vigil; Worthies.*

5. Eupolis of Athens (acme 445-410 B.C.)
Wrote: *Autolycus; Chieftains; Days of the New Moon; Demes; Dippers; Flatterers; Friends; Goats; Golden Race; Maricas; Prospaltians; Slackers; The Cities.*

6. Phrynichus of Athens (acme 429-405 B.C.)
Wrote: *Connus; Cronus; Ephialtes; Hermit; Muses; Mystics; Revellers; Tragedians; Welders.*

7. Aristophanes of Athens (see below).

8. Platon of Athens (ca. 450-385 B.C.)
Wrote: *Adonis; Alliance; Ambassadors; Amphiareus; Cleophon; Europa; Festivals; Hyperbolus; Laïus; Islands; Phaon; Spartans; The Log Night; Zeus Reviled.*

ARISTOPHANES OF ATHENS (446-385 B.C.)

1. Greatest writer of Old Comedy; only playwright in this genre whose plays have survived.

2. Little known of him; most of his plays were written during the Peloponnesian War.

3. Wrote ca. 40 plays.

EXTANT PLAYS

Acharnians (425 B.C.)	*Lysistrata* (411 B.C.)
Knights (424 B.C.)	*Thesmophoriazusae* (411 B.C.)
Clouds (423 B.C.)	*Frogs* (405 B.C.)
Wasps (422 B.C.)	*Ecclesiazusae* (392/391 B.C.)
Peace (421 B.C.)	*Plutus* (388 B.C.)
Birds (414 B.C.)	

ACHARNIANS

Prologue (lines 1-203)

The scene is the Pnyx at Athens; nearby are the houses of Dicaeopolis, Euripides, and Lamachus. Dicaeopolis, a "good" Athenian citizen, is seen sitting alone in the Pnyx. He reviews his joys and woes while waiting for the Assembly to convene. His principal interest is the restoration of peace with Sparta. When the Assembly finally goes into session, Amphitheus proposes peace negotiations with Sparta. He is quickly silenced. An embassy just returned from Persia gives an absurd report on the wonders of that country.

Disgusted, Dicaeopolis commissions Amphitheus to negotiate a private truce for him and his family with Sparta. Another absurd report is given by an embassy sent to the Thracian Sitalces. Dicaeopolis feels a drop of rain, and the meeting is instantly adjourned.

Amphitheus returns from Sparta, pursued by the Acharnian charcoal burners, who form the Chorus. They are opposed to peace. Amphitheus offers Dicaeopolis three samples of truces: a 5-year, 10-year, and 30-year type. He chooses the 30-year truce. Dicaeopolis then leaves to celebrate the rural Dionysia.

Parodos (204-236)

The Chorus is searching for the man who dared to conclude a truce with Sparta.

Episodes (237-625)

Dicaeopolis comes out with his family and begins the phallic procession in honor of Bacchus, to celebrate peace. The Chorus spies him and begins to stone him. He rushes inside and brings out a basket of charcoal. Using this "fellow-citizen" of the Acharnian charcoal burners as a hostage, he manages to plead his case—but with his head on a block.

In order to arouse their pity he decides to go for aid to Euripides. He knocks on the door of his house, and Euripides is revealed lying on a bed. Dicaeopolis begs for and receives the tattered costume and accessories of one of Euripides' most wretched and pitiable heroes.

Dicaeopolis, with his head on a block, now delivers an eloquent speech, in which he reviews the causes of the Peloponnesian War and absolves the Spartans of sole blame.

The Chorus is now divided in its sympathies. The die-hards summon their champion, the general Lamachus, who appears in full battle array. Dicaeopolis routs him with subtle arguments, proclaims the end of all the war boycotts, and goes into his house.

Parabasis (626-718)

The Chorus proclaims the services of Aristophanes to Athens, particularly his alerting the citizens to foreign flattery. "Never lose him who will always fight for the cause of justice in his comedies." The ode sings of the Muse of Acharnae, urges the case of the aged against the young, and supports the cause of peace.

Episode (719-970)

Dicaeopolis returns, and marks out the confines of his market place, which he declares open to all Greeks. A Megarian arrives with his daughters and laments the distress caused by Pericles' harsh decrees against the Megarians. He disguises his daughters as little pigs and sells them to Dicaeopolis for garlic and salt. An informer appears, and threatens to denounce the Megarian. Dicaeopolis drives him off.

A prosperous Boeotian enters, and offers many provisions for sale. Nicarchus, an informer, enters and denounces the Boeotian. He is promptly seized and bound, and packed in hay to be carried off by the Boeotian. Lamachus sends a slave to ask Dicaeopolis for some food, but gets a refusal.

Stasimon (971-999)

The Chorus proclaims the blessings of peace.

Exodos (1000-1234)

A herald enters and announces the gay Anthesterian banquet, a feast of plenty. Another herald informs Lamachus that the generals have ordered him to depart at once on an expedition. Gloomily Lamachus prepares, with an eye on the feast he is not permitted to enjoy. Dicaeopolis and Lamachus go off in different directions, the former to the feast, the latter to war.

Lamachus returns, wounded. Dicaeopolis comes back drunk, escorting two courtesans. The groans of Lamachus alternate with Dicaeopolis' amorous roistering. The Chorus hails the triumph of Dicaeopolis.

INTERPRETATION

1. This play is a plea for peace with Sparta during the Peloponnesian War.

2. It burlesques the Athenian assembly and satirizes the gullibility of the people.

3. Euripides is exposed to ridicule.

KNIGHTS

Prologue (lines 1-246)

The scene is before the house of Demos (The People). Two slaves (representing the generals Demosthenes and Nicias) have just been whipped because of the malice of the Paphlagonian (representing Cleon, the powerful leader of the extreme democrats). They seek a way out of their troubles. Their master Demos is under the domination of a new slave, the Paphlagonian tanner, who flatters him, and panders to his wishes. He has made him the prey of soothsayers, and constantly incites Demos against his other slaves, who are mistreated as a result.

In their despair Demosthenes and Nicias decide to drink wine and formulate a plan. As they begin, Demosthenes hits upon a happy idea. They will steal the oracle book of the Paphlagonian and thus outsmart him. From the oracle book they discover that a leather-monger (Cleon) is destined to be overthrown by a sausage-monger.

Just then a sausage-monger enters, and they greet him as the savior of Athens. Demosthenes tells him he is destined to rule

Athens because he comes of disreputable parents, has a little education, is generally ignorant and without scruples. Demosthenes also instructs him how to be a demagogue. His cause will be championed by the Knights and all good people who hate Cleon. Just then Cleon appears threateningly. As the sausage-monger tries to run away, Demosthenes summons the Knights.

Parodos (247-275)

The Chorus of Athenian Knights (a conservative group who manned the cavalry) enters, chases Cleon and abuses him. Cleon appeals to the Popular Assembly for help.

Pro-Agon (276-302)

Cleon and the sausage-monger gird themselves for the *Agon* by hurling accusations and counter-accusations against each other.

Agon (303-460)

The Chorus, the sausage-monger and Demosthenes assail Cleon, calling him a disturber of the state, imposer of unjust tribute on the Allies, a cheat, deceiver of citizens and Allies alike. The sausage-monger claims to be as low born as Cleon. Cleon defends his skill in speaking to the people, in controlling the generals, moulding the stupid Demos to his will through masterful shamelessness and skill at informing.

Episode (461-497)

The sausage-monger is hailed by the Chorus as the new star of Athens. Cleon threatens to accuse him of treason before the Council, and rushes out. Demosthenes helps the sausage-monger gird for the battle of words before the Council.

Parabasis (498-610)

The Chorus addresses the audience, commenting on their withdrawal of favor from other comic writers, and bespeaks their goodwill toward Aristophanes. They praise the good old days of their fathers, who won victory after victory for Athens, fighting not for food and pay, but for the welfare of their city.

Episode (611-755)

The sausage-monger enters to announce he has been victorious over the Paphlagonian before the Council. He outsmarted him at his own game of playing upon the weaknesses of the people. Cleon enters and a battle royal develops between him and the sausage-monger. Then Demos appears, and they begin to vie for his favor.

Second Agon (756-941)

The Paphlagonian recounts all he has done for Demos' welfare: granted him money without end that he extorted from the citizens, defended him in battle and performed other noteworthy services, including the capture of Pylos from Sparta, ferreted out the subversives. He is exceedingly obsequious.

The sausage-monger offers Demos comforts, peace and plenty of food, exposing Cleon's peculations and deceit. Finally he gives him a pair of shoes and a tunic. Demos is completely won over.

Episode (942-1262)

Demos gives the sausage-monger his signet ring, making him his minister. The Paphlagonian and the sausage-monger now compete again for Demos' favor by citing their oracles. Demos prefers those of the sausage-monger.

Then the two leave to bring offerings of food and drink for Demos. The latter now reveals to the Chorus that he is not as stupid as he seems, and that he plays one off against the other for his own advantage. Again the sausage-monger is victorious. He is now confirmed in his position as minister to Demos, and we learn that his true name is Agoracritus (Choice of the Agora).

Second Parabasis (1263-1314)

The Chorus addresses the audience, abusing well-known individuals in Athens.

Exodos (1315-1408)

Agoracritus reenters, dressed as befits his new position. He has an important announcement—he has boiled Demos in magical herbs and rejuvenated him, so that he lives in the good old days of the past. Demos, transformed, enters, talking of peace, the days of Athenian glory, integrity in government and the law courts. Agoracritus presents to Demos, to have and to hold, the lovely maiden Peace, whom Cleon has been hiding all this time. Cleon is to get the sausage-monger's job, and he will have to face those whom he wronged most deeply—the Athenian Allies.

INTERPRETATION

    1. Attack on the political leader Cleon and his war policy.

    2. Satire on demagogues.

    3. Plea for return to limited democracy of the early part of the Fifth Century.

CLOUDS

Prologue (lines 1-262)

Strepsiades, an old Athenian gentleman, lies tossing on his bed, worried about the debts which his son has incurred because of a mania for chariot racing. His son, Phidippides, talks in his sleep about the races. Still unable to fall asleep, Strepsiades tells of his happy early life in the country, and how his difficulties began when he married an elegant city lady. After their son was born, they quarreled about his name; his wife insisted on a name which had some reference to "horse." So they called him Phidippides (Son of Sparer of Horses), and he grew up with a passion for horses.

Suddenly Strepsiades has an idea. He wakens his son, and asks him to enroll in the school of Socrates, the Athenian philosopher, next door, in order to learn how to win lawsuits, for he expects to be sued for his son's debts. He hopes that the education in clever speaking will help him evade payment. When Phidippides refuses because school will ruin his tan, Strepsiades, despite his old age, decides to enter the school himself.

He knocks on the door of the Thinkery of Socrates, and is rebuked for disturbing the studies of his disciples. He hears about

Socrates' subtle ideas, and is eager to join the school. He sees other disciples, who are pale and disposed in various odd positions, studying a variety of subjects. Then he finally spies the master himself suspended in a basket from the roof of the Thinkery. He learns that Socrates cannot think unless he is in a rarefied atmosphere. Socrates is informed of Strepsiades' desire to learn to talk well enough to be able to evade payment of his debts.

Parodos (263-509)

As Socrates prays to Air, Ether and the Clouds, his special divinities, the Chorus of Clouds enters. The frightened Strepsiades watches the Chorus sing and dance. He learns that they are the goddesses who inspire tricky rhetoric, windy talk, and aid quacks and impostors. Socrates teaches Strepsiades about the nature and power of the Clouds, and that there is no Zeus. It is the Clouds, according to Socrates, that cause rain, thunder and lightning, not Zeus. Strepsiades is convinced, and swears to accept no gods but Chaos, the Clouds, and the Tongue. He is ready to undergo all difficulties in order to learn sufficient eloquence to outwit his creditors. Socrates administers a preliminary examination, in which Strepsiades reveals that his main interest is evasion of debts, and then they enter the Thinkery.

First Parabasis (510-626)

The Chorus, addressing the audience, expresses Aristophanes' conviction that this is his best play, airing his views on the writing of comedy, and his pride in his art. They ask the audience for divine worship of the Clouds, recounting their services to the Athenians. Finally they attack the politician Cleon.

Episodes (627-888)

Socrates rushes out, incensed at Strepsiades' stupidity and bad memory. Strepsiades comes out, and is required to lie on a bed while he is being instructed by Socrates. It is obvious that the old man is not interested in learning for its own sake, but only for the material reward he may gain from his knowledge. His major interest is the art of false reasoning. After an unsuccessful lesson in the gender of nouns, Strepsiades is ordered to lie on the bed to ponder. He is assailed by bugs, and howls in pain. After a silence, he reveals his innermost thoughts to Socrates: he can only think of ways of outwitting his creditors, but at these thoughts he is quite ingenious. Socrates is, however, finally disgusted with him, and dismisses him from the school because of his bad memory.

Strepsiades then decides to drive his son out of his home unless he enrolls in the Thinkery. He tries to teach his son some of his newly acquired knowledge. Phidippides thinks it all quite foolish, but is rapidly inducted into the school.

First Agon (889-1112)

Phidippides is instructed by Just Cause and Unjust Cause, two teachers in the Thinkery. They quarrel and debate with each other, as each elaborates on his own merits. Just Cause exemplifies truth, justice, uprightness; Unjust Cause material success and modern ways. Each delivers a formal speech expounding his virtues. Just Cause discourses on the old education which emphasizes honesty, justice, modesty, discipline, good health through physical training, morality, good manners, temperance, and respect for elders. Unjust Cause presents the merits of the new (Sophistic) education, which teaches how to discover loopholes in the laws, how to win arguments through clever speaking, how to talk oneself out of difficult situations, and the propriety of taking enervating hot baths, and practicing sexual looseness and intemperance. Just Cause finally acknowledges defeat on a technicality. Phidippides is to be instructed to talk cleverly by Unjust Cause.

Second Parabasis (1113-1130)

The Chorus addresses the judges of the contest in comedy, and asks that the prize be awarded to this play.

Episode (1131-1320)

Several days elapse. Strepsiades comes to inquire about his son's progress in the Thinkery, and learns from Socrates what a brilliant student Phidippides has turned out to be. Overjoyed, he greets his son deliriously. Phidippides gives an exhibition of his ability to split hairs and quibble in the manner of the Sophists. A money-lender arrives to collect a debt from Strepsiades. He refuses to pay him because he makes an error in gender. Another money lender is driven off by Strepsiades with the aid of the little skill which he himself has acquired.

Some time later, in the midst of a meal, Strepsiades rushes out of his house, howling with pain and indignation because his son Phidippides has just beaten him.

Second Agon (1321-1452)

Strepsiades and his son debate on the justice of a son beating his father. It is revealed that they have quarreled over the merits of Euripides, with Phidippides defending him. He argues that he was just in beating his father, because his father beat him when he was a child, and his father is now in his second childhood. Strepsiades admits defeat. Phidippides then undertakes to prove that it is also just to beat one's mother.

Exodos (1453-1510)

This is too much for Strepsiades. He suddenly admits that he has ruined his son by following the path of evil, and he regrets his errors. Rushing to the Thinkery, he begins to demolish and burn the school with the aid of his slaves, mocking and driving out Socrates and his disciples.

INTERPRETATION

1. Satire of the "new education" of the Sophists and on scientific speculation as destructive of traditional religion and morality.
2. Attack on intellectuals as making bad citizens.
3. Caricature of the philosopher Socrates.

WASPS

Prologue (lines 1-229)

The scene is before the house of Philocleon in Athens. Sosias and Xanthias, slaves of Philocleon, an admirer of the demagogue Cleon, are sleepily trying to stand guard in front of the house to prevent the old man from getting out. His son Bdelycleon, who mounts guard on the roof, wants to prevent his father from indulging in his passion for jury service.

Xanthias explains to the audience the mania of Philocleon for the courts. His son is brokenhearted. All previous efforts to keep Philocleon away from the courts have failed. Finally, Bdelycleon surrounded the house with a huge net, and decided to maintain a permanent guard.

Philocleon makes a series of frantic efforts to escape and get to court on time: he ferrets about the stove-chamber like a rat; then pretends he is the smoke coming out of the chimney. Failing in this, he asks Bdelycleon to let him go sell his ass. His son, trying to deprive him of this excuse, fetches the ass himself, only to find the old man clinging to the belly of the ass like Odysseus escaping from the Cyclops' den. At length they lock him into the house again and pile stones against the door, but soon Philocleon climbs beneath the tiles of the roof, pretending to be a bird ready to fly away.

Parados (230-315)

The Chorus of Jurymen dressed as Wasps enters to summon Philocleon to join them.

Episode (316-525)

Philocleon greets his fellow-jurymen and begs for assistance. While Bdelycleon falls asleep, the old man, though toothless, manages to gnaw his way through the net and let himself down the window with a rope. Bdelycleon awakes and with his slaves seizes his father to prevent his escape. The Chorus comes to Philocleon's aid, and a wild tussle takes place.

Agon (526-727)

Father and son debate the pros and cons of jury service. Philocleon argues that jurymen wield great power and are courted by the politicians. He describes the court scenes, the devious arguments and devices employed by plaintiffs and accusers. Jurymen decide the fate of people. They enjoy the favor of Cleon and other demagogues, who cater to them. The pay is good, and Philocleon thereby has the respect of his wife and daughter, if not his son Bdelycleon.

Bdelycleon assails the "disease so inveterate and widespread in Athens." The pay of the jurymen is but a tiny part of the state budget. The fees paid are mere crumbs given by the demagogues to the people. The jurymen are but slavish tools in their hands.

Episode (728-1008)

Philocleon is finally convinced, and the Chorus concedes victory for Bdelycleon. He promises to feed his father and to permit him to hold trials at home over his slaves, with all the paraphernalia for judging cases.

Philocleon tries the dog Labes for stealing some cheese. The court procedure and atmosphere is travestied in this scene. Two people costumed as dogs, strongly resembling the demagogues Cleon and Laches, are brought in. One is the plaintiff, the other the defendant. Bdelycleon skillfully pleads the case of the dog, bringing in Labes' puppies. Philocleon, despite his intentions and usual practice, acquits the dog. Horrified at his error, Philocleon swoons and is taken inside.

Parabasis (1009-1121)

The Chorus addresses the audience, and on behalf of Aristophanes reproaches them for not having due respect for the many services the author rendered Athens; in particular they criticize the cool reception given to his play the *Clouds* the year before. They then glorify the jurymen of the past, who fought at Marathon and under Cimon, and explain why they are dressed as stinging wasps.

Episode (1122-1264)

Bdelycleon and Philocleon come out, on the way to a banquet. The son instructs his father on how to behave like an Athenian gentleman.

Second Parabasis (1265-1291)

The Chorus abuses a number of prominent Athenians, including Cleon.

Episode (1292-1449)

Xanthias returns to report the monstrous misbehavior of Philocleon at the banquet. He became drunk, insulted all the guests, ate too much, and was boisterous.

Philocleon enters, quite drunk and holding a nude flute-girl, whom he has stolen from the guests. The abused guests have followed him. The old man becomes amorous with the girl, to his son's disgust. Philocleon is accused by a number of people—of theft, malicious mischief, assault and battery. Bdelycleon carries the old man into the house.

Stasimon (1450-1473)

The Chorus praises the character and behavior of Bdelycleon.

Exodos (1474-1537)

Philocleon soon emerges again, and indulges in a wild dance, in which the Chorus joins.

INTERPRETATION

1. This play satirizes the abuses of the Athenian judicial system.
2. It ridicules the fondness of Athenians for law suits, and exposes the use of the law courts by the demagogues to deceive the people.
3. Attack on the demagogue Cleon.

PEACE

Prologue (lines 1-300)

The scene is before the farmhouse of Trygaeus; nearby is the palace of Zeus. Two slaves of Trygaeus, an Athenian citizen, are shown kneading cakes of dung and feeding them to a dung-beetle, which Trygaeus is keeping in his stable. The slaves are revolted at their task of feeding the gluttonous, disgusting monster.

Trygaeus has despaired of securing peace through the usual means, and so has decided to take matters into his own hands. He is determined to go directly to Zeus himself to save Greece from mutual destruction. His previous attempt to climb to Zeus' palace on ladders failed, and he suffered a broken head. And so he obtained the dung-beetle, on which he intends to fly to heaven economically.

Trygaeus is revealed astride the dung-beetle. He wants to save all Greece. As he flies off, his little daughter bids him farewell. Soon Trygaeus is at the door of Zeus' palace. He is greeted rudely by Hermes, who informs him that Zeus and the Olympian gods, because of their anger at the Greeks, have moved as far away as possible. They have left War and Tumult in their palace to rule over the Greeks in their stead.

War has cast Peace into a deep pit, and piled stones on her. Now War has prepared a huge mortar, and intends to grind up the cities of Greece. Soon the monster War enters with his huge mortar. One by one he throws products representing various Greek cities into the mortar. He calls his slave Tumult to fetch a pestle. But he cannot find one, for both Athens and Sparta have lost theirs—Cleon and Brasidas died recently. Frustrated, War goes out to make a pestle for himself.

Trygaeus realizes he must rescue Peace quickly from the pit, and summons laborers and farmers from all parts of Greece to help him.

Parodos (301-345)

The Chorus of laborers and farmers from various Greek states enters, elated at the prospect of restoring peace.

Episodes (346-728)

Hermes objects to the efforts to free Peace, but is soon appeased with promises of prayers and sacrifices. The Chorus and Trygaeus begin to lift the stones. There ensues typical Hellenic rivalry, confusion, and working at cross purposes. Finally Peace is drawn out of the pit, together with Opora (Harvest) and Theoria (Embassy). Trygaeus and the Chorus adore Peace, and Hermes tells them why she disappeared for so long—because of the misdeeds of the Greeks and the evils wrought by Cleon, Brasidas and the informers. Hermes bestows Opora on Trygaeus as his wife; Theoria is to be brought to the Senate. Trygaeus descends to earth with the two ladies.

Parabasis (729-818)

The Chorus addresses the audience, expounding Aristophanes' distinction as a comic playwright ("he has built up for us a great art"), and attacking a tragic poet and his sons. They pray to the Muse for peace.

Episodes (819-1126)

Trygaeus comes in with Opora and Theoria. He begins to enjoy peace. He then instructs his slave to prepare Opora for the wedding. But first Theoria, completely nude, is presented to the Senate. Preparations for a great feast are begun. Trygaeus prays to Peace to bring friendship and prosperity again to all the Greeks.

Trygaeus and his slave are roasting meat, when the soothsayer Hierocles appears. He utters prophecies purporting that the war cannot possibly be stopped, and tries to obtain a share in the feast. Trygaeus drives him off.

Second Parabasis (1127-1190)

The Chorus hails peace and its pleasures.

Exodos (1191-1359)

A sickle maker enters. His business is now booming, and he therefore offers a sickle and casks to Trygaeus as wedding presents.

A group of persons hard hit by the outbreak of peace appear. They include an armorer, crest maker, breastplate manufacturer, trumpet maker, helmet maker, polisher of lances. Their spokesman, the armorer, tries to unload surplus war products on Trygaeus. He promptly rejects their offer and drives them off.

The sons of Lamachus and Cleonymus sing snatches of songs reminiscent of their fathers. Trygaeus declares the beginning of the feast. Opora is brought out, and Trygaeus and the Chorus sing a marriage song.

INTERPRETATION

1. This play attacks the leaders of the war parties in Athens and Sparta and their supporters.

2. It is a plea for peace and Panhellenic harmony.

BIRDS

BACKGROUND

In the year this play was produced a mighty Athenian naval force carrying the cream of Athens' army was engaged in the ambitious but fruitless effort to capture the island of Sicily and annex it to the Athenian Empire (see p. 7).

Prologue (lines 1-259)

Pisthetaerus, an old Athenian adventurer, and Euelpides, a fellow-Athenian, are seen in a desolate spot, each holding in his hand a bird, which has been serving as a guide to the kingdom of the birds. The two Athenians are discouraged. Euelpides explains that they have abandoned Athens for a quieter country. As they call upon Epops, the mysterious hoopoe (lapwing), his servant Trochilus enters, and they are seized by uncontrollable fear. When Epops appears, they explain their mission: they want his advice on where to find a quieter, more peaceful city to live in than Athens, a place where there is no money with its attendant selfish motives and disunity. He makes several suggestions, which they reject. Suddenly Pisthetaerus is struck with an idea. Why do not the birds build their own city between the sky and earth? They will thus become masters of gods and men alike, by intercepting the smoke

of sacrifices made by men to the gods. Epops excitedly summons
his wife, Procne, and the other birds.

Parodos (260-450)

The birds of the Chorus begin to arrive one by one. Pisthetaerus
and Euelpides comment on them, with topical allusions to contemporary personages in Athens. As the Chorus inquires why they
have been summoned, and spy the two men, they threaten to tear
them into pieces. They rush to attack, but are stopped by Epops.
He asks the two Athenians to explain their plan to the birds, after
a truce has been declared.

Agon (451-675)

Pisthetaerus and Euelpides set out to "sell" their project to the
birds. They argue that the birds were the first creatures of the universe, and that they once ruled all lands. They discourse on the
importance of birds to man. Having stirred up the pride of the
birds, they propose the building of a new city between earth and
heaven. When this is completed an ultimatum will be sent to the
gods and men demanding submission to the birds and divine worship from men of the birds as superior to all. The birds are completely won over. They are prepared to follow Pisthetaerus.

Parabasis (676-800)

The Chorus comes forward and addresses the audience. They
give the audience a lesson in the origin of birds and their importance to man. They next invite the spectators to come to live with
them and enjoy a life without legal restrictions such as exist in
Athens. They finally expatiate on the advantages of having wings.

Episode (801-1057)

Pisthetaerus and Euelpides return, having sprouted wings. They
decide to name the new city Cloudcuckooland, and supervise the
construction work. Prayers are devised for the new bird-gods. Various quacks and impostors arrive: a poet to celebrate the city in
verse, a prophet with oracles, a mathematician to do surveying

work, an Athenian government inspector, and a dealer in decrees, but they are all driven off.

Second Parabasis (1058-1117)

The birds proclaim their divinity, and issue a decree setting forth penalties for those who injure birds in any way. They discourse on the carefree happiness of birds, and ask that the prize for the best play in the current competition be awarded to them, offering blessings to the Athenians, or evil if it is not.

Episodes (1118-1705)

A messenger describes how the wall of the city was constructed and completed by the birds. A second messenger announces that an interloping god has entered the new realm. It is Iris, the messenger of the gods. She is shocked at the arrogance of the birds. Pisthetaerus threatens the gods with war, ordering that the city be closed to the gods and that smoke from men's sacrifices be intercepted.

A herald arrives from earth and presents Pisthetaerus with a golden crown. Many humans are desirous of dwelling in Cloudcuckooland. Pisthetaerus orders wings prepared for their reception. Several men arrive seeking wings to aid them in their activities, a parricide, a poet, an informer.

The Titan Prometheus, the benefactor of mankind, masked and hiding under an umbrella, so as not to be seen by Zeus, arrives. He has come to offer his help as an informer, and tells them that the gods are starving and that there is dissension between the Olympian gods and the foreign (Treballian) gods. He advises Pisthetaerus that when peace envoys are sent by the gods he should demand, as tokens of submission, the sceptre of Zeus and the hand of Basileia (Royalty), Zeus' housekeeper, in marriage.

Poseidon arrives with Heracles, now a minor divinity, and a Treballian god. They come as ambassadors of peace. Advised by Prometheus, Pisthetaerus states his terms. There are long, drawn-out negotiations. Heracles, having been offered dinner, immediately votes to accept the terms. Poseidon dissents. The Treballian god talks gibberish, but it is interpreted by Heracles and Pisthetaerus as a vote for peace. The terms are finally accepted, and preparations are made for Pisthetaerus' wedding to Basileia and for the wedding feast.

Exodos (1706-1765)

Pisthetaerus and Basileia enter in divine splendor, Pisthetaerus holding Zeus' lightning and thunderbolt. As the Chorus of birds adores them and joyfully sings the wedding song, the couple fly away to Zeus' palace where they are to reign.

INTERPRETATION

1. Escapist, utopian fantasy.
2. Perhaps criticism of grandiose imperialistic schemes of Athens (Sicilian Expedition of 415 B.C.).

LYSISTRATA

BACKGROUND

In 411 B.C. Athenian fortunes during the Peloponnesian War were at a very low ebb. The disastrous defeat in Sicily in 413 B.C. had severely weakened the city and empire, and Athens was on the verge of revolution.

Prologue (1-253)

The scene is Athens, beneath the Acropolis. Lysistrata, an Athenian woman, impatiently awaits a group of women she has asked to meet her. Calonice arrives, and is informed by Lysistrata that the future of all Greece depends on its women. Myrrhine arrives, then Lampito from Sparta, accompanied by a Boeotian and a Corinthian woman. Lysistrata proclaims her scheme to bring an end to the Peloponnesian War—all the women of Greece must agree to a sex strike.

There is vigorous objection to the idea from the other Athenian women, but they finally reluctantly agree. Lysistrata's plan is further elaborated: all the women of Greece are to heighten their allure in every way but deny themselves to their men until they bring about permanent peace. The old women of Athens are to seize the Acropolis with its war treasury housed in the Parthenon. Under

Lysistrata's direction they all swear a solemn oath to abstain from sex until war ends. Shouts are heard: the women have succeeded in capturing the Acropolis.

Parodos (254-386)

A semi-chorus of old men of Athens enters with fire-pots to smoke out the women. Another semi-chorus, of old women, enters with pitchers of water to extinguish the fire-pots. They abuse each other, and the women empty their pitchers on the men.

Pro-Agon (387-475)

An Athenian magistrate enters with four policemen. He has come to obtain money from the treasury in order to procure additional naval equipment. The policemen are ordered to force the gates of the Acropolis.

Lysistrata comes out of the Acropolis to negotiate. The magistrate orders her arrested. The women guard her and beat off the policemen.

Agon (476-613)

Lysistrata and the magistrate debate the issue: he assails the women for trespassing on the concerns of men; she proclaims, "War shall be the concern of women." He belittles women; she declares they have acquired experience in managing affairs through household duties, and have a great stake in politics and peace. The magistrate retires ignominiously.

Parabasis (614-705)

The semi-chorus of old men assails the interference of women. The semi-chorus of old women boasts of women's services to the state in bearing children. The two semi-choruses engaged in a mock battle, abusing each other.

First Episode (706-780)

After an interval of a few days, Lysistrata comes out from the Acropolis. The women are trying to desert. Their excuses are varied: some declare they have household chores to look after;

one pleads that she is about to have a baby. Lysistrata succeeds in holding them together through the force of her personality.

First Stasimon (781-828)

The Choruses of men and women abuse each other.

Second Episode (829-1013)

Lysistrata spies an Athenian. It is Cinesias, Myrrhine's husband. Lysistrata encourages Myrrhine to use every feminine wile on her husband, but to frustrate his desires. He has brought their baby with a view to luring her home. Myrrhine leads him on with every enticement, but finally runs back into the Acropolis.

A Spartan herald arrives to announce that conditions in Sparta are no better, and that he has been sent to arrange a truce. Lampito and the Spartan women have all banished their husbands until peace is made in all Greece. The Athenian magistrate, alarmed at the general conspiracy of the women, hastens to inform the Council.

Second Stasimon (1014-1071)

The semi-chorus of men begs for reconciliation with the women; the semi-chorus of women expresses eager willingness. They both join in a plea for peace.

Third Episode (1072-1188)

Spartan ambassadors arrive to sue for peace. Athenian ambassadors enter. They all call for Lysistrata.

Lysistrata appears with a female statue representing Reconciliation. She proclaims the worth of women, and reads them a lesson in Panhellenism and the need for peace. The minds of the men are on more mundane matters, but all eagerly agree to peace, and enter the Acropolis to sacrifice and exchange sacred oaths.

Third Stasimon (1189-1215)

The Chorus, now merged into a single group, sings a joyful song.

Exodos (1216-1321)

There has taken place a banquet to celebrate the declaration of peace. The Athenians and Spartans joined in the festivities in complete harmony. The Spartan and Athenian envoys now appear, followed by Lysistrata and all the women. A chorus of Spartans sings and dances joyously a national dance; then a chorus of Athenians responds in similar fashion. All then leave for their homes, together with their women, singing and dancing.

INTERPRETATION

1. Utopian plea for peace between Athens and Sparta and for an end to the Peloponnesian War.
2. Plea for Panhellenism.

THESMOPHORIAZUSAE

Women Celebrating the Thesmophoria

Prologue (lines 1-294)

The scene is before the house of the tragic poet Agathon; nearby is the Thesmophorion. Euripides, the famous tragedian, and his father-in-law Mnesilochus come to Agathon for help. They summon him out, but must await his pleasure, for he is now composing. It appears that Euripides is in trouble: the women of Athens at a meeting this very day at the Thesmophorion are planning to punish Euripides with death for his insults to their sex in his tragedies. Euripides hopes to induce Agathon to go to the Thesmophorion dressed as a woman, and support Euripides.

The effeminate Agathon finally appears on the *eccyclema*, lying in his bed, surrounded by feminine toilet articles. Euripides explains his need to Agathon, but the latter firmly refuses. Mnesilochus then volunteers, and Euripides removes all obvious traces of his masculinity. Euripides borrows clothing from Agathon, dresses Mnesilochus like a woman, and sends him off to the meeting.

Parodos (295-379)

The scene shifts to the Thesmophorion. Mnesilochus enters, trying to act as womanly as possible. The Chorus of women celebrating the Thesmophoria pray for blessings to women.

Quasi-Agon (380-530)

A woman speaks in detail of the indignities Euripides has heaped on women in his plays. She moves that he be put to death. Another woman seconds the motion. Mnesilochus pleads the case eloquently, pointing out the numerous sins of women which Euripides has not mentioned.

Episodes (531-784)

The women are infuriated, and begin to punish the disloyal speaker, employing violent methods, when the well-known pederast Clisthenes, also dressed as a woman, enters. He has come to inform the women that there is a man in their midst. The women promptly investigate, and presently Mnesilochus is exposed as the intruder. Clisthenes hurries off to report the sacrilege to the magistrates.

Mnesilochus exercises his wits to discover a means of escape. The women threaten to burn him to death. He decides to send a message to Euripides to rush to his aid, and writes it on wooden statues, which he scatters about, imitating a character in one of Euripides' plays who wrote a message on oars which he cast into the water.

Parabasis (785-845)

The Chorus addresses the audience, maintaining the superiority of women over men.

Episode (846-946)

Euripides has not come, and Mnesilochus decides to recite lines from the part of Helen in Euripides' play of that name. Euripides promptly enters dressed as Menelaüs and reciting lines from Menelaüs' part in the *Helen*.

A magistrate enters with a Scythian policeman, and Euripides hastily retreats. Mnesilochus is arrested and bound to a post, still dressed as a woman, as an object of ridicule.

Stasimon (947-1000)

The Chorus sings a joyous song of praise to various gods, including Artemis, Hermes, Pan and Bacchus.

Episode (1001-1135)

Mnesilochus tries another device. He quotes a lament from Euripides' *Andromeda,* while Euripides, impersonating Echo in the wings, repeats the final word or phrase of everything Mnesilochus and the policeman say. Finally Euripides enters disguised as Perseus rushing to the rescue of Andromeda in distress. But he fails to induce the barbarian policeman to release Mnesilochus.

Stasimon (1136-1159)

The Chorus prays to Athena and the Thesmophoriae.

Exodos (1160-1231)

Euripides returns disguised as a procuress, bringing a flute-girl and a dancing-girl. He makes his peace with the Chorus, promising never again to malign women. The girls, with the assistance of Euripides, distract the policeman with pleasures. Soon he goes off-stage with the dancing-girl. Euripides promptly releases Mnesilochus, and they both run off.

When the policeman returns the Chorus obligingly sends him off in the opposite direction.

INTERPRETATION

This play ridicules Euripides and Agathon as writers of tragedy.

FROGS

BACKGROUND

Near the end of the Peloponnesian War the democrats, faced with internal unrest because of continued Athenian reverses, and fearful of subversion, exiled the conservative families.

Prologue (lines 1-208)

Dionysus, god of wine, enters disguised as Heracles with lion skin and club, but also wearing the formal tragic costume. His slave, Xanthias, is on a donkey, and carries a bundle of luggage on his shoulder. After an attempt at a few ribald jokes, Xanthias complains about carrying the bundles, but Dionysus insists that the donkey is carrying Xanthias—and therefore the bundles, too. They arrive at the house of the hero Heracles, and knock. When Heracles sees Dionysus' odd costume, he roars with laughter. Dionysus reveals that he is consumed by a great passion for the dead tragic poet Euripides. He is bent on going to Hades to bring him back to Athens, for contemporary tragedians are not as clever and tricky as Euripides was. He asks Heracles for directions to Hades, for Heracles once made the journey to seize the three-headed watchdog of the Underworld, Cerberus. Heracles playfully suggests three ways to reach Hades quickly: all of them involve suicide. Heracles then tells him the usual route, emphasizing the horrors and difficulties, in order to frighten Dionysus.

As Xanthias again complains about the bundles, a funeral passes by. Dionysus hails the dead man, and asks him to take the bundles along with him to Hades, but the dead man asks too high a transportation fee, and Xanthias shoulders the bundles again. The two go on their way, and reach the banks of the River Styx. They see the old squalid ferryman of the River Styx, Charon, but he refuses to take Xanthias, because he is a slave and had not seen military service. After Xanthias departs on foot, Charon requires Dionysus to do the rowing.

First Parodos (209-270)

As he does, he hears the Chorus of Frogs, singing and keeping rhythm with his rowing, using the repeated refrain, *brekekekex coax coax*.

Episode (271-353)

After reaching the other side of the River Styx, Dionysus pays his fare to Charon, and meets Xanthias. They are both frightened by the darkness and by the sights of the Underworld. Dionysus in fear rushes to his priest sitting in the seat of honor in the audience, and begs for protection. They hear flute playing and watch in hiding.

Second Parodos (354-459)

The Chorus of Initiates enters, singing a hymn to Dionysus, invoking his presence. With many satirical topical allusions to living persons, the Chorus asks all uninitiated to depart. They sing hymns to Athena, Demeter, and Dionysus, asking them to guide them in their joyful celebration. Dionysus then comes out of hiding, and joins in the wild, orgiastic dance. The Chorus assails well-known Athenians of the time, and finally gives directions to Dionysus how to enter Hades' palace.

Episode (460-673)

Dionysus knocks on the door of Hades' palace. Aeacus, one of the judges of the Underworld, appears, and taking him for Heracles, runs to summon guards to arrest him for theft. Dionysus is terror-stricken. In fear he offers to change costumes with Xanthias and carry his bundles. When the exchange has been made, one of Persephone's maids appears and joyfully welcomes Xanthias, thinking him Heracles, to a feast and entertainment. Dionysus now, asserting that he was merely fooling before, forces Xanthias to change costumes with him again. After this is effected, a landlady of an inn appears, accuses Dionysus, thinking him Heracles, of having failed to pay his enormous hotel bill when he was last in Hades, and threatens to summon her lawyer. Dionysus and Xanthias change costumes once again.

Aeacus now arrives with his guards to arrest Heracles. Xanthias, overpowered, offers Dionysus, as his slave, for questioning by torture. At this point, Dionysus reveals his true identity. Since there is doubt as to who is the god and who the slave, it is decided to test this by whipping each. Since both cry out in pain, and Aeacus is at a loss, he decides to take them both to King Hades for identification of the true god. Dionysus suggests it would have been a good idea to have thought of that before the whipping was administered.

Parabasis (674-737)

The Chorus praises the Athenians, and abuses the politician Cleophon. They urge an amnesty for the reactionary revolutionaries of some years ago, who are in exile or have been disfranchised. They then gibe at a political figure called Cligenes. Finally they urge the Athenians to honor the older citizen families above the newer ones, as pure coins are more valued than debased ones.

Episode (738-894)

Aeacus reappears, having found out the real Dionysus. He and Xanthias have become quite intimate. A noise of quarreling is heard, and Aeacus reveals that Aeschylus and Euripides are competing for the privilege of eating free at Hades' table. Aeschylus had had the place of honor for some time, but, since Euripides' recent arrival, popular opinion had swung to Euripides, particularly because the rather large number of disreputable and lowborn people in Hades naturally favored Euripides. To end the dissension, Hades has proclaimed a contest as a trial of their skill. Sophocles has deferred to Aeschylus. The contest is to consist of the weighing of lines in a scale from the works of the two contestants. Dionysus is to be the judge.

As the Chorus sings in anticipation of the mighty verbal battle in the making, Euripides, Aeschylus and Dionysus come out. After the contestants warm up with a few trial gibes at each other, the Chorus prays to the Muses for aid. Before the duel begins, Aeschylus prays in an orthodox fashion to the goddess Demeter; Euripides, however, to Ether, his own tongue, and other esoteric concepts.

Agon (895-1098)

Euripides begins by attacking Aeschylus for having employed superhuman characters far removed from realistic people, and for using silent, veiled characters merely for effect. He assails him, too, for his long, difficult words, his bombastic language, which is often obscure and pompous, his excessively long choral odes, and his dwelling so much on warlike themes.

In turn, Aeschylus attacks Euripides for his prosaic style, his excessive realism in language, characters and plots. Realism is criticized as inviting immorality among the citizens. Particularly, Euripides' realistic treatment of the illicit and abnormal in relations between the sexes is assailed as a corrupting influence. His formal, explanatory prologues are censured as monotonous. In addition, his elevation of humble people and his debunking of heroes of the past have a harmful effect on the audience.

It is conceded by both that the function of the dramatist is to improve the citizen body. Aeschylus accuses Euripides of corrupting them through his rationalism, clever rhetoric and sophistry, which he rejects as diminishing the value of citizens as soldiers, from whom unquestioning obedience is required. Aeschylus had instilled patriotism among the Athenians; Euripides' realism corrupts them. Aeschylus asserts that only noble and idealized aspects of life should be depicted in the theater. Euripides' excessive emphasis on pathos and human weaknesses, and his religious unorthodoxy can only have a harmful effect.

Episode (1099-1499)

Euripides continues his attack on Aeschylus, emphasizing his obscurity and repetitiousness. Aeschylus retorts with an attack on Euripides' prologues, which he asserts are monotonous and so formalized that it is possible to fit the rhythm of the phrase "a bottle of oil" at the end of each of them. When Euripides points to the monotony of Aeschylus' music, which is noisy and pompous, concentrating on military themes, Aeschylus repudiates Euripides' newfangled, sensuous music, as well as his commingling of realistic language with traditional tragic style.

The scale is now brought out, and each of the contestants quotes a verse from one of his plays into the balance. In each of three trials Aeschylus wins, for the meanings of the words he chooses involve weighty objects or ideas, while those of Euripides, on the contrary, suggest lightness and intangible Sophistic intellectuality. At this point Hades arrives to learn who the winner is. But Dionysus still finds it difficult to decide. He then proposes to grant victory to the one who can give the best practical advice for saving the city from its difficulties in the Peloponnesian War. Euripides is vague and sophistic; Aeschylus decisive and vigorous, recommending an increase in the fighting potential against the enemy. Dionysus is on the point of deciding in favor of Aeschylus when Euripides reminds him that he came to Hades explicitly to bring him back to Athens. Dionysus chooses Aeschylus, quoting to Euripides his own famous

line from the *Hippolytus,* "My tongue has sworn . . ." Hades invites Aeschylus and Dionysus to a farewell dinner.

Exodos (1500-1533)

After dinner Hades sends Aeschylus off to earth, urging him to
aid his city, and giving him death-dealing gifts for a number of
specific individuals in Athens. He asks Aeschylus to tell these persons that Hades wants to see them soon. Aeschylus asks that
Sophocles succeed him at the place of honor at Hades' table, and
that Euripides be forever excluded. The Chorus bids Aeschylus
bon voyage.

INTERPRETATION

1. Fantasy on literary criticism. (Aristophanes is thus the first
extant literary critic in the history of literature.)
2. Satire on Euripides as a dramatist and moralist; some criticism of Aeschylus.
3. Attack on realism in the drama as tending to encourage immorality and lack of patriotism among the citizens.
4. Political theme: plea for national unity and recall of conservative political exiles.

ECCLESIAZUSAE

Women in Parliament

Prologue (lines 1-284)

The scene is a public square in Athens, before two houses, one
belonging to Praxagora. The time is before dawn. Praxagora, an
Athenian woman, awaits the arrival of other Athenian women.
They have formed a secret conspiracy to seize control of the government from the men. One by one the women appear, carrying
men's clothing. They receive instructions on masculine behavior
from Praxagora and attach false beards they have obtained. Praxagora outlines the arguments she will use, stressing the corruption of
existing governments and the evils wrought by demagogues.
They will move that control of the government be handed over

to the women, who will then establish a new, perfect order of society. Praxagora leads them off to the Assembly.

Parodos (285-311)

The Chorus of Women comments on the decay of civic devotion.

Episode (312-477)

Blepyrus, Praxagora's husband, enters in distress, wearing his wife's clothing. He awoke with the need to relieve himself, but could not find either his clothing or his wife. The man next door reports that his wife and clothing are gone too.

Soon Chremes, a friend of Blepyrus enters, and reports of amazing goings-on in the Assembly. It was heavily attended by a large group of pale persons, looking like shoemakers. A very beautiful young man, after an eloquent speech, moved that the government be turned over to the women, and the motion was enthusiastically carried. "It is the one and only innovation that has not yet been tried at Athens." Blepyrus looks forward to a life of pleasant leisure.

Second Parodos (478-503)

The Chorus, led by Praxagora, hastens back. They remove their masculine attire and their beards before the men realize the deception by which the women seized the government.

Episode (504-729)

Blepyrus gratuitously informs Praxagora of what has taken place in the Assembly. Praxagora outlines the new society to be established. All private property is to be abolished and everything, including women, is to be held in common by all. To avoid the danger that the prettiest women will monopolize the men, a law will be passed obligating men to sleep first with the ugly women. A similar law will be in effect to protect old men and ugly men. Lawsuits will end, for there will be no private property. They will live like one big happy family, eating common meals in public dining halls. In fact, Praxagora declares it will be possible to abolish prostitution. Blepyrus is delighted, and proud of being the dictator's husband. Praxagora prepares to go to the market place to supervise the redistribution of property.

Choral Interlude

(Provision is made for a choral piece here, but none was written by the author.)

Episode (730-876)

Chremes returns with his property and arranges everything in a line. A citizen arrives and tells Chremes he has no intention of contributing his property to the common store until he sees whether the others do. A female herald enters to announce a public feast for all. The citizen hastens to obey the law, and eagerly goes off to the banquet, intending to share in the feast without contributing his property.

Choral Interlude
Episode (877-1111)

The scene shifts, and the two houses now represent the abodes of two prostitutes. An old prostitute, heavily decked out with cosmetics, and a young beautiful courtesan recount their allure to men. A young man enters eagerly desirous of the young girl; but he knows, to his disgust, that he must first lie with the old woman. Despite his resistance and arguments, the law which requires young men to lie with old women before young ones cannot be disobeyed. He has already resigned himself, when the young girl rescues him and he starts to enter her house. Now an even older and uglier hag claims him. She is soon joined by still another old woman, even more frightful. They fight over him, and pull him back and forth. Finally, he is dragged off by the two old women.

Choral Interlude
Exodos (1112-1183)

The Chorus invites the audience to join the communal feast, and appeals to the judges to award the prize to this play.

Blepyrus and the Chorus depart joyously to the feast.

INTERPRETATION

1. This play, which exhibits many characteristics of the Middle

Comedy, satirizes the social and economic panaceas in the air during the Fourth Century.

2. It also satirizes democracy and the demagogues it spawned in Athens.

PLUTUS

Prologue (lines 1-252)

The scene is a public square in Athens, before the house of Chremylus. A ragged and blind old man enters followed by Chremylus and his slave Cario. Chremylus and Cario have been following the old man for a long time, and Cario is becoming impatient. Chremylus consulted the Delphic oracle on how his son might be successful in life and still remain principled. He was instructed by the oracle to follow the first man he met after leaving the temple. It turned out to be a blind, dirty old man.

Cario, in desperation, finally demands to know why they are following the old man. Chremylus reveals to his slave the oracle's injunction. He must persuade the blind man to accompany him home.

They demand of the old man that he reveal who he is. Reluctantly he tells them he is Plutus, the god of wealth. He was afflicted with blindness by Zeus because of the god's jealousy of mankind. Ever since, he has been unable to distinguish the good from the evil, and has been mistreated by all humans to whom he revealed his identity.

Chremylus has an idea. What if Plutus' blindness is healed? Would not all the ills of mankind be cured? Plutus is at first skeptical, but Chremylus convinces him of his power, "the sole cause of both good and evil." Chremylus then sends Cario to fetch the farmers who are his friends to share in the gifts of Plutus. Chremylus escorts Plutus into his house.

Parodos (253-321)

Cario brings in the Chorus of rustics. They learn that Plutus is in Chremylus' house and that they too will become rich. They dance in ribald joy.

First Episode (322-453)

Chremylus comes out to greet his neighbors. Blepsidemus, a friend of Chremylus, arrives. He is suspicious of Chremylus' sudden riches, word of which has begun to spread. When Blepsidemus is promised a share, he enthusiastically agrees to help in the restoration of Plutus' sight. They decide to take Plutus to the Temple of Asclepius, god of healing. Suddenly a horrifying woman enters. She is the goddess Poverty. They are terrified when they learn who she is.

Quasi-Agon (454-626)

Chremylus and Poverty debate on whether she or Plutus is of greater benefit to humanity. Chremylus argues that if Plutus regains his eyesight, he will reward only the good and shun the evil, and thus all will eventually become honest, rich and pious. Hunger, filth, poverty are not worthy of man.

Poverty counters that, if this happened, no one would want to work, and there would be no slaves, either. The good things of life would not be produced, and thus riches would be of no avail. Poverty and hunger are necessary to the best interests of humans, and the fount of all blessings. Riches cause degeneracy and lead to injustice.

Poverty is beaten in argument and departs with threats. Chremylus and Blepsidemus hasten to take Plutus to the Temple of Asclepius.

Choral Interlude

Second Episode (627-770)

Cario returns with joyful news, and reports to Chremylus' wife the miraculous cure that has been wrought: Plutus can see again!

Choral Interlude

Third Episode (771-801)

Plutus returns overjoyed at his restored eyesight and the Utopia about to be established.

Choral Interlude

Fourth Episode (802-958)

A Just Man enters. He is now for the first time happy, and wants to thank the god. An Informer enters. Times are indeed bad for him; he has been ruined. Cario strips the Informer of his cloak and shoes and dedicates them to Plutus. The Informer threatens to denounce the god.

Choral Interlude

Fifth Episode (959-1096)

An Old Woman, dressed as a young girl, comes to see Plutus. Her gigolo has no need of her any longer. The youth enters, and shows insolent independence of her.

Choral Interlude

Exodos (1097-1209)

Hermes enters and declares that the gods have lost their power: humans do not make sacrifices or pray to them any more. Hermes himself is starving, and there is no use any longer for the rascally tricks on which he used to thrive. Hermes deserts to the service of the new god.

A Priest of Zeus arrives. He too is starving, because there are no sacrifices being made. He too deserts to the new god. Plutus comes out, followed by the Old Woman. She is assured that the young man will return to her.

A procession to install Plutus on the Acropolis begins.

INTERPRETATION

1. This play belongs to the Middle Comedy.
2. It is a Utopian fantasy in which a better life through the elimination of economic injustice is portrayed.

LOST PLAYS OF
ARISTOPHANES

Aiolosicon; Amphiareus; Anagyrus; Babylonians; Centaur; Banqueters; Cocalus; Daedalus; Daughters of Danaüs; Farmers; Frying Pan Club; Gerytades; Heroes; Lemnians; Merchant Ships; Old Age; Phoenician Women; Poetry; Rehearsal; Telemesses; The Islands; The Storks; Triphales; Seasons; Women Under Canvas.

TECHNIQUE AND STYLE OF ARISTOPHANES

1. Serious satire on contemporary issues, achieved through exaggeration and caricature.

2. Unsurpassed comic imagination.

3. Unparalleled combination of exquisite lyric poetry with obscenity, of seriousness and high purpose with low comedy.

4. Ribald jests and vulgar farce.

5. Method: direct exposition through parabasis, allegory, and real persons and events; highly topical.

6. Plots: loosely constructed.

7. Characters: generalized, subordinated to plot and humor.

8. Style: varied, but essentially Attic in simplicity and grace; extraordinary poetic genius.

BASIC THOUGHT OF ARISTOPHANES

1. Central theme: the welfare of the city-state of Athens.

2. Criticism of intellectuals as being a bad influence on the citizens; particular dislike of the Sophists and Euripides.

3. Conservative traditionalist: enemy of new ideas and movements.

4. Critic of the weaknesses of Athenian democracy, of radical social and economic theories, of demagogic leaders of the democratic party, and of their imperialistic war policy.

CHAPTER SEVEN

DRAMA IN THE FOURTH CENTURY

DECAY OF THE CITY-STATE

1. Greece never recovered from the loss of wealth and manpower caused by the Peloponnesian War.

2. Growing economic, political, and social crisis:

    a. Inflation; growing gap between large number of poor and few rich.

    b. Fierce internal class struggle in many Greek city-states.

3. Distress and disillusionment caused growing individualism (concern for self and family), in contrast with citizenship ideal of Fifth Century; increasing detachment from affairs of government on the part of many; avoidance of civic responsibilities.

4. Increase in militarism.

5. Government: revival of democracy in many states; numerous oligarchies; military despots supported by professional armies.

DECAY OF GREEK POWER

1. Spartan Hegemony (404-371 B.C.)

    a. Development of coalition against Sparta headed by Thebes, Athens and Corinth.

    b. Victory of Thebes over Sparta; end of Spartan invincibility.

2. Theban Hegemony (371-362 B.C.)

    a. Coalition against Thebes, led by Athens and Sparta.

    b. Defeat of Thebes.

    c. Exhaustion, chaos, confusion in Greece, bordering on anarchy.

3. Hegemony of Macedon

    a. Rise of influence of Macedon, military monarchy north of Hellas, whose leaders had become Hellenized.

    b. Philip II, King of Macedon (358-336 B.C.)

    c. Alliance of Athens and Thebes, headed by Demosthenes, against Philip of Macedon.

    d. Defeat of Greek forces by Philip in 338 B.C.; loss of Greek freedom; political bankruptcy of city-state form of government.

4. Alexander the Great (336-323 B.C.)

    a. Succeeded his father Philip at age of 20; tutored by Aristotle.

    b. Conquest of Persian Empire.

    c. Policies and achievements of Alexander:

        i. Spread of Hellenism over Asia and North Africa.

        ii. Racial and cultural fusion of upper classes of natives with Greco-Macedonian conquerors.

    d. New type of culture, Hellenistic, characterized by fusion of Greek and Oriental cultures, and large monarchies with little or no political freedom.

DECLINE OF TRAGEDY AND OLD COMEDY

1. In the catastrophic environment of the Fourth Century B.C., tragedy ceased to be a significant, dominant literary form.

2. Growing individualism and interest in momentary pleasure destroyed the appeal of classical Greek tragedy to contemporary audiences.

3. A new type of audience, largely an intellectual élite, maintained an interest in the theater.

4. The impact of Euripides on Greek tragedy tended to alter the character of the drama:

a. Through his realism he brought tragedy down to earth, thus destroying the validity of the use of subject matter derived from myths.

b. His emphasis on romantic love became a dominant influence on the drama.

c. His frequent relegation of the chorus to the role of performing dramatically irrelevant odes was the forerunner of its eventual complete elimination.

d. His use of melodrama and situational plots was not in the mainstream of classical Greek tragedy.

5. The Dionysiac cult, whose principal adherents were among the lower classes, particularly those who made their livelihood from the soil, now began to lose its appeal and to be replaced by cults with an emphasis on the hereafter. Constant economic distress was fatal to the optimism inherent in the worship of Dionysus.

6. Tragedy continued to be written by literary hacks:

a. Fictional and historical plots became more frequent.

b. Revivals and imitations of Fifth Century plays were common.

c. Many tragedies were written that were not intended for production but to be read ("closet dramas").

d. Artificiality and mechanical adherence to traditional forms were the rule.

e. Rhetoric replaced exploration of social, religious, political and ethical problems, and interest in character portrayal. Aristotle: "The older poets made their characters speak like citizens; the poets of the present day make them speak like rhetoricians."

f. Tragedy was finally divorced from the Dionysiac cult and became completely secularized.

7. For similar reasons, and because of increasing restrictions on freedom and the self-censorship by writers of comedy, Old Comedy could not survive. Aristophanes' last few plays belong to the Middle Comedy (see above, pp. 168-173). Old Comedy withered with Athenian democracy.

WRITERS OF
FOURTH CENTURY TRAGEDY

1. Astydamas. Wrote *Parthenopaeus; Hector.*
2. Polyidus. Wrote *Iphigenia.*
3. Chaeremon. Wrote *Centaur; Oeneus.*
4. Carcinus. Wrote *Thyestes; Medea; Oedipus; Alope; Aerope.*
5. Theodectes. Wrote *Oedipus Rex; Lyncaeus.*
6. Moschion. Wrote *Themistocles* (an historical drama); *Men of Pherae.*

RHESUS

(This play, included in the manuscripts of Euripides, is generally believed to be the work of an unknown Fourth Century playwright.)

BACKGROUND

The *Rhesus* retells in dramatic form an incident in the Tenth Book of the *Iliad* of Homer. After Hector drove the Greeks back to their camp on the shore, Dolon was sent by the Trojans during the night to reconnoiter. A similar mission was undertaken by Odysseus and Diomedes against the Trojans.

Prologue and Parodos (lines 1-86)

The scene is set before Hector's tent on the battlefield. The Chorus of Trojan sentinels enters. They summon forth Hector and request him to rouse the Trojans and their allies. They have observed intense activity and huge fires in the Greek camp. Hector suspects that the Greeks are planning flight from Troy during the night. He decides to prevent this, in order not to be cheated of his hopes of destroying utterly his Greek foes.

First Episode (87-223)

Aeneas, a Trojan chief, and Dolon enter. When they hear of Hector's intentions, they counsel caution. First a Trojan spy must be sent to discover the Greek plans. Hector agrees. Dolon volunteers for the dangerous mission, asking as his reward the horses of Achilles. He leaves to disguise himself as a wolf.

First Stasimon (224-263)

The Chorus prays to Apollo for the success of brave Dolon's mission.

Second Episode (264-341)

A shepherd enters to report good news to Hector—that his ally Rhesus of Thrace is approaching with a large army. Hector at first repudiates the assistance of this late-comer in the war, especially since victory seems at hand, but the Chorus counsels acceptance of his aid.

Second Stasimon (342-387)

The Chorus sings a song of welcome to the famed Rhesus. May he help to free Troy from the Greeks!

Third Episode (388-526)

Rhesus enters in his chariot, drawn by his famed white horses. He is chided by Hector for not rendering aid ten years ago. Rhesus defends himself, asserting the need to defend Thrace from the war-ring Scythians to the north. As soon as he defeated them, he set out to aid the Trojans. Now that he has come, boasts Rhesus, the war will soon be over, for he will himself destroy the Greeks, and, moreover, carry the war to their homeland across the seas. The Chorus cautions him not to be too proud. Hector briefs him on the nature of the enemy and on their chieftains.

Third Stasimon (527-564)

The Chorus, on the lookout for Dolon's return, is apprehensive of the enemy during the night. They leave to summon new guards to take over the watch.

Fourth Episode (565-691)

Odysseus and Diomedes enter on reconnaissance. Earlier they caught Dolon, terrified him into betraying the array of the Trojans, as well as their password, and then slew him. They had hoped to trap Hector in his tent and slay him, or Aeneas, or Paris. Suddenly

Athena ppears and tells them of the coming of Rhesus. She advises them where to find him, to slay him and steal his famed white horses as a trophy. They see Paris coming, but are told that they are not fated to kill him. They depart to find Rhesus.

Paris has come to see Hector, for he suspects spies in their midst. Athena, pretending to be his favorite divinity Aphrodite, deceives him into complaisance. Meanwhile, Rhesus has been slain, and Odysseus rushes in, pursued by the Chorus. He deceives them with his knowledge of the password, and escapes into the darkness.

Fourth Stasimon (692-727)

The Chorus now suspects that the intruder was Odysseus.

Exodos (728-996)

A wounded charioteer enters to announce the slaying of Rhesus. He describes in detail how the spies killed Rhesus and stole his horses. Hector enters and assails the guards for neglect of duty. The charioteer accuses Hector of murdering Rhesus because he coveted his horses. Hector, of course, denies this, suspecting Odysseus as the intruder. He orders the wounded charioteer taken to his palace.

Suddenly the Muse Terpsichore, mother of Rhesus, appears on high with the body of Rhesus in her arms. She bewails the fate of her son, and curses Odysseus, Diomedes, and Helen. She relates the lineage and greatness of her son. Knowing his coming doom, she had warned him not to go to Troy. Athena is to blame, for it was she who guided Odysseus and Diomedes to the deed. She then predicts the coming death of Achilles. As the day dawns, Hector prepares for battle.

INTERPRETATION

1. This play, the weakest of the extant thirty-three Greek tragedies, is a melodrama, superficial and episodic, retelling the well-known legend of Dolon and Rhesus.

2. "Pride goeth before a fall."

MIDDLE COMEDY (400-338 B.C.)

1. Over 40 authors and the titles of over 600 plays of this transitional form are known. But only two plays are extant: the *Ecclesiazusae* and the *Plutus* of Aristophanes.

2. The leading playwrights in Athens were foreigners and professional writers: Antiphanes; Xenarchus; Eubolus; Timocles; Anaxandrides; Alexis; Amphis; Anaxiles; Epicrates.

3. The Chorus and Parabasis characteristic of Old Comedy dwindle away.

4. The Dionysiac cult is ignored in this dramatic form.

5. Reduction of political and other topical references, as well as obscenity and personal abuse.

6. Emphasis on situation.

7. Emphasis on pleasures of food, sex, courtesans.

8. Tendency to realism in plot and use of everyday speech.

9. Burlesquing of a myth is the dominant type of plot in the Middle Comedy.

10. Chorus is present but performs transferable musical and dancing interludes.

CHAPTER EIGHT

NEW COMEDY: MENANDER

HELLENISTIC AGE (323-30 B.C.)

1. At the death of Alexander the Great in 323 B.C. his great empire disintegrated, various parts falling into the hands of his leading generals.

2. Hellenistic states:

    a. Large monarchies, kingdoms of Macedonia, Seleucid Syria, Ptolemaic Egypt, Pergamum, and federations of cities replaced the numerous independent, now politically outmoded city-states of the Hellenic world.

    b. Political freedom and the citizen-soldier ideal came to an end.

    c. With the loss of interest in public affairs there developed extreme individualism, greater emphasis of personal economic and social concerns.

    d. The concept of a world society (*cosmopolis*) replaced devotion to the city-state (*polis*).

3. Alexander's conquests and policies brought into being a new *Hellenistic* culture, shared by the upper classes of Greece and the Oriental world, involving a fusion of Greeks and non-Greeks, of Greek culture and Oriental culture.

4. With the decline of Greece Athens became a kind of "univer-

sity center;" new cultural centers sprang up outside of Hellas, especially Alexandria, Pergamum, Antioch, Rhodes, Syracuse.

5. Endless disastrous warfare and struggles for power among the great Hellenistic powers; severe economic crises, resulting in increasing impoverishment of the masses everywhere, and concentration of wealth in the hands of the few; intense class struggles, frequent disastrous revolutions.

6. This political and economic instability led to intellectual confusion, uncertainty of the future, fears, moral decay, depopulation.

7. Roman Intervention: annexation of Macedonia to Roman Empire (147 B.C.); Greece nominally free, but subject to Roman governor of Macedonia; growth of Roman protectorate over Hellenistic states; gradual absorption of Hellenistic states into Roman Empire by war and diplomacy; Egypt annexed in 30 B.C.; Greece becomes Roman Province of Achaea in 27 B.C.

8. Hellenistic Philosophy

a. Stoicism: individual happiness can be achieved through reason and virtue, inner peace; everything is predestined; self-sufficiency and tranquillity can be attained by complete suppression of emotion and by freedom from external circumstances and material things, by accepting whatever happens, and enduring pain and suffering with resignation.

b. Epicureanism: individual happiness can be achieved through mental calm and tranquillity, banishment of fear of gods and death through knowledge of science and nature (atomic theory); the highest good is pleasure, which is mental calm; physical pleasures should be enjoyed in moderation; marriage, politics, wealth and power should be avoided.

HELLENISTIC LITERATURE

1. Literature largely escapist, written for small cosmopolitan intellectual élite; divorced from politics and social and economic problems.

2. Numerous works of research, scholarship, science.

3. New Comedy (see below).

4. Alexandrianism: preoccupation with literary polish; emphasis on form rather than content; artificiality; pedantic erudition, especially mythological; emphasis on romantic love. The outstanding Alexandrian poets were: Callimachus (*Epigrams*); Apollonius (*Argonautica*); Aratus (*Phaenomena*); Theocritus (*Idyls;* father of pastoral poetry).

NEW COMEDY (330-150 B.C.)

1. The principal dramatic form of the Hellenistic period. Its spirit is panhellenic, cosmopolitan, epicurean; its aim is entertainment for an educated, leisure-class audience.

2. New Comedy is heavily indebted to the techniques and thinking of Euripides, and also evolved from the Middle Comedy.

3. Comedy of manners: emphasis on the private affairs of leisure-class Greeks.

4. Realism in plot and speech.

5. The plot frequently is based on the difficulties that beset lovers; it always has a happy ending, and usually a reversal from the difficulties through a conventional recognition scene.

6. Fixed types (stock characters): the parasite, courtesan, loyal slave, knavish slave, boor, foundling, twins, miser, bold adventurer, etc.

7. No connection with Dionysiac cult.

8. Structure: explanatory prologue, followed by five acts.

9. There is a chorus, but it entertains the spectators between the acts.

10. Complete illusionism—no parabasis.

ADAPTATION OF GREEK THEATER

1. Probably introduction of raised stage.

2. The orchestra, with the altar of Dionysus eliminated, is now a semicircle, but no longer used.

3. The parodos is eliminated, since formal entry and exit of a chorus are not part of the play.

4. The scene usually represented two houses separated by an

alley. All the action took place before these houses. Interior scenes could not be shown.

LEADING WRITERS
OF NEW COMEDY

1. About seventy writers are known; they had an output of about 1400 plays.

2. The outstanding playwrights in Athens were almost all foreigners.

3. Philemon of Syracuse (ca. 361-263 B.C.). Wrote about 100 plays, including *The Ghost; Merchant; Myrmidons; Palamedes; Treasure.*

4. Diphilus of Sinope (ca. 340-289 B.C.). Wrote about 100 plays, including *Lot Drawers; Suicide Pact; Heracles; Theseus; Sappho; Telesias.*

5. Apollodorus of Carystus (dates unknown). Wrote *The Claimant; Mother-in-Law.*

6. Menander (see below).

MENANDER OF ATHENS (ca. 342-291 B.C.)

1. Father of the New Comedy.

2. Wrote over 100 plays:

   a. Only one entire play is extant, having been discovered in Egypt in the 1950's—*The Grouch.*

   b. Parts of three other plays were unearthed in Egypt about 50 years ago: *The Arbitration* (more than half preserved); *The Shearing of Glycera; The Girl from Samos.*

   c. Nine of his plays survive in the imitations of the Roman dramatists Plautus and Terence.

   d. Other typical titles: *Brothers; Eunuch; Double Deceiver; Hero; Hated Man; Farmer; Ghost; Flatterer; Flute Player; Necklace; Physician; Soldier; Twins; Selfish Person; Gay Ladies; Maiden Possessed; Self-Tormentor; Woman of Andros; Woman of Perinthos; Women at Luncheon.*

THE GROUCH

(This play, the only complete play of Menander extant, was un-earthed from the sands of Egypt in the 1950's. The manuscript, inscribed in codex form about A.D. 200, is now in the Bodmer Library, Geneva, Switzerland. Prof. Victor Martin has edited the first modern edition of the play. *The Grouch* was produced in 317/316 B.C., when Menander was about twenty-five years old. It contains 969 verses, and has the following structure: Act I; Choral Interlude; Act II; Choral Interlude; Act III; Choral Interlude; Act IV; Choral Interlude; Act V.

At the date of publication of this volume the complete text of the play was not yet at hand. Hence only a brief summary of the plot can be made available at this time.)

The scene is set at Phyle, at the foot of Mt. Parnes in Attica, before the houses of Cnemon and Gorgias. Nearby is the sanctuary of Pan and the nymphs.

The prologue is spoken by the god Pan. This genial divinity, whose cult is characterized by gaiety and rustic good-fellowship, has decided to punish Cnemon, an old misanthrope who lives near the sanctuary. Cnemon is an ill-tempered, unsociable, cantankerous person, who hates neighbors, strangers and relatives alike. He lives a solitary life with his daughter and an old woman servant. Previously he had been married to a young widow with a son named Gorgias, but his dour personality caused her to leave him. His step-son Gorgias, who now lives next door to Cnemon, is a well-balanced, intelligent young man with a sincere concern for his mother.

Pan is angry with Cnemon because of his unsociability and dourness, and particularly because he has neglected an important feature of his cult, namely, love. The misanthrope has, in fact, no intention of permitting his daughter to marry anyone. The girl is sweet, ingenuous, virtuous, and pious to the nymphs. The god Pan, pitying her, decides that she shall have a happy marriage.

Through Pan's intervention, Sostratus, a wealthy young man, while on a hunting trip sees Cnemon's daughter and falls passionately in love with her at first sight. Sostratus declares his love to Cnemon and asks for his daughter's hand in marriage, but is angrily rejected by Cnemon. Despite his stern rebuff, Sostratus persists undaunted in his efforts to win his lady love.

Things remain at a gloomy impasse for the young pair, until Cnemon accidentally falls into a well, from which he is rescued by his stepson Gorgias and Sostratus. In begrudging gratitude he resigns his parental authority to Gorgias, and authorizes him to give his daughter in marriage to Sostratus.

Despite Pan's triumph over Cnemon, he remains, however, basically unreconstructed. He decides now to live entirely apart from all humans as a hermit. Nevertheless, though he remains a misanthrope at heart, he is caught up by the exciting preparations for the wedding, and, despite his irascible and vigorous resistance, is forced to join in the marriage feast.

All ends happily for the young people, and Gorgias is rewarded by receiving the hand of Sostratus' sister in marriage.

(Minor characters in the play are: Chaereas, a parasite; Pyrrhias, Daus, and Getas, slaves; Sicon, a cook; Simice, an old woman servant; Callipides, Sostratus' father. The Chorus consists of revellers, worshippers of Pan.)

THE ARBITRATION

BACKGROUND

Pamphila, the daughter of Smicrines, an Athenian businessman, had the misfortune of being violated by a drunken youth at a festival. Months later she was married to a young Athenian, Charisius. Five months later, while her husband was out of town, Pamphila gave birth to a son. The child was promptly exposed, but the husband learned about the child through his slave Onesimus. Though he is in love with his wife and basically a person of philosophic interests and strict morals, Charisius takes up with a harp-girl, Harbrotonon, and begins to live an extravagant, riotous life. Smicrines, upon learning of his son-in-law's behavior, seeks to induce Pamphila to leave her husband, but without success. Meanwhile, the baby has been found by Davus, a goatherd, who gave it to Syriscus, a charcoal burner.

Act I

[In large part lost. There was probably an explanatory prologue giving the antecedent facts.]

Cario, the cook of Chaerestratus, the neighbor of Charisius, leeringly inquires of Charisius' slave, Onesimus, why his master has left home for Harbrotonon, the harp-girl whom he is entertaining lavishly at Chaerestratus' house. Chaerestratus enters and sees Smicrines, who arrives in agitation because he has heard of Charisius' extravagances and fears that his daughter's dowry is being squandered. Smicrines goes in to talk to his daughter; Chaerestratus departs to inform Charisius of his father-in-law's presence.

Act II

Smicrines reappears, indignant at Charisius' behavior. Two slaves enter, Syriscus, the charcoal burner, who belongs to Chaerestratus, and Davus, the goatherd. Syriscus' wife is carrying a baby. The two slaves are arguing over the possession of a necklace and trinkets which were found with the baby. Smicrines agrees to arbitrate the dispute. Davus tells of finding the baby in the fields and giving it to Syriscus, whose own child had recently died. Syriscus, in a clever speech, argues like a trained lawyer. Smicrines rules for Syriscus, on the ground that the trinkets should go with the child. Smicrines departs.

Onesimus enters and sees a ring among the trinkets which he recognizes as belonging to Charisius, who lost it sometime ago while he was drunk. Syriscus agrees to permit Onesimus to show the ring to his master, Charisius.

Act III

Onesimus is reluctant to show the ring to Charisius because he knows it would reveal him as the father of the foundling, and thus add to his troubles. Harbrotonon enters, indignant because Charisius pays no attention to her. When she learns of the ring, she reveals that she was present at the festival the year before when a rich, beautiful young girl was violated. She thinks of a stratagem to win from Charisius an admission that he is the father of the foundling. She will show him the ring, pretend that she is the girl he attacked while he was drunk. This will give them time to find out the identity of the girl.

[Smicrines returns, increasingly more indignant at what he has learned of Charisius' extravagance. Meanwhile, Harbrotonon's ruse has worked perfectly: Charisius has acknowledged the baby as his own. The party in Chaerestratus' house immediately breaks up, and the cook leaves in high dudgeon. Smicrines learns about the baby, believing it to be Harbrotonon's, and that Charisius intends to purchase the slave girl Harbrotonon from her master and set her free. Simias, Charisius' friend, and Chaerestratus try to mollify Smicrines, but he insists he will now take his daughter home and sue for divorce.]

Act IV

[Smicrines talks to his daughter Pamphila, but he is astounded to find that she is not eager to leave her husband. He argues with her, but she will not forsake her husband. She considers marriage an indissoluble bond, despite her unhappiness over Charisius' behavior. Charisius, meanwhile, has overheard the conversation. Smicrines leaves in a rage.]

Harbrotonon enters with the baby. As Pamphila looks on in anguish, Harbrotonon recognizes her as the girl who was violated at the festival. Pamphila recognizes the trinkets on the baby, and learns that Charisius is the father. The two women go into Pamphila's house.

Charisius, meanwhile, completely humbled by Pamphila's loyalty to him, has been raging against himself in remorse over his behavior toward Pamphila. Onesimus enters, fearful of being blamed for the mess. As he hides, Charisius comes out and soliloquizes on his own baseness and Pamphila's nobility.

[Harbrotonon enters and tells Charisius she is not the mother of the child. Believing he has been made the dupe of a fraud, Charisius

is furious. Onesimus weakly blames Harbrotonon.] At this point
Harbrotonon reveals the truth—that the child is really the baby of
Pamphila and Charisius.

[Charisius is convinced and is reunited with Pamphila.]

Act V

[Harbrotonon and Onesimus probably obtain their freedom. Smicrines has been summoned, and is indignant when he hears that a
reconciliation has taken place between his daughter and Charisius.]

Smicrines is twitted by Onesimus, who is made bold by his
newly-acquired freedom. Then he reveals that the baby is Smicrines'
grandson. All ends happily.

THE GIRL FROM SAMOS

(Less than half of this play has survived in fragmentary form.)

[Demeas, a well-to-do affable Athenian citizen, lives next door
to Niceratus, poor but proud Athenian citizen. Niceratus has a
lovely daughter, Plangon, but no dowry to marry her off. In the
absence of both Demeas and Niceratus on business, Plangon had a
love affair with Demeas' adopted son Moschion, and a baby was
born. Demeas has a mistress, Chrysis, a girl from Samos. She was
a refugee expelled from Samos during political upheavals, together
with other Athenians. She came to Athens and was taken in by
Demeas. He could not marry her because she could not prove
Athenian citizenship. In Demeas' absence she too bore a child,
which, presumably, died soon after. When it was learned that
Demeas and Niceratus were returning, it was decided to conceal the
birth of Plangon's baby by having Chrysis pretend to be its mother.
Demeas, somewhat disturbed at finding himself the "father" of an
illegitimate child, agrees to keep the baby.

Because of some obligation to Niceratus, Demeas arranges for
his son to marry Plangon without a dowry. Parmeno, Demeas'
slave, is sent to buy provisions for the wedding. But a number of
complications soon arise that delay the wedding.]

Demeas tells the audience that his suspicions have been aroused
because he overheard a talkative woman inside refer to the baby as

Moschion's. He is furious because he thinks that Chrysis and his
son have deceived him in his absence. His slave Parmeno arrives
with provisions for the wedding. Demeas questions him but Parmeno's answers are evasive, thus increasing Demeas' suspicions. He
believes that Chrysis must have seduced his son, whose character
has been flawless. He rushes into the house in a blaze of anger,
drives out Chrysis with the baby, and slams the door in her face.
She cannot understand why.

Niceratus returns with his contribution to the wedding feast and
sees Chrysis in tears. [He takes her and the baby into his house.
Meanwhile, Demeas has discovered that Plangon is really the baby's
mother. When he tells Niceratus that the baby is his daughter's, it is
Niceratus' turn to be furious. He thinks he will have an unwed
daughter and illegitimate child on his hands. And he supposes that
Demeas has decided to break off the marriage.] Demeas hears
Niceratus storming inside. Chrysis has refused to give up the baby.
Niceratus becomes a raving maniac. Chrysis rushes out with the
baby, pursued by the irate Niceratus. Demeas protects her and
sends her into his house. Finally Demeas informs Niceratus that
his son Moschion is the father and that the marriage will take place
today, as previously decided.

Moschion broods over his father's suspicions that he had an affair
with Chrysis, and plans to chasten his father by threatening to leave
home and go abroad. Parmeno returns, and Moschion sends him
inside for a cloak and sword. He comes out joyfully and reports
that preparations for the wedding are taking place. But Moschion
decides to settle matters with his father.

[It is likely that Moschion in the end discovers that he is not
Demeas' son, but a foundling; Chrysis is recognized as Moschion's
sister, and as a citizen can marry Demeas. Moschion, of course,
marries Plangon.]

THE SHEARING OF GLYCERA

(Less than half of this play is preserved, in fragmentary form.)

Act I

[The scene is before the houses of Moschion and Polemon. Polemon, a prosperous Corinthian soldier, has been away to the wars. He returns suddenly to find his mistress Glycera, a foundling, embracing Moschion, a wealthy fashionable young man living next door. Moschion lives with a wealthy lady, Myrrhine, who he thinks is his mother, though he is in reality a foundling, too, and the twin brother of Glycera. She is aware of their relationship, but Moschion is not. When Polemon saw Moschion kissing Glycera, he rushed in in a fury and cut off her hair.]

The character Misapprehension appears and tells the audience about the origin of the twins, how they were exposed, and found by a woman, who took the girl but gave the boy to Myrrhine. When the woman became poverty-stricken, she entrusted the girl to the Corinthian soldier, who was madly in love with her. Before she died the woman told the girl who she is and that her twin brother is Moschion. The girl has kept the secret because she does not want to spoil Moschion's happy, prosperous life. The young impetuous Moschion finds Glycera very attractive, and last night, when he saw her standing at the door, he stole a kiss just as Polemon was arriving.

Act II

Sosia, Polemon's sergeant, enters. He has been sent by the heart-sick Polemon, who is staying in the country with friends, to fetch some of his clothing. In reality Polemon wants to know what Glycera is doing. Glycera decides to enlist the aid of her neighbor Myrrhine, and for this purpose sends her slave Doris next door. [Myrrhine agrees to take Glycera in.] Davus, Moschion's slave, decides to inform his master at once about the wonderful opportunity to fulfill his attraction for Glycera.

Act III

Moschion returns with Davus, who claims to have facilitated his master's amours by persuading the girl to come to their house. Moschion sends Davus inside to learn whether Glycera is really to be his. Davus returns with bad news: Myrrhine wants Moschion to stay out of the way. They go inside, anyway.

Sosia returns at Polemon's instructions, to find out what Glycera is doing. When he finds her gone, he berates the other slaves, and thinks she has gone to her lover next door. He sees Davus and accuses him of helping to keep his master's girl next door. Davus informs him that Glycera took refuge with Myrrhine.

Polemon returns, together with Sosia and others, including an elderly friend Pataecus. They have come to regain Glycera for the soldier. Sosia, drunk, urges force; Pataecus recommends negotiations. Polemon sends away the entire band he brought with him. He asserts he always considered Glycera his wife, and wants to die now that she has left him. They go inside Polemon's house.

Moschion comes out of his house, quite unhappy. [There is a lacuna in the text. Moschion realizes that he was wrong about Glycera's intentions, and has overheard some talk of his own identity and that of Glycera.]

Glycera assures Pataecus that she did not leave Polemon for Moschion. She is angry with Polemon because of his suspicions and mistreatment of her. She wants to break with him permanently.

[Glycera asserts she is freeborn and can prove it.] She asks Doris to bring a casket out. Pataecus examines the contents and soon recognizes that Glycera is his own daughter. Moschion overhears everything and realizes he is Glycera's twin brother. Glycera learns that her mother died in childbirth, and when Pataecus became poverty-stricken soon after, he had the babies exposed. [Moschion comes out, and father and children are reunited.]

Polemon cannot live without Glycera. He now knows that there was nothing between Glycera and Moschion. Pataecus leads out Glycera, who has changed her mind, and bestows her on Polemon as his lawful wife. Pataecus decides to marry off his son Moschion, too. [The ending is lost.]

TECHNIQUE AND STYLE OF MENANDER

1. Exquisite perfection of style; purity of language.
2. Sparkling wit and sophistication.
3. Master of plot and character portrayal.
4. Realism; pathos.
5. Frequent epigrammatic statements.

CHAPTER NINE

ROMAN DRAMA

ROMAN CIVILIZATION: THE REPUBLIC (509-30 B.C.)

1. The city of Rome was at first ruled by kings (753-509 B.C.), the first of whom was the mythical Romulus; the monarchy was ended by a revolution in 509 B.C. which resulted in the establishment of a republican form of government.

2. The Republic was governed by annually elected officials; but the Senate, consisting of high ex-officials, became the decisive political power.

3. Despite legal and political advances made by the plebeian class, the Republic remained essentially aristocratic, being dominated by the Senatorial Order.

4. Territorial Expansion:

   a. Conquest of Italy (500-272 B.C.); the Romans dominated all Italy south of the Rubicon River, ruling a fusion of Italic peoples, Etruscans, Greeks and Gauls.

   b. Conquest of Western Mediterranean (264-146 B.C.); defeat and destruction of Carthage in disastrous Punic Wars; first annexation of overseas provinces—Sicily, Corsica and Sardinia, Spain, Africa.

   c. Conquest of Eastern Mediterranean (200-30 B.C.); Roman annexation of Greece, Macedonia, Asia Minor, Syria, Judea, Egypt.

EARLY ROMAN LIFE

1. Family and Character Training

a. Large household (*familia*) ruled by head called *paterfamilias;* purity and solidarity of family life.

b. Suppression of individualism through inculcation of *pietas* —obedience to *paterfamilias,* devotion to state, submission to gods.

c. Patriotism; physical toughness; military courage.

d. Conservatism: respect for traditions of ancestors.

e. Roman women subordinated to men, but their status in the family and in society was far higher than that of Greek women.

2. Economy

a. No extremes of wealth.

b. Basically agricultural; commerce and industry negligible.

c. Problem of landless poor partially solved by distribution of conquered lands and establishment of citizen colonies in Italy.

d. Slaves relatively few in number.

3. Religion

a. Family religion: worship of vague protective spirits (*numina*), who were supposed to guard the landed property, other possessions and welfare of the household; *paterfamilias* acts as priest of the family.

b. State religion: worship of anthropomorphic divinities borrowed from Etruscan and Greek religion which were supposed to protect the entire state and its territories; religion controlled by various priestly officials.

EFFECTS OF ROME'S CONQUESTS

1. Economic: growth of large estates in Italy owned by Senators; worked by slave gangs consisting of war captives; ruin of Italian peasants, who flocked to Rome; increase in wealth and luxury side by side with widespread economic distress; growth of commerce and industry.

2. Social: besides the wealthy Senatorial Order, the poverty-stricken city masses (*plebs*), the numerous slaves, the ubiquitous

freedmen, there emerged a new powerful class, the Equestrian Order, composed of financiers and businessmen.

3. Political: supreme power of the Senate.

4. Religious: confusion, skepticism, superstition, decay of the native religion. The traditional agricultural family religion served no purpose in urban life; the state religion became a political tool of the Senate; growing individualism was not satisfied by the community spirit of early Roman religion and by its cold formalism and stress on exact ritual. The void was filled by Greek speculation and by a variety of Greek and Oriental mystery cults characterized by emotionalism and the promise of blessedness in the afterlife.

5. Family life: breakdown of solidarity and purity of family life; growth of individualism in the matrix of traditional collective living; collapse of Roman *pietas;* moral and ethical barrenness; growth of profligate living, divorce, childlessness.

6. Cultural: adoption by the Romans of Greek (Hellenistic) culture, its individualistic spirit, religious ideas, literature, art, philosophy, educational system, amusements, language. "Captive Greece made her barbarian captor captive." The principal effect was a marked emphasis on the individual and striving for personal aggrandizement, wealth, power.

DECAY OF THE REPUBLIC (133-30 B.C.)

1. General political, social, economic, and imperial crisis.

2. Supremacy of the Senate was challenged by reformers and military leaders supported by professional volunteer armies.

3. Attacks on the Roman Empire; revolt of Italians; slave uprisings; widespread piracy.

4. Violent internal revolutions and civil wars; growth of personal political power of war lords, e.g. Marius, Sulla, Pompey the Great, Julius Caesar, Antony, Octavian (Augustus).

5. Final destruction of the power of the Senatorial Order by Caesar and Octavian (the later Augustus).

6. The Roman Republic came to an end because the Senate was unable to solve the deep political, social and economic contradictions engendered by the Roman conquests of the civilized world,

because the city-state of Rome was not adapted to ruling a great empire, and because the continuous warfare and upheavals of this century impelled most people to sacrifice the little liberty they enjoyed for peace and security.

ROMAN LITERATURE

1. Early Period (240-70 B.C.)

a. Translation of Homer's *Odyssey* by Livius Andronicus, a Greek from S. Italy.

b. Epics on Roman national themes by Naevius and Ennius.

c. Adaptations and imitations of Greek New Comedy by many writers.

d. Adaptations and imitations of Greek tragedy by many writers.

e. Creation of a new literary type, Satire, by Lucilius.

2. Golden Age—Ciceronian Period (70-43 B.C.)

a. Lucretius' *De Rerum Natura* (*On the Nature of Things*), didactic epic on Epicurean philosophy.

b. Catullus' lyric poems.

c. Cicero's oratorical writings, popularizations of Greek philosophy, and letters.

d. Caesar's historical works (*Gallic War; Civil War*).

e. Sallust's historical works (*Jugurtha; Catiline*).

EARLY ITALIAN POPULAR COMEDY

A variety of pre-literary dramatic forms existed among the Italic peoples before the influx of Greek influences. These were essentially broad farces, rather crude in technique, with lively slapstick plots, satire, indecencies, and prominence of song and dance.

1. Fescennine Verses: improvised rude banter by masked entertainers at harvest festivals and weddings; jesting, obscenity, abuse.

2. *Satura*: dramatic miscellany; the evidence indicates the possible existence of a dramatic musical medley, consisting of dialogue, gestures, and music.

3. *Fabula Atellana*: a popular rustic farce, short plays with song

and dance, featuring the stock characters Maccus (stupid clown), Bucco (glutton and braggart), Pappus (foolish old man), and Dossennus (cunning swindler).

4. Mime: a type of farce, including dancing and gesticulation, with much obscenity and indecent situations; adultery was a popular theme.

GREEK INFLUENCE

Roman drama is largely derivative. Most of Roman dramatic productions were translations, imitations and adaptations of Greek plays.

1. Roman tragedy is essentially a reworking of the plays of Aeschylus, Sophocles, mostly Euripides.

2. Roman comedy borrowed heavily from the Greek New Comedy. It was this dramatic form, rather than Aristophanic comedy, which influenced the Romans, because it is cosmopolitan and universal in subject matter, whereas Old Comedy is not only too topical for transfer to another milieu, but its sharp political and personal satire would not have been tolerated by the Roman ruling class.

Roman adaptations of the New Comedy were called *fabula palliata*—"comedy in Greek dress." Roman writers of comedy frequently practiced *contaminatio*—the process of combining two plots from Greek originals into one Latin play. Roman dramatists, such as Plautus, added the native elements of song, dance, and broad farce to the Greek New Comedy.

GOLDEN AGE OF ROMAN DRAMA (240-140 B.C.)

1. Livius Andronicus (ca. 284-ca. 204 B.C.)

a. From Tarentum in S. Italy; actor, and tutor in family of Roman senator. In 240 B.C. he produced a Greek tragedy and a Greek comedy at the festival commemorating the end of the First Punic War. (He also translated the *Odyssey* into Latin, and composed lyrics from the Greek.)

b. Titles of nine tragedies and three comedies are known, all adapted from Greek originals. Wrote: *Achilles; Aegisthus; Ajax*

Bearing a Whip; Andromeda; Danaë; Trojan Horse; Hermiona; Tereus.

    2. Gnaeus Naevius (ca. 270-ca. 201 B.C.)

        a. First native dramatist. He was imprisoned and exiled for literary attacks on members of Senatorial families. (He also wrote a native historical epic, *Bellum Punicum, "The Punic War."*)

        b. Titles of seven tragedies from the Greek are known: *Andromache; Danaë; Trojan Horse; Hector Departing; Hesione; Iphigenia; Lycurgus.*

        c. Naevius created the native historical play (*fabula praetexta*). Two titles are known: *Clastidium; Romulus.*

        d. Titles of thirty-four comedies in Greek dress are known, e.g.: *The Concubine; The Charcoal Woman; Female Charioteer; Flatterer; The Gifts; Madmen; Demetrius; Deceit; Potter; Gymnasticus; Lampadio; The Lion; Masked Woman; Quadruplets; Stalagmus; Struck With a Spear; Branded Man; Terentilla; Triphallus.*

        e. Comedy in native dress, e.g., *Ariolus.*

    3. Quintus Ennius (239-169 B.C.)

        a. First great Roman poet. A half-Greek, half-Italian from S. Italy, he was the teacher and friend of aristocratic Roman families. (He also wrote poetic miscellanies, *Saturae,* and an epic on Roman history, the *Annals.*)

        b. Wrote some comedies; also native historical plays, e.g., *Ambracia; Sabine Women.*

        c. Titles of about twenty tragedies are known, e.g.: *Achilles; Ajax; Alcmeo; Alexander; Andromacha; Athamas; Cresphontes; Erechtheus; Eumenides; Ransoming of Hector; Hecuba; Iphigenia; Medea; Melanippe; Nemea; Phoenix; Telamo; Telephus; Thyestes.*

    4. Marcus Pacuvius (ca. 220-ca. 130 B.C.)

    Twelve titles of tragedies are known, including *Paulus* (an historical play); *Judgment of the Armor; Niptra; Antiopa; Chryses.*

    5. Lucius Accius (170-ca. 86 B.C.)

        a. Fifty titles of tragedies are known, including: *Achilles; Aegisthus; Children of Agamemnon; Alcestis; Alcmeo; Alphesiboea; Amphitryo; Andromeda; Children of Antenor; Antigona;*

Judgment of the Armor; Astyanax; Athamas; Atreus; Bacchae; Chrysippus; Clytaemnestra; Deiphobus; Diomedes; Epigoni; Epinausimache; Erigona; Eriphyla; Eurysaces; Hecuba; Hellenes; Io; Medea; Melanippus; Meleager; Minos; Myrmidons; Neoptolemus; Night Alarm; Oenomaüs; Children of Pelops; Philoctetes; Children of Phinias; Phoenician Women; Partisans; Telephus; Tereus; Thebais; Trojan Women.

   b. Roman historical plays, e.g., *Brutus; Descendants of Aeneas.*

   6. Plautus (see Chapter Ten).
   7. Terence (see Chapter Eleven).
   8. Caecilius Statius (ca. 219-166 B.C.)
      a. Insubrian Gaul who came to Rome as slave and was freed.
      b. Forty titles of comedies are known, including: *Plocium; Carine; Dardanus; Ephesio; The Hermaphrodite; Imbrians; The Maniac; The Merchant; The Nurse; The Supposititious Child; The Woman of Andros; The Woman of Chalcis.*

PRODUCTION OF ROMAN PLAYS

   1. Produced always at public festivals on various occasions during the year. About 200 B.C. there were dramatic presentations for five to eleven days a year; in the Augustan Age for forty days.
   2. Plays were produced by managers of companies of actors under contract with state officials employing funds appropriated by the Roman government. The playwright was paid for the use of his play.
   3. Actors (*histriones*) were mostly slaves and freedmen.
   4. Musical accompaniment by flutist.
   5. There was no chorus.
   6. Audience consisted of all classes, and included women.
   7. Admission was free during the Republic.

ROMAN THEATER

   1. Modification of Greek theater of the Hellenistic period.
   2. No permanent theater in Rome until 55 B.C., when the The-

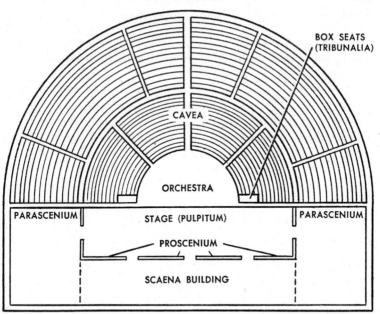

PLAN OF A
TYPICAL ROMAN THEATER

ater of Pompey, with seating capacity of 9,000, was built. Before
then temporary wooden structures were used.

3. Formal seating arrangement: first fourteen rows of orchestra
reserved for Senatorial Order; behind them sat members of the
Equestrian Order; remainder of seats for Plebeians.

4. Box seats on sides of orchestra for officials presiding at the
games.

5. Long wooden stage with *scaena* containing dressing rooms
for actors. In comedy the scene usually represents three houses
from which characters enter and exit. Between two of the houses
was a narrow street representing an alley (*angiportum*) where
characters concealed themselves to eavesdrop. There were also two
projecting wings providing side entrances and exits. In tragedy the
scene represents a palace, house, or other appropriate backdrop.

6. There is no evidence of a drop curtain.

CONVENTIONS OF ROMAN COMEDY

1. All action staged out of doors, before the houses of the characters. Indoor scenes are described by actors or acted out before the houses.

2. Action is continuous. There is no drop curtain, and no act or scene divisions. There is no evidence for the five act law in the Roman theater, though Horace in a famous passage in the *Ars Poetica* recommends its use. The traditional division of Roman plays into five acts is the work of later editors.

3. Conventionalized acting; use of masks and wigs.

4. Poetic form always employed.

5. Asides and soliloquies frequent; eavesdropping common.

6. Violations of dramatic illusion permitted for comic effects.

7. No lighting effects—all scenes acted in broad daylight.

DECLINE OF ROMAN DRAMA

1. After Accius few tragedies were written for the stage. The Roman preference for spectacular effects, rhetoric, horror and sensationalism had a deleterious effect on the composition and production of tragedy. The nine tragedies of Seneca and one Roman historical play, the *Octavia* (see Chapter Twelve), are the only extant Roman tragedies.

2. In the field of comedy, after Terence a new form became popular, the *fabula togata*—"comedy in native dress." This was the dominant form between ca. 150-50 B.C. Seventy titles are known. The themes were taken from the lives of ordinary Italians of the lower classes in country towns. These plays were lively, often indecent, satirical farces. The outstanding writers of *fabulae togatae* were Titinius (wrote *The Fuller's Trade; The Bearded Man; The Woman of Setia; Quintus*); Afranius (wrote *Divorce; Letter; The Sisters-in-law; The Stepson; Vopiscus; Pretender; The Fire*); and Atta (wrote *Aedile's Games; Hot Springs; Aunt; Mother-in-law; Medley*).

3. Revival of the *fabula Atellana,* which was now given literary form.

4. About the middle of the First Century B.C. the mime, now elevated to literary form, also became popular.

5. Beginning 22 B.C. pantomime—acting and dancing in dumb show—acquired vogue, and was highly popular throughout the period of the Empire.

6. Under the despotic conditions of the imperial period the mime and pantomime steadily degenerated. Sordid themes, vulgar obscenity and indecent language prevailed.

7. Because of their obscenity these popular dramatic forms came under vigorous attack by the Christians. Finally, all theatrical performances were abolished by the Emperor Justinian in the Sixth Century A.D.

CHAPTER TEN

PLAUTUS

TITUS MACCIUS PLAUTUS (ca. 254-184 B.C.)

1. From Sarsina in Umbria.

2. Employed in theatrical productions; became trader, lost everything; worked in mill.

3. Became most successful Roman comic playwright.

4. Wrote over 100 comedies (20 are extant), all adaptations of the plays of Demophilus, Diphilus, Menander, Philemon and other writers of New Comedy.

5. Originality: combined Greek New Comedy with native Italic farce and own dramatic genius to create comedy of farce.

EXTANT PLAYS

Amphitryon

Asinaria
  (Comedy of Asses)

Aulularia
  (Pot of Gold)

Bacchides
  (Two Bacchides)

Captivi
  (The Captives)

Casina

Cistellaria
  (The Casket)

Curculio

Epidicus

Menaechmi
  (Twin Menaechmi)

Mercator
  (The Merchant)

Miles Gloriosus   Pseudolus
   (Braggart Soldier)   Rudens
Mostellaria   (The Rope)
   (Haunted House)   Stichus
Persa   Trinummus
   (Girl from Persia)   (Three Penny Day)
Poenulus   Truculentus
   (Carthaginian)

AMPHITRYON

(This play is the only extant travesty on a mythological theme in
Roman comedy. The Greek source is unknown.)

Prologue

The scene is the front of the house of Amphitryon in Thebes.
Mercury, disguised as Sosia, slave of Amphitryon, announces that
this will be a tragicomedy. Jupiter is in love with Alcmena, wife of
Amphitryon, general of the Theban army. She is pregnant by both
Jupiter and Amphitryon. Jupiter, disguised as Amphitryon, is now
inside with Alcmena.

Act I

Sosia, Amphitryon's slave, enters from the harbor. Amphitryon,
having concluded the war in which he has been engaged, has just
landed with his army. Sosia was dispatched in the middle of the
night to tell Alcmena the good news. He describes in detail the
battle against the enemy and Amphitryon's great victory.

The night, it seems to Sosia, is unusually long. Mercury, intent
on keeping Sosia out of the house, accosts him, threatens him as an
intruder, liar and madman, and beats him. He, says Mercury, is
Sosia; and he reveals accurate knowledge about the recent battle
and victory. Sosia is astounded; what is worse, the other person
looks just like himself.

Mercury announces that Alcmena will this day bear two sons in
one birth, one by Jupiter, one by Amphitryon. Jupiter and Alcmena
enter. He declares he must return to his troops. She complains of

his short visit—just a few hours during the night. He gives her the
cup he says he won as a trophy from the slain king of the enemy. As
Jupiter departs with Mercury, he bids the long-delayed dawn to
appear.

Act II

Amphitryon and Sosia enter. Amphitryon is angry with Sosia,
disbelieving his report on his recent experience in front of the
house; he asserts he is either a scheming rascal or insane. Alcmena
enters aglow with love and regretful of her husband's rapid departure. It is no wonder she is surprised to see him back so soon.
Amphitryon cannot understand her references to his recent visit.
When he disclaims this, she reminds him of her recent warm greet-
ing and their night together. He thinks her quite mad. She tells him
accurate details about the battle, and, what is more, shows him the
trophy cup. He is amazed, and in a fury at her infidelity threatens
to divorce her. He is determined to get to the bottom of all this, and
departs to fetch her kinsman Naucrates to testify to his presence on
shipboard during the entire night.

Act III

Jupiter appears to explain that he will eventually rescue Alcmena
from her difficulty. He takes the form of Amphitryon, and accosts
Alcmena, who is indignant at her husband's recent treatment of her.
He pretends it was all a joke to test her. He apologizes and swears
an oath that he does not believe her to be unfaithful. He summons
Sosia and sends him to call the pilot Blepharon to dine with him.
Then he orders Mercury to keep Amphitryon out while he amuses
himself with Alcmena.

Act IV

Amphitryon, unable to find Naucrates anywhere, returns. Mercury appears on the roof disguised as Sosia, and mocks Amphitryon, who threatens severe punishment.

[At this point there is a lacuna in the manuscripts. Alcmena
comes out, has another argument with Amphitryon, and returns to

the house. Sosia brings in the pilot Blepharon. Jupiter and Amphitryon confront each other and there is a violent dispute. Blepharon is puzzled; he cannot decide who the real Amphitryon is.]

Blepharon leaves and Jupiter enters the house because Alcmena has suddenly become ill. Amphitryon, completely deserted, falls into a towering rage. As he rushes to break down the door and kill everyone inside, a peal of thunder is heard.

Act V

Bromia, Alcmena's maidservant, enters completely worn out by all that has recently happened She reports that, when Alcmena was in labor, there was lightning and thunder, and a mighty voice assured Alcmena of aid. Then she gave birth to two sons. Suddenly Bromia sees Amphitryon lying on the ground in terror. She reassures him, tells him of Alcmena's giving birth and of the remarkable occurrences at the time. One of the boys is unusually strong (it is Hercules). In his crib he was attacked by two snakes, which he promptly strangled.

Then a voice called on Alcmena and revealed that her lover is Jupiter, that Hercules is his son, and that Amphitryon is the father of the other boy.

Amphitryon is content, and plans offerings to Jupiter. Jupiter then appears on high, and reveals the truth to him. Amphitryon enters the house to rejoin his wife.

THE COMEDY OF ASSES

(Adapted from a play of the Greek writer Demophilus.)

Prologue

The scene is before the houses of Demaenetus and Cleareta in Athens. The Prologue gives a bare introduction to the play.

Act I

Demaenetus, an old Athenian gentleman, who fears his wife, and his slave Libanus enter. Demaenetus' son Argyrippus has fallen in love with Philaenium, who lives next door. She is the daughter of

Cleareta, a procuress. Demaenetus is indulgent with his son, and is seeking a way to obtain the money needed to pay for the girl without his wife's knowledge. He urges Libanus to cooperate with his other slave Leonida in devising a scheme to steal the money from his wife. They depart to see what they can do.

Argyrippus is thrown out of Cleareta's house because he has no money. He is furious with Cleareta, but she is stubbornly business-like—"no credit," "first come, first served," she says. For a set sum of money he can marry her. Argyrippus leaves to try to raise the money.

Act II

Libanus has not been able to think of a deception to obtain the money. Leonida arrives with good news. Some asses were recently sold by the family's steward Saurea, and the money is being brought to the house by the purchaser. It amounts to exactly the sum Argyrippus needs. Leonida will impersonate the steward and thus obtain the money for the lovesick lad. Leonida hurries to tell Demaenetus.

The dealer in asses arrives with the money. Leonida reappears and pretends he is the steward Saurea. The dealer, however, is cautious and wants to pay the money only to Demaenetus. They all depart for the Forum to look for him.

Act III

Philaenium berates her mother Cleareta for keeping her sweetheart away from her. She loves Argyrippus and is heartbroken, but is obedient and goes inside again with her.

Libanus and Leonida return. With the aid of Demaenetus, who vouched for Leonida as Saurea, they obtained the money. Argyrippus comes out of Philaenium's house. She is weeping, and Argyrippus and Philaenium talk of suicide. Another suitor, Diabolus, has just offered Cleareta the necessary sum of money for Philaenium, and intends to pay it today. At this point Libanus and Leonida produce the money, and demand and receive in return a kiss from Philaenium. Argyrippus is forced to carry Libanus on his back. Argyrippus is then informed that Demaenetus cooperated to make his son happy. However, the father desires a share in Philaenium's affections.

Act IV

Diabolus and a Parasite enter. They are bringing the money to obtain Philaenium for Diabolus, and prepare the contract. They enter the house but come out hastily, for they have seen Demaenetus kissing Philaenium. Diabolus instructs the Parasite to inform Artemona, Demaenetus' wife.

Act V

A banquet is prepared to celebrate Argyrippus' and Philaenium's reunion. Demaenetus is lecherously attentive to Philaenium, and his son is somewhat unhappy about sharing his beloved with his father. Artemona then appears with the Parasite; she knows all. She listens, undetected, while Demaenetus offers to steal a mantle from his wife for Philaenium, and she sees him kissing her. Then Demaenetus reveals his intense dislike for his wife. At this point Artemona confronts him. Deflated, he meekly agrees to come home, while Argyrippus goes into Philaenium's house.

THE POT OF GOLD
(Based on an unknown Greek original)

Prologue

The scene is a street in Athens, before the houses of Euclio and Megadorus; nearby is the Temple of Faith. The Household God of Euclio, an old Athenian gentleman, reveals that there is a treasure of gold buried in the house. The god, after several generations, has decided to reveal it to the miserly Euclio, a poor man, because he has a pious daughter, Phaedria. She, it seems, has been seduced by Lyconides. The god's purpose is to facilitate the marriage of Phaedria to Lyconides through the treasure.

Act I

Euclio, suspicious of everyone, drives his old slave woman Staphyla out of the house. He fears that the treasure will be discovered and stolen. Staphyla does not understand her master's present behavior. He goes in to make sure the gold is still there, returns to caution Staphyla to permit no one to enter the house, and departs. Eunomia, mother of Lyconides, urges her confirmed old bachelor brother Megadorus to marry. He is a rich man, and expresses a liking for Phaedria, even though she is poor.

Act II

Euclio returns, and rushes into his house to check on the safety of his treasure. He comes out again, and Megadorus asks for Phaedria's hand in marriage without a dowry. Reluctant and suspicious, Euclio agrees. The marriage is to take place that very day.

Euclio berates Staphyla as a blabber, suspecting her of telling about the treasure. He instructs her to prepare a marriage feast for Phaedria and Megadorus; she is deeply disturbed because she knows of Phaedria's condition. Strophilus, slave of Megadorus, brings cooks, a music girl and food for the wedding.

Euclio returns from the Forum with a little incense and a few flowers he has bought. When he sees the preparations, he fears people are searching for his gold.

Act III

Euclio has beaten the cook and his assistants, and driven them out of his house. He fears to have anyone inside. Then he decides to take the pot of gold out of the house, and orders the cook and flute-players inside again. Megadorus enters and soliloquizes on the advantages of marrying a poor girl who does not expect luxuries. Euclio is overjoyed. Megadorus tells him to prepare for the wedding feast. Euclio then takes the pot of gold and hides it inside the Temple of Faith.

Act IV

Lyconides' slave has been sent to find out as much as he can about the rumored marriage of Phaedria to his uncle Megadorus. He hides, and hears Euclio talking to himself about where he has hidden the gold. When Euclio leaves, he goes into the temple. Ever uneasy, Euclio rushes back into the temple and drags out the slave, accusing him of theft, though the slave did not actually find the pot of gold. Euclio brings the pot out of the temple and decides to bury it in a field outside the city walls. The slave follows him.

Lyconides has told his mother Eunomia of his affair with Phae-dria, and begs her to stop the marriage. Suddenly Phaedria's voice is heard: she is in labor.

Lyconides' slave has dug up the pot of gold, and goes to hide it at home. Euclio enters frantic—the pot of gold has been stolen. Lyconides enters, and hearing Euclio's angry tones, thinks he has learned about his affair with his daughter. He confesses guilt guard-edly, and Euclio thinks he has stolen the gold. When the misunder-standing is cleared up, Lyconides confesses to seducing Phaedria at a festival when he was drunk. He asks to marry her. Meanwhile, Phaedria has had a baby, and Megadorus has renounced her hand in favor of his nephew Lyconides.

Act V

Lyconides' slave returns and confesses to Lyconides that he stole Euclio's pot of gold.

[The rest is lost. Apparently Lyconides restored the pot of gold to Euclio, who then bestowed it on Lyconides and Phaedria as a dowry.]

THE TWO BACCHIDES

(Based on a Greek original by Menander, *The Double Deceiver*)

Prologue and Act I

The scene is Athens, in front of the houses of Bacchis and Nicobulus. [The beginning of the play is lost, but can be recon-structed as follows. Two years before, Nicobulus, an old Athenian gentleman, had sent his son Mnesilochus to Ephesus to collect a debt for him. On his journey he stopped over at Samos, where he fell in love with the courtesan Bacchis. She, however, was hired for a year by a soldier, Cleomachus, and taken to Athens. Mnesilochus then wrote his friend Pistoclerus in Athens begging him to seek out the girl Bacchis and obtain her release from Cleomachus. An Athenian courtesan, also named Bacchis, tells Pistoclerus that her twin sister, Bacchis of Samos, has arrived in town. Pistoclerus is delighted at finding Mnesilochus' girl so quickly.]

The two sisters greet one another. Bacchis of Samos desires to return to Samos after the year is over, but needs money to do this. Bacchis of Athens wants Pistoclerus to pretend to be engaged to her when the captain Cleomachus comes. She wants to give a banquet of welcome to her sister. Pistoclerus, smitten with her, offers to pay the expenses, and goes off to obtain the food, drink and flowers. He soon returns, aided by Lydus, slave of his father Philoxenus and his own personal tutor. Lydus is suspicious of what is going on, and is horrified when he learns of his ward's interest in Bacchis. They enter her house.

Act II

Chrysalus, slave of Nicobulus and Mnesilochus, returns from Ephesus. He learns from Pistoclerus that Bacchis of Samos loves Mnesilochus and that money is needed to free her from the captain. Chrysalus undertakes to provide this. He has, in fact, brought a large sum from Ephesus belonging to his master Nicobulus, and will devise a stratagem to use it to win Bacchis for Mnesilochus.

Nicobulus enters and is greeted by Chrysalus. He reports that Nicobulus' debtor in Ephesus paid the money to Mnesilochus but then tried to steal it back. Therefore, they decided to leave it in the Temple of Diana at Ephesus for safekeeping, under the care of a certain Theotimus. Nicobulus goes to look for his newly arrived son Mnesilochus. He has decided to go to Ephesus himself to retrieve his money.

Act III

Lydus comes out of Bacchis' house as from a den of iniquity. He decides to tell Philoxenus about his son. Mnesilochus arrives from the harbor, happy at the news about his beloved Bacchis and Chrysalus' scheme. He overhears Lydus and Philoxenus talking. Pistoclerus' father is far less disturbed than the strait-laced, old-fashioned Lydus at his son's behavior. They greet Mnesilochus. Lydus informs him of his friend's conduct, telling him of his love affair with a girl from Samos called Bacchis. Mnesilochus' faith is shattered. They suppose he regrets his friend's behavior, and leave it to him to extricate Pistoclerus. Mnesilochus, quite bitter, confesses the deception to his father and returns the money. Then he meets Pistoclerus, who tells him that there are twin sisters called Bacchis. Mnesilochus, astounded, goes into Bacchis' house.

Act IV

The Parasite enters with a slave of the soldier Cleomachus. He knocks at Bacchis' door and tells Pistoclerus that Cleomachus demands money or Bacchis. Pistoclerus drives them away.

Mnesilochus is grieved at mistrusting his friend and at letting the money out of his grasp. Chrysalus returns and is told that the money has been given to Nicobulus. Mnesilochus begs Chrysalus to devise another scheme to obtain money. Chrysalus instructs Mnesilochus to write his father a letter accusing Chrysalus of laying another plot to obtain the money from him for Mnesilochus to spend on girls. He is to beg his father in the letter not to flog Chrysalus but to bind him and lock him up in the house. They don't understand what he is up to, but trust him and go inside Bacchis' house for the banquet.

Chrysalus' purpose is to anger Nicobulus by this means. He succeeds, and then taunts Nicobulus, telling him that his son Mnesilochus is in mortal danger and needs help. He shows him the two couples banqueting. Chrysalus informs him that his son's life is in danger because of the girl with him.

At this point Cleomachus enters, and Chrysalus confides to Nicobulus that this is the girl's husband. When he hears Cleomachus threatening violence, he fears for his son's life. Chrysalus says he can buy him off with a sum of money. Cleomachus accepts Nicobulus' oral assurance that he will pay the money. Then Chrysalus decides to deceive Cleomachus by swearing that the girl and Mnesilochus are not inside but have gone elsewhere. Thereupon Cleomachus goes in search of the girl. Chrysalus goes into Bacchis' house and Nicobulus into his own.

Chrysalus returns with another letter from Mnesilochus. It begs Nicobulus to give Chrysalus a sum of money to save his life, declares that Chrysalus deserves gratitude for leading him to repent his misdeeds, and states that he needs a similar sum of money to pay off the women. Nicobulus agrees, and brings out the money. He goes off to give the money to the captain, and supplies Chrysalus with an equal sum to give to his son. Chrysalus goes into Bacchis' house.

Philoxenus, father of Pistoclerus, is still indulgent with his son's love affair, but hopeful that Mnesilochus has succeeded in bringing him to his senses.

Act V

Nicobulus returns from the Forum. He has discovered the deception from the captain, and is furious with Chrysalus for having made a fool of him. He is greeted by Philoxenus, shares concern for their sons, and together they bang on Bacchis' door. The twin sisters appear and mock the old men. They then decide to lure the fathers of their sweethearts inside by their wiles and persuasions. Philoxenus is an easy mark; Nicobulus more stubborn. When he begins to weaken, they offer to return the sum of money he gave to Bacchis. He agrees, and pardons his son and Chrysalus. In a gay mood they all enter Bacchis' house for an evening of merriment.

THE CAPTIVES
(Based on an unknown Greek source)

Prologue

The scene is in front of the house of Hegio, in a town in Aetolia, Greece. The Prologue introduces Philocrates, a young noble war captive from Elea, and his slave Tyndarus. Hegio, an old Aetolian gentleman, who has bought up the captives, is actually the father of Tyndarus. Hegio had two sons, one of whom was stolen as a young child by a slave and sold to Philocrates' father, who gave him to his own son as a playmate. Later Hegio's second son was taken prisoner of war by the Eleans. Therefore Hegio has been buying up many Elean war captives to find one that he can exchange for

his son. The two captives, Philocrates and Tyndarus, have ex-
changed dress and names to enable Philocrates to escape to his
home.

Act I

Ergasilus, the parasite of Hegio's captive son Philopolemus,
hopes that his patron will be ransomed, for he is in need of suste-
nance. Hegio cautions his slave overseer to treat Philocrates and
Tyndarus well, but to guard them carefully. Ergasilus expresses to
Hegio his longing for his son Philopolemus. Hegio invites him to
dinner.

Act II

The slave overseer brings in Philocrates and Tyndarus, who are
impersonating each other. Tyndarus is devoted to his master, and
is prepared to do anything to help him. Philocrates cautions him to
act in every way like the master, so as not to give away the deception. Hegio questions the captives about the importance and wealth
of Philocrates' family. He is convinced by Tyndarus to send Philocrates, whom he thinks the slave, to Elea to arrange for the exchange
of captives. If he does not return, the penalty is to be a large sum
of money as the price of the slave. Philocrates receives careful
instructions about his mission. Slave and master exchange affec-
tionate farewells, and Hegio is moved to tears. Philocrates departs
for Elea, and Tyndarus is meanwhile to be guarded carefully.

Act III

The parasite Ergasilus laments his troubles—he has had difficulty
scrounging a good meal.
Hegio enters with Aristophantes, a young Elean captive who is
a friend of Philocrates. He is now also a slave of Hegio, who is
bringing him to meet Philocrates. Tyndarus, having seen Aristophantes, rushes out in alarm, fearing he will be betrayed by him.
Tyndarus, when addressed by his own name, declares that Aristophantes was always thought to be mad. He stoutly maintains he
is Philocrates. Aristophantes' anger mounts, and he finally succeeds

in convincing Hegio, to Tyndarus' despair, that he is not Philocrates.

Hegio at once orders Tyndarus to be bound. He admits the
deception, and declares that he is happy to have served his master
faithfully by restoring him to freedom and father. He is prepared
to die. Now Aristophantes regrets the exposure. Hegio orders Tyndarus to be put into heavy chains and forced to perform hard labor
in the quarries. Once deceived, Hegio decides not to trust anyone
again.

Act IV

Ergasilus, overjoyed, is the bearer of important news for Hegio.
First he instructs Hegio to prepare a large feast; then he tells him
that he has just seen his son Philopolemus with Philocrates in the
harbor. With them is also Hegio's slave Stalagmus, the one who
stole his little son many years before and ran away. Ergasilus receives the run of the house and a promise of many banquets, as
Hegio rushes off to the harbor. Ergasilus enters Hegio's house.
There is consternation as he begins to devour everything in sight.

Act V

Hegio enters with his son Philopolemus, Philocrates and the slave
Stalagmus. Hegio is grateful to Philocrates for restoring his son to
him, and agrees to release Tyndarus to Philocrates. When the
young men go inside to refresh themselves, Hegio questions Stalagmus, and discovers that he sold his other son to Theodoromedes of
Elea, father of Philocrates. Hegio summons Philocrates, and it is
soon revealed that Tyndarus is Hegio's long-lost son.

Tyndarus is brought in, still in his quarry clothes. He is astounded by the reception he gets, and soon learns the reason. His
chains are promptly removed and put on Stalagmus.

CASINA

(Based on a Greek original by Diphilus, *The Lot Drawers*)

Prologue

The scene is in front of the houses of Lysidamus and Alcesimus
in Athens. The Prologue tells that Lysidamus, an old Athenian

gentleman, and his son Euthynicus are both in love with Casina, the sixteen year old slave girl of Lysidamus' wife Cleustrata. In order to possess her without his wife's knowledge, Lysidamus has arranged for his slave overseer Olympio to marry the girl. Similarly, the son has arranged for his armor-bearer Chalinus, a slave, to ask to marry the girl. Cleustrata, however, favors her son's plans. When Lysidamus discovered that his son was also in love with the girl he sent him abroad on business.

Act I

Olympio and Chalinus enter. Chalinus is following Olympio everywhere. Each hopes to marry Casina in order to foster his master's love affair. Cleustrata comes out of the house and tells her friend Myrrhina, wife of her neighbor Alcesimus of her unhappiness over the behavior of her reprobate of a husband, Lysidamus. Myrrhina advises her to be indulgent.

Act II

Lysidamus, very debonair and reeking of perfume, soliloquizes on his love for Casina. Cleustrata gives him a dressing down. He requests that Olympio be married to Casina. She is adamant, and he suspects she knows his plans. Lysidamus offers Chalinus his freedom if he foregoes marriage with Casina, but he rejects the offer. Lysidamus then decides to have the two slaves draw lots for the girl. Meanwhile, Cleustrata has tried to get Olympio to withdraw, to no avail.

Chalinus, extremely unhappy, overhears Lysidamus planning to enjoy Casina in the house of his neighbor Alcesimus. He plans to have his neighbor's wife help with the wedding and sleep that night at his own house. Olympio is sent off to buy delicacies for Lysidamus and Casina; Chalinus hurries inside to inform Cleustrata.

Act III

Lysidamus arranges with Alcesimus for the use of his house that night. Cleustrata, who now knows all, tells Alcesimus that she will not need his wife's help with the wedding. When Lysidamus returns,

Cleustrata decides to plague him: she informs him that Alcesimus has had a quarrel with his wife Myrrhina and will not send her to help with the wedding. Alcesimus, confused, agrees to send his wife to Lysidamus' house.

Pardalisca, Cleustrata's slave woman, rushes out in feigned terror, and pretends to Lysidamus that Casina has suddenly gone insane and is threatening everyone with a sword. Casina, she declares, swore that she would kill the person she should sleep with this night, and asserted that she is especially enraged with Olympio and Lysidamus. He tells her to urge his wife to beg the girl to put down the sword so that he can come back into the house.

Olympio and the cook Chytrio return with the provisions, and enter the house.

Act IV

Pardalisca enters. Inside they have arranged a plan to disguise Chalinus as Casina and marry him to Olympio. There is much bustle inside, but no banquet will be prepared.

Lysidamus tells Cleustrata that he is planning to accompany the new bride and groom to the country to establish them on his farm. Olympio comes out dressed as a bridegroom. He and Lysidamus begin to sing a wedding song. Chalinus, veiled and dressed as a bride, followed by Pardalisca and Cleustrata, appears. They give Chalinus to Olympio and go inside. The two men eagerly take the "bride" into Alcesimus' house.

Act V

Myrrhina, Cleustrata and Pardalisca come out. They cannot stop laughing at the deception. Soon Olympio rushes out and tells the audience that he tried to enjoy "Casina" first. He confesses to the women about the difficulties he had in the bedroom, and how he was beaten by the "bride." Lysidamus then rushes out, half undressed, pursued by Chalinus. He is ashamed at what has happened to him. When Lysidamus is confronted by Cleustrata, Olympio hastens to confess. Lysidamus begs forgiveness of his wife. She accedes.

The Epilogue informs the audience that a happy ending awaits
Casina. She will be revealed as the long-lost daughter of the man
next door, and, as a citizen, will be able to marry Lysidamus' son,
Euthynicus.

THE CASKET

(Based on a Greek original by Menander, *The Women at Luncheon*. The extant text of *The Casket* is very much mutilated.)

Act I

The scene is in front of the houses of Alcesimarchus and
Demipho in the Greek city of Sicyon. Selenium, a courtesan's
daughter, is the mistress of Alcesimarchus, a young gentleman of
Sicyon. She comes out of his house with the courtesan Gymnasium
and her mother, a procuress, who is somewhat tipsy. Selenium
believes herself to be the daughter of the procuress Melaenis, friend
of Gymnasium's mother. Selenium is in love with Alcesimarchus,
and has never given herself to anyone else. Alcesimarchus is in love
with her, too, but his father insists he marry the daughter of
Demipho, who lives next door. Therefore, Selenium decides to
leave Alcesimarchus' house and go back to her mother. She asks
Gymnasium to stay there and look after things for her.

The procuress confides to the audience that Selenium was a
foundling, whom she gave many years ago to Melaenis. The latter
brought her up as her own child.

The god Succor speaks a delayed prologue. He tells how a young
maiden of Sicyon was once ravished by a merchant from Lemnos
at a festival of Bacchus. She bore a baby girl, who was promptly
exposed. The procuress found it and gave it to Melaenis. The man
subsequently married, but his wife died. He then came back to
Sicyon and married the girl he had previously violated. The slave
who was given the baby to expose has for years been trying to
locate the woman who picked it up.

Act II

Alcesimarchus returns from the country, where he has been kept
by his father for six days in order to separate him from his beloved

Selenium. [Several hundred lines are at this point very fragmentary.]

Alcesimarchus' slave listens to him reproaching himself for his treatment of Selenium. He is quite beside himself with worry over losing Selenium. Gymnasium advises him to go to see Selenium's mother.

Alcesimarchus' father enters. He has come to persuade Selenium to give up his son. He mistakes Gymnasium for Selenium, as she carries out the role. The old gentleman finds her exceedingly attractive. Alcesimarchus returns with Selenium and Melaenis. Selenium refuses to forgive him, and leaves. Melaenis, too, rejects him because he promised to marry her daughter, but he has only trifled with her. In a fury he rushes into the house.

Lampadio, a slave of Demipho, rushes in, and tells Demipho's wife Phanostrata that he has found the woman who picked up her baby many years before. Melaenis, who is listening in a doorway, hears that the procuress gave the baby to herself. She accosts Lampadio, and learns that Selenium is the daughter of Demipho and Phanostrata. She goes to fetch Selenium.

Act III

Melaenis returns with Selenium and her slave woman Halisca. Melaenis has brought a casket of trinkets which were left with the baby. These will serve to identify her.

At this point Alcesimarchus comes out of his house with a sword, threatening suicide. Selenium rushes to him, and, overjoyed, he carries her across the threshold into his house. Halisca, who is holding the casket, drops it and follows Melaenis inside.

Act IV

Lampadio returns, finds the casket, and gives it to Phanostrata. She immediately recognizes the trinkets. Halisca comes to recover the precious casket, and Phanostrata reveals she is the mother of Selenium. They all go into Alcesimarchus' house.

Act V

Demipho enters and learns that Selenium is his daughter. All ends well, for there is no doubt that Alcesimarchus will now marry

Demipho's newly-recovered daughter Selenium instead of his other daughter.

CURCULIO

(Based on an unknown Greek original)

Act I

The scene is before the houses of Cappadox and Phaedromus in the Greek city of Epidaurus; nearby is the Temple of Aesculapius. The time is just before daybreak. Phaedromus, a young man of Epidaurus, enters with his slave Palinurus and several other slaves carrying wine and food. He is going to court Planaesium, a slave girl belonging to the pimp Cappadox, who lives next door. He is madly in love with Planaesium, and she returns his love. Planaesium, despite her surroundings, has managed to retain her chastity. Cappadox wants a large sum of money for the girl, and Phaedromus is trying to raise the sum.

They sprinkle Cappadox's door with wine, and presently out comes Laena, Cappadox's old slave woman, who is a tippler. They give her wine to drink, and soon she brings out Planaesium. The lovers embrace ecstatically. Soon they hear Cappadox coming. The girl and the men return to their respective houses.

Act II

Cappadox has spent the night in the Temple of Aesculapius in the hope of curing himself of his many ailments, but in vain.

Palinurus goes to buy provisions for lunch, and greets the pimp. Cappadox decides to go back to the temple. Palinurus rushes back and summons Phaedromus. He has just seen Phaedromus' parasite, Curculio, who was sent to Caria to raise the needed money.

Curculio arrives, fainting with hunger, and is promised a meal. He reports that his mission has been unsuccessful. But while in Caria he met a captain, Therapontigonus, who told him that he recently bought a girl, now living in Epidaurus, from the pimp Cappadox. (The girl is, of course, Planaesium.) The money for her has been deposited with the Epidaurian banker Lyco, and the captain has made arrangements for the girl to be turned over to a person who brings a letter to Lyco sealed with the captain's ring. Thereupon Curculio stole the ring and ran off. The three now decide to write a letter to Lyco and seal it with the captain's ring.

Act III

The banker Lyco passes by. Curculio pretends he has been sent by the captain Therapontigonus with a letter. It instructs the banker to turn over to the bearer the girl as well as jewelry and clothing purchased by the captain. Just then Cappadox comes out of the temple. He goes to fetch the girl in exchange for the money.

Act IV

Curculio comes out with Planaesium, the clothing and jewelry. Lyco reminds Cappadox that, should the girl prove to be freeborn, the money is to be returned to him. Planaesium is weeping, not knowing her destination. Curculio takes her into Phaedromus' home. Cappadox returns to the temple.

Therapontigonus suddenly arrives to claim his property. When he hears what has happened, he accuses Lyco of mishandling his funds. As Lyco leaves, Cappadox comes out and receives the brunt of the captain's anger. The soldier realizes that Curculio has tricked him. They depart.

Act V

Curculio tells that when Planaesium saw the ring she snatched it from him and asked him where he got it. She said it once belonged to her father. The captain enters, and when he spies Curculio demands the girl or the money. Soon it is revealed that Planaesium is really his sister. She too has a ring, which he recognizes and thus completes the identification.

Since Planaesium is thus proven to be freeborn, she is to marry Phaedromus, and Therapontigonus can now reclaim his money from Cappadox. When Cappadox returns, he is seized by the captain, and finally hands over the money. Thus all ends well.

EPIDICUS

(Based on an unknown Greek original)

Act I

The scene is before the houses of Periphanes and Chaeribulus in Athens. Thesprio, the orderly of the young Athenian soldier Stratippocles, runs in from the harbor, followed by Epidicus, slave of Stratippocles' father Periphanes. Stratippocles has just arrived from the war, but is afraid to see his father, for he has fallen in love with a young captive, and has borrowed money from a moneylender to buy her.

Epidicus is stunned, because before he left to join the army Stratippocles commissioned him to buy from a pimp a certain music girl with whom he was in love. Epidicus' chagrin stems from the fact that in Stratippocles' absence he had convinced his father, Periphanes, to provide the money to buy the music girl Acropolistis. This he achieved by persuading the gullible Periphanes that Acropolistis is Telestis, an illegitimate daughter of Periphanes, born of a youthful indiscretion.

Stratippocles enters with his friend Chaeribulus. He tells his friend of the lovely young war captive, whose innocence is still preserved. Stratippocles needs a sum of money to pay off the moneylender. Epidicus greets Stratippocles, who tells him that he is no longer in love with Acropolistis. It is now up to Epidicus to get rid of Acropolistis, posing as Telestis, and to raise the necessary money for the moneylender. They all go into Chaeribulus' house.

Act II

Periphanes comes in with an old friend, Apoecides. Periphanes has a problem. He has been thinking of marrying the mother of his illegitimate daughter Telestis. Epidicus accosts Periphanes and pretends that Stratippocles is in love with a music girl Acropolistis and intends to buy and free her. For this purpose he borrowed money from a moneylender. Urged by Periphanes, Epidicus suggests a plan —Periphanes is to select a wife for his son, buy the music girl Acropolistis for himself, on the pretense that he himself is in love with her, then sell her to another soldier, who, says Epidicus, is in love with her. Periphanes, convinced, goes in to get the money.

Act III

Stratippocles and Chaeribulus enter. Epidicus comes out with the money, and turns it over to Stratippocles to pay off the money-lender. He himself intends to hire another girl, a clever music girl, who is to pretend she is Acropolistis, Stratippocles' sweetheart, and that he has just bought her.

Act IV

Periphanes sees his friend Apoecides coming with a music girl, supposedly bought by Epidicus. He has her taken inside and locked in a room. Then Apoecides hurries off.

A soldier enters looking for Periphanes. He has been told that Periphanes just bought his sweetheart, and he wants to pay for her. When the music girl is brought out, he rejects her because he knows that she is not Acropolistis. He departs. Periphanes realizes that he has been duped by Epidicus.

Philippa, a woman from Epidaurus, whom Periphanes wronged in his youth, enters seeking Periphanes. Philippa and Periphanes recognize each other. She tells him their daughter Telestis was recently captured in war. When he tells her that Telestis is inside, Philippa asks to see her.

Acropolistis comes out, and Philippa declares she is not her daughter. Periphanes now knows that he was doubly deceived by Epidicus. He goes off to look for his rascally slave.

Act V

Stratippocles comes out looking for the moneylender who is to bring the captive girl he bought. Epidicus knows he is being hunted and tries to hide. The moneylender arrives, and Stratippocles goes for the money. Epidicus recognizes the girl as Periphanes' illegitimate daughter Telestis, and tells her Stratippocles is her half-brother. The moneylender receives his money and departs. They all go inside.

Periphanes and Apoecides enter. Epidicus accosts them, surrenders at once to Periphanes, and is tied up. He insolently and confidently admits everything. He urges Periphanes to go inside to see for himself why he is so sure of himself. Periphanes, having been told about the recovery of Telestis, unties Epidicus, agrees to set him free, and even begs his pardon.

THE TWIN MENAECHMI

(The Greek original of this play is unknown. It is a Comedy of Errors, exploiting the technique of recognition to the full.)

Prologue

The Prologue gives the audience the background. A Syracusan merchant had twin sons. On one occasion he took one of his young sons, Menaechmus, with him on a business trip to Tarentum. There the lad of seven was kidnapped by a merchant from Epidamnus in Greece. The father, brokenhearted, soon died. Thereupon the boys' grandfather changed the name of the other twin to Menaechmus. The merchant of Epidamnus, being childless, adopted the kidnapped boy, made him his heir, and married him off. At his death, Menaechmus fell heir to a large fortune. Meanwhile, the other twin has been searching for his twin brother for years.

Act I

The scene is Epidamnus, a Greek seaport on the west coast of Greece. Peniculus, a parasite who is always hungry, enters with a view to scrounging a meal from Menaechmus. Just then Menaechmus I comes out of his house berating his wife for nagging him about his misbehavior. When she slams the door in his face, he reveals that he has stolen a garment from his wife to give to the courtesan Erotium, who lives next door. Peniculus accosts him, and is promptly invited to a dinner party at Erotium's house.

Erotium appears, and Menaechmus presents the dress to her as a gift. He requests her to have a dinner prepared for the three of them. Meanwhile he and Peniculus will go into town until all preparations are completed. Erotium orders her cook, Cylindrus, to market for the feast.

Act II

Menaechmus II, accompanied by his slave Messenio, enters. He has just arrived by boat at Epidamnus in his long search for his twin brother. Messenio cautions him that Epidamnus is notorious for its drinkers, swindlers, and disreputable women. Menaechmus II quickly retrieves his purse, which Messenio has been carrying.

Cylindrus returns from marketing, and greets Menaechmus II, believing him to be the friend of his mistress. The "Comedy of Errors" has begun. Messenio warns his master to beware of the local swindlers.

Erotium reappears to announce that everything is ready. Menaechmus II is indeed astounded when she invites him in to dinner and other pleasures. He is amazed that she knows his father's name and his birthplace. After hesitating, he decides to accept her invitation, but first gives Messenio his purse for safekeeping.

Act III

Peniculus returns looking for Menaechmus I. He is dejected because, while he was in town serving on a jury, Menaechmus left. He fears for his meal. Menaechmus II comes out of Erotium's house, happy and drunk, carrying the dress of Menaechmus I's wife. He has offered to have it taken to an embroiderer's for additional embellishment. Peniculus confronts him, indignant at having lost his meal and entertainment. When Menaechmus II denies knowing him, he threatens to tell "his wife" everything.

A slave girl of Erotium comes out and requests Menaechmus II to take a bracelet to the goldsmith's for repairs. He is delighted to obtain more loot.

Act IV

Menaechmus I's wife enters with Peniculus, who has told her all. Menaechmus I returns from town, unhappy because he was unduly detained on some urgent business. As Peniculus eggs her on, his wife assails him for stealing her dress and giving it to Erotium. She finally leaves, shutting him out of their house. He knocks on Erotium's door. When he begs her to return the dress, and denies having received the dress and bracelet from her, she thinks he is trying to cheat her, and slams the door in his face.

Act V

Menaechmus II returns, having failed to find Messenio. The wife of Menaechmus I comes out again, and seeing Menaechmus II with her dress demands it. When he repulses and insults her, she threatens to divorce him. She decides to call her father.

Her old father, summoned by a slave, comes to find out about his daughter's difficulties. He is realistic, expects marital squabbles and infidelity on the part of the husband. He condones everything Menaechmus has done, but not the stealing of his daughter's dress. He sees Menaechmus II, who ridicules the old man. Since he is believed to be insane, when he denies knowing him, Menaechmus II decides to act the part in order to frighten him off. The old man decides to get a doctor, and Menaechmus hurries off.

The doctor, a typical quack, hurries in to see the patient. Meanwhile, Menaechmus I reappears, and the doctor tries to examine him and prescribe for his illness. When Menaechmus I expresses indignation, the doctor requests the old man to bring some slaves to fetch him to his clinic.

Messenio returns looking for his master. The old man returns with four slaves, who seize Menaechmus I. Messenio comes to the rescue, believing Menaechmus I to be his master, and helps beat them off. Messenio then starts off to bring Menaechmus II's purse and luggage. Meanwhile, he runs into his master, and they both confront Menaechmus I. Messenio immediately sees the resemblance, and slowly and methodically assists the twins to recognize each other.

After prolonged questioning by Messenio, the twins are reunited. Messenio is promptly granted his freedom. Menaechmus I decides to dispose of his property in Epidamnus, including his wife, and return with his brother to Syracuse.

THE MERCHANT

(Based on the Greek original *Emporos* by Philemon)

Act I

The scene is before the houses of Demipho and Lysimachus in Athens; nearby is an altar of Apollo. Charinus, a young Athenian, son of Demipho, tells how his father sent him on a business trip to Rhodes two years before. There he fell in love with a girl, the courtesan Pasicompsa, whom he made his mistress. Years before he had had another love affair with a courtesan in Athens, and as a consequence had been sent off on a commercial venture to Rhodes. When he fell in love with Pasicompsa, he bought her and returned to Athens with her. His father must not know.

Acanthio, Charinus' slave, comes running in to tell him that his father Demipho boarded the ship in the harbor and met Pasicompsa. Acanthio pretended that Charinus bought the girl as a maid for his mother. But Demipho took an immediate liking to the girl, and desires her for himself.

Act II

Demipho tells the audience of a dream he had the night before. He believes it has some connection with the girl he just met on the ship and with whom he fell madly in love. His neighbor Lysimachus comes out, and Demipho confides to him that he has fallen in love.

Charinus returns, disturbed at the mess he is in, and fearful of his father's reaction. He greets his father, who begs him not to tell his mother that he bought Pasicompsa as a maid for her. Demipho pretends he wants to buy the girl for a friend of his. Charinus asserts that a young man has commissioned him to buy a girl just like her for him. They bid for the girl. Demipho outbids him, and thrusts aside all obstacles Charinus seeks to put in his way. He rushes off to the harbor.

Eutychus, son of Lysimachus and friend of Charinus, enters. He offers to help his friend by buying the girl for him.

Act III

But Demipho has been faster. He got Lysimachus to act on his behalf and buy the girl. Lysimachus brings in the beautiful, charming, sophisticated Pasicompsa. She thinks Charinus has brought her back for himself, and is delighted. Lysimachus decides to keep her in his house for Demipho, while his wife is in the country.

Demipho returns anticipating the pleasures in store for him. Demipho plans a catered dinner at Lysimachus' house that night. The two old men go to arrange for the dinner.

Charinus enters, extremely depressed. Eutychus returns with the bad news—the girl was sold to someone and is gone. Charinus is desperate. He decides to leave home and go abroad somewhere.

Act IV

Dorippa, Lysimachus' wife, returns home unexpectedly, to discover another woman in her home—a courtesan, at that. Lysimachus returns and greets Dorippa with fear. He keeps Demipho's secret, while she accuses him of bringing in a mistress in his absence. The caterer arrives with provisions, and Lysimachus, unable to explain, sees his difficulties multiplying. Dorippa threatens divorce. Eutychus returns, having failed to find the missing girl.

Act V

Lovesick Charinus comes out with his luggage, prepared to leave home. Eutychus dissuades him by telling him his mistress is in his house, but that his mother thinks she is Lysimachus' girl. They go inside Lysimachus' house.

Eutychus comes out and sees Demipho and Lysimachus. He informs Demipho that Pasicompsa is his son's mistress. Demipho is contrite, and abandons the girl to his son. All ends well.

THE BRAGGART SOLDIER
(From a Greek original, *The Braggart,* author unknown)

Act I

The scene is before the houses of Pyrgopolynices and Periplectomenus in Ephesus. Pyrgopolynices, the braggart soldier, enters with his parasite Artotrogus and his orderlies. He orders his armor kept polished, and boasts of his military exploits. No one is deceived by his bragging. Artotrogus prefers to talk of food. It is made plain that Pyrgopolynices is a lecher, and thinks that all women are crazy about him. They all depart for the Forum.

Act II

Palaestrio, slave of the young Athenian Pleusicles, is now in the power of Pyrgopolynices. He tells the audience that his master and a courtesan in Athens were in love with each other. In his absence from Athens Pyrgopolynices came there, met the courtesan's mother, a procuress, and by trickery brought the girl Philocomasium to Ephesus against her will. Thereupon Palaestrio sailed to tell his master what had happened, but pirates captured the ship, and by a coincidence Palaestrio was given as a gift to the same Pyrgopolynices. The girl and Palaestrio pretended not to know each other. Palaestrio managed to get a letter off to his master urging him to come to Ephesus. Pleusicles is now in Ephesus, staying next door with a friend of his father, the old bachelor Periplectomenus. Palaestrio dug a hole in the adjoining wall, and thus provided a secret passage for the lovers to meet.

Periplectomenus enters, and orders his slaves to permit no one on his roof. It appears that one of Pyrgopolynices' slaves had been on the roof and had seen Philocomasium and Pleusicles kissing. The girl is to be told to go back and deny that she has left the house. Palaestrio has conceived a cunning deception: he will say Philocomasium's twin sister has arrived with a lover and that they are staying next door.

Sceledrus, the soldier's slave who saw the lovers together, enters. He tells Palaestrio, who goes inside and returns with the information that Philocomasium is in the soldier's house. The girl appears from Pyrgopolynices' house, thoroughly briefed on what to say. She accuses Sceledrus of defaming her. She tells him she dreamed last night that her twin sister came to Ephesus. Now she goes in, and soon comes out of Periplectomenus' house, taking the role of her pretended twin sister, Dicea. She asserts she arrived in Ephesus the

evening before with her lover, an Athenian youth, to look for her
twin sister. Sceledrus is skeptical, and tries to seize her and drag
her into the soldier's house. She escapes into Periplectomenus'
house. Palaestrio pretends to agree with Sceledrus' suspicions.
Sceledrus goes inside the soldier's house, and to his amazement
finds Philocomasium there. He is now convinced that there is a twin
sister.

Periplectomenus enters, and accuses Sceledrus of mistreating his
guest and spying on her. Sceledrus is invited into the house to see
the "twin sister." Sceledrus comes out, astounded at the likeness of
the two girls. He apologizes to Periplectomenus, and is advised to
hold his tongue about the whole matter.

Act III

Palaestrio, Periplectomenus and Pleusicles come out. Periplectomenus is a bachelor and happy in his lot. Palaestrio has thought
of a neat trick to deceive the soldier and make it possible for Philocomasium to escape with Pleusicles to Athens. Periplectomenus is
to hire a young, attractive, clever courtesan, who is to pretend to
be Periplectomenus' wife. The girl is also to pretend to be madly in
love with Pyrgopolynices. Palaestrio will give the soldier a ring,
supposedly from her as a token of her love. Then they will trap him
in "adultery."

Periplectomenus returns with the courtesan Acroteleutium and
her maid Milphidippa. They have already been briefed about the
plan, but Palaestrio insists on explaining it all over again. The go-
betweens in the pretended love affair are to be the maid and Palaestrio, who goes off to fetch the soldier.

Act IV

Pyrgopolynices returns with Palaestrio. He hands the soldier the
ring, and informs him of the love of the beautiful married lady next
door. The soldier is eager. Palestrio advises him to get rid of Philocomasium at once by telling her to leave his house immediately.
Pyrgopolynices agrees.

Milphidippa comes out, tells of Pyrgopolynices' charms, and

says her mistress is in torment for love of him. Pyrgopolynices goes inside to tell Philocomasium to leave.

Acroteleutium, Milphidippa and Pleusicles come out. Pleusicles is to disguise himself as a ship captain, and pretend that Philocomasium's mother has just arrived and wants Philocomasium to come home with her. Pyrgopolynices comes out, and reports that Philocomasium has consented to leave after "spirited objections." The soldier agreed to give her jewelry, clothing and Palaestrio as a gift.

Acroteleutium plays her part well, enjoying every moment. Pyrgopolynices is informed that she has turned her old husband out of her house and wants to live with him only always. He assures her he will be in soon.

Pleusicles comes in, disguised as a ship captain, and states he has come from Philocomasium's mother to bring her home. Palaestrio brings out Philocomasium with all her luggage. "Reluctantly" she and Palaestrio, both pretending devotion to the soldier, bid him tearful farewells. Prygopolynices enters Periplectomenus' house.

Act V

Periplectomenus and his slaves drag out Pyrgopolynices. He has been caught "in adultery." They beat him. He admits his guilt, begs for mercy, and entreats them not to unman him for his offense.

Sceledrus enters, and tells him the ship has sailed and that the ship captain was Philocomasium's lover. Pyrgopolynices now realizes that he was duped by Palaestrio, but good-naturedly concedes he deserved it.

THE HAUNTED HOUSE

(From a Greek original, *The Ghost,* probably by Philemon)

Act I

The scene is in front of the houses of Theopropides and Simo in Athens. Grumio, a country slave of Theopropides, an Athenian gentleman, summons another of his master's slaves, Tranio, and berates him for assisting the master's son in squandering the

master's property in his absence. Tranio is indifferent and goes off
to buy provisions for another banquet.

Philolaches, son of Theopropides, enters somewhat drunk. He
was a model young man, but as soon as he became twenty-one, he
began to change. He became lazy, immoral, and fell in love. He
steps into the alley between the houses.

Philematium, his mistress, comes out of Theopropides' house
with her maid Scapha, and prepares her toilet, as Philolaches
watches. She is devoted to him. We learn that Philolaches bought
her and set her free to be his mistress. Scapha urges her to think of
herself and provide herself with other lovers, but Philematium is
true to Philolaches. He finally comes out and greets his sweetheart.

Callidamates, his friend, arrives with his girl friend, the courtesan
Delphium. He is drunk, but ready for another round of drinking,
eating and general merriment at Philolaches' expense. Couches are
brought on stage, and a drinking party begins.

Act II

Tranio comes rushing back with food and bad news. Philolaches'
father has just returned from abroad. Philolaches is aghast. He
cannot face his father, because he has been squandering his money,
and has bought a mistress. They clean up the evidence of the
banquet and take the drunken Callidamates and the girls inside.
Tranio has a plan. The house is to be locked up tight and no one is
to answer. Tranio will manage the rest.

Theopropides enters, happy to be home after three years in
Egypt. He knocks, but no one answers. Tranio welcomes him and
tells him that no one has been inside the house for seven months
because the house is haunted by the ghost of a murdered man,
killed by the previous owner of the house. He gives details of the
ghost's activities, and Theopropides runs away in terror.

Act III

Misargyrides, a moneylender, comes to collect interest from
Philolaches on the money lent to buy the girl, the food and the
drink. Tranio plans to forestall him in some way, when he spies

Theopropides. The latter had gone to the man who sold him the house, and the former owner scotched the story of a murder. Tranio is indeed in a fix. He decides to deal with Misargyrides first. The moneylender demands his interest and raises a tumult. Tranio tells Theopropides that Philolaches borrowed the money to buy a house because the old house is haunted. Theopropides tells the moneylender he will take care of the matter the next day. Tranio informs Theopropides that his son bought the house of Simo, his next door neighbor.

Just then Simo enters, and Tranio takes him aside and begs him not to tell Theopropides about the debauchery that took place in his master's house. He also asks him to permit Theopropides to look over Simo's house. He agrees. Theopropides examines the exterior and then goes in, as Simo leaves on business.

Act IV

Phaniscus and Pinacium, slaves of Callidamates, have come to fetch their master home. They knock on Philolaches' door but there is no answer. Just then Theopropides and Tranio come out of Simo's house. The old man is delighted at what he has seen, praises his son's good business sense, and agrees to pay the moneylender the sum he thinks was borrowed to buy the house. He sends Tranio to fetch his son. Tranio sneaks into the house by the back door.

Theopropides now spies Callidamates' slaves, and soon learns about the goings-on in his house and about his son's immoral behavior in his absence. Theopropides is furious. When Simo returns, he learns also that Simo has not sold his house to Philolaches. Simo offers his assistance.

Act V

Tranio spies Theopropides with some of Simo's slaves. He realizes that trouble is brewing, but brazens it out. In the confusion he seeks refuge at an altar in the street. Callidamates, now sober, returns to try to make peace with his friend's father. Philolaches is, he says, ashamed of his behavior, and is repentant. His friends have agreed to repay all the money squandered by Philolaches. Theopropides forgives his son, and is also persuaded, reluctantly, to pardon Tranio.

THE GIRL FROM PERSIA
(From a Greek original by an unknown author)

Act I

The scene is before the houses of Toxilus' master and of Dordalus in Athens. Toxilus, a slave, is deeply in love with the courtesan Lemniselenis, who belongs to the pimp Dordalus. Toxilus' master is away. He needs money today to buy the girl. Sagaristio, a friend, also a slave, promises to try to raise the money for him.

Saturio, Toxilus' parasite, arrives. Toxilus has a plan. He persuades Saturio to lend him his daughter for a little while. They will get someone to disguise himself as a foreigner, pretend that the daughter is a kidnapped foreign girl, sell her to the pimp, and thus secure the money. Then they will disclose that she is freeborn, and thus regain her. The parasite agrees.

Act II

Sophoclidisca, the maid of Lemniselenis, assures her that she will deliver a letter to her sweetheart Toxilus. Toxilus comes out and sends his young slave Paegnium with a letter and a message to his beloved next door. The two slaves deliver the letters.

Sagaristio returns with good news. His master sent him to buy some oxen and gave him a sum of money, which he is promptly bringing to his friend Toxilus. Toxilus comes out with Sophoclidisca and tells her to assure his sweetheart that all will be arranged. Sagaristio gives him the purse.

Act III

Saturio returns with his daughter dressed up as a Persian girl. She is opposed to participation in the affair, but will obey her father. They go into Toxilus' house.

The pimp Dordalus enters, and Toxilus gives him the money. The girl is to be set free by legal process and then brought to Toxilus.

Act IV

Toxilus sends Sagaristio, dressed as a Persian, and Saturio's daughter, also in Persian dress, toward the harbor. Dordalus enters, and Toxilus gives him a letter to read. This letter was supposedly sent from Persia by his master recommending the bearer to Toxilus and asking him to arrange for the sale of a girl the man owns. Dordalus is wary of buying a slave without a legal title.

Sagaristio brings in Saturio's daughter. The pimp is very much impressed with her and buys her. Dordalus gives the money to Sagaristio, who departs quickly. Saturio comes out, asserts the girl is his daughter, and that she is freeborn. Then he hales Dordalus to court.

Act V

Toxilus prepares a celebration banquet on stage for himself, his sweetheart Lemniselenis and Sagaristio. Dordalus returns in a fury because he has lost his money. He realizes that Sagaristio was the one disguised as the Persian. They all have fun mocking Dordalus, who retires admitting defeat.

THE CARTHAGINIAN

(From a Greek original, author unknown)

Prologue

The scene is before the houses of Agorastocles and Lycus in Calydon. The Prologue tells the audience that the son of a Carthaginian was stolen when he was seven years old. The man died and left his cousin Hanno his heir. The boy was sold to a rich Calydonian who wanted children but hated women. The Calydonian adopted the boy (Agorastocles), and when he died made him his heir.

The uncle of Agorastocles, Hanno, is still alive. His two daughters with their nurse were kidnapped, too, as very young children, and all sold to a pimp, Lycus, who now dwells next door to Agorastocles. The young Agorastocles is deeply in love with one of the girls, while a soldier loves the other. Hanno has been searching for his daughters ever since they were kidnapped. He has just arrived in Calydon. It happens, too, that the man who adopted Agorastocles was a friend of Hanno.

Act I

Agorastocles confesses to his slave Milphio that he is hopelessly in love with the courtesan Adelphasium, who belongs to the vile pimp Lycus next door. Milphio has a plan to deceive Lycus. They will send Agorastocles' slave overseer Collybiscus with a sum of money to Lycus' house. He is to say he is a stranger desirous of a girl to enjoy. Then Agorastocles will break in, accuse the pimp of theft (since the money belongs to Agorastocles), and will thus recover double the value of the gold and the slave.

Adelphasium and her sister Anterastilis come out on their way to a festival of Aphrodite. Agorastocles accosts Adelphasium, who is angry with him because he has made many promises to free her, but has not succeeded. The girls leave; Agorastocles and Milphio plan further details of the deception of Lycus.

Act II

Lycus enters, followed by Antamoenides, a braggart soldier, who is in love with Anterastilis and wants to buy her.

Act III

Agorastocles brings in several counsellors to aid him in accusing Lycus of being party to a theft.

Milphio and Collybiscus enter. The latter is dressed as a stranger. Lycus comes out and is accosted by the counsellors, who introduce Collybiscus to Lycus as a wealthy foreigner looking for fun in complete privacy. Collybiscus gives him the money and goes inside with Lycus.

Lycus comes out, and is accused of having Agorastocles' slave in his house. Agorastocles recovers the money and his slave, and plans legal action. Lycus goes to consult his friends.

Act IV

Milphio accosts the pimp's slave Syncerastus, who hates Lycus and wants to cooperate in ruining him. He reveals that Adelphasium and her sister Anterastilis are freeborn Carthaginians. Thus a suit can be brought against Lycus on the claim that the girls are freeborn. Milphio hurries to tell his master.

Act V

Hanno arrives from the harbor in search of his daughters. He is looking for the house of his old friend Antidamas, who is now dead, for he wants to greet his son Agorastocles. Hanno overhears talk of two freeborn Carthaginian girls who were kidnapped. Agorastocles reveals that he, too, is a Carthaginian by birth. On further questioning, it is revealed that Hanno is Agorastocles' uncle.

Milphio has a new plan. Hanno is to claim the two girls of Lycus as his long-lost kidnapped daughters. At this point Gidennis, the nurse of the girls, comes out. She recognizes Hanno. He has come just in the nick of time, for the girls were about to begin a career as prostitutes.

Agorastocles asks for the hand of Adelphasium in marriage, and the request is granted. Hanno reveals to the girls who he is, and thus the whole family is reunited.

The soldier Antamoenides comes out of Lycus' house, and threatens Hanno for embracing his sweetheart Anterastilis. Then he learns who Hanno really is.

Lycus returns, and is confronted by Hanno, who claims the girls as his freeborn daughters. Lycus is completely ruined, and surrenders everything.

PSEUDOLUS

(From a Greek original, author unknown)

Act I

The scene is before the houses of Callipho, Simo, and Ballio, in Athens. Calidorus, son of Simo, is in love with the courtesan Phoenicium, who belongs to the pimp Ballio. He tells his troubles to his father's slave Pseudolus, and shows Pseudolus a letter from his sweetheart. She shares his love and begs for his aid. The pimp Ballio has sold her to a Macedonian soldier for twenty minae. The soldier paid fifteen down and left a token of identification. When a messenger comes with a similar token and the balance still due, she is to be sent away to the soldier. The day set for the transaction is tomorrow.

Calidorus does not have a penny. Pseudolus promises to help. Ballio comes out with a whip. He shakes it at his slaves and courtesans, and warns them to earn their keep. It is his birthday, and he wants specially good results today.

Pseudolus and Calidorus accost Ballio and ask for a few days' delay until they can raise the cash for Phoenicium; but the pimp is hardhearted. He declares that he has already sold her. He is willing, however, to sell her to Calidorus if he pays twenty minae before the soldier's representative brings the balance.

Pseudolus begins to formulate a plan. Simo, Calidorus' father, and his friend Callipho enter. Simo has heard that his son wants to free his mistress and needs money for this. Callipho is understanding, but Simo is stern. Pseudolus comes out and is accused of plotting to pilfer twenty minae from Simo. Pseudolus is brazen about it, and predicts that Simo will willingly give him the money. He asserts he will swindle the pimp out of Calidorus' sweetheart. Callipho persuades Simo to promise the money if Pseudolus succeeds.

Act II

Pseudolus comes out of Simo's house. Harpax, the slave of the Macedonian soldier, arrives with the token and the balance due Ballio for the girl. Pseudolus accosts him, pretends he is Surus, Ballio's slave, and states that Ballio is not at home. Harpax gives him a letter with the token from the soldier. He then goes off to an inn, requesting to be called as soon as Ballio returns.

Just then Calidorus returns with his friend Charinus. The latter can supply the five minae and a clever rascal to play the part of Harpax.

Act III

Ballio returns with a cook and provisions for his birthday party. He is suspicious of Pseudolus, and goes in to warn his household not to trust him.

Act IV

Pseudolus arrives with Simia, slave of Charinus' father. He is disguised as Harpax. Ballio comes out and Simia hands him the soldier's letter with his seal. Ballio is quickly deceived, and soon Simia comes out leading Phoenicium. They go off with Pseudolus to the Forum.

Ballio boasts to Simo that Pseudolus will not get the girl, and promises Simo he will give him twenty minae as a gift if Pseudolus succeeds.

At this moment the real Harpax arrives, offers the balance of the payment due for the girl, and demands her for the soldier. Ballio thinks this a ruse of Pseudolus, but finally discovers that this is the real Harpax, and that Pseudolus has indeed succeeded.

Act V

Pseudolus comes in drunk, and demands of Simo the twenty minae he promised. He tells Simo that Phoenicium is now a free woman, and is together with his son. Simo, with respect for Pseudolus' cleverness, gives him the money, and agrees to join him for a drink.

THE ROPE

(This play is based on a comedy of the Greek author Diphilus)

Prologue

The prologue is spoken by the constellation Arcturus. We are informed that Daemones, an old man from Athens, had lost his fortune, and is now living on a farm at Cyrene, in North Africa. Daemones had a daughter, Palaestra, who was stolen in Athens as a child and sold to a procurer, Labrax, who brought her to Cyrene. A youth from Athens, Plesidippus, fell in love with her and agreed to buy her, giving Labrax a deposit. Meanwhile, a friend of the procurer, Charmides, urged Labrax to take his girls Palaestra and Ampelisca to Sicily, where huge profits were assured. A ship was chartered, and the procurer, Charmides and the girls sailed from Cyrene. Arcturus caused a violent storm which wrecked the ship not far from shore.

Act I

The scene is the seacoast of Cyrene. Sceparnio, the slave of Daemones, comes out of the cottage to repair the damage done to the house by the storm. Plesidippus arrives with three friends to visit the nearby shrine of Venus, where the procurer had asked him to meet him. Daemones enters, and is greeted by Plesidippus. Suddenly they notice survivors from the shipwreck struggling in the water, and Plesidippus and his friends hurry to the shore. Daemones and his slave go into the cottage.

Palaestra appears, exhausted and wet, but safe. She is soon joined by Ampelisca, who has also survived. As they pray at the altar of Venus, the priestess of the temple, Ptolemocratia, warmly welcomes them inside.

Act II

Three fishermen, passing by on their way to fish, sing and dance a delightful number. Trachalio, Plesidippus' slave, enters looking for his master. He sees Ampelisca, whom he knows, and learns of the procurer's deception and the shipwreck. He hears that Palaestra is distressed because a casket containing tokens of identification had been lost with the ship.

Ampelisca goes to obtain water from the cottage. Suddenly she spies the procurer Labrax and his Sicilian friend Charmides, who have also survived, and she rushes back to the temple to tell Palaestra the bad news.

Labrax and Charmides enter, shaking with cold. They are quarreling about the disaster. Sceparnio has brought the water inside the temple, and unwittingly reveals to the procurer and his friend that two shipwrecked girls are in the temple. They rush inside to retrieve Labrax's property.

Act III

Daemones enters. Trachalio rushes out of the temple shouting for help for the two women, who, together with the priestess of the temple, are being roughly handled by Labrax. Daemones summons his slaves, and they rush to the rescue. Palaestra and Ampelisca come out to take refuge at the altar. Daemones protects them from Labrax, learns that Palaestra was born of free Athenian parents. Trachalio goes off to fetch his master Plesidippus. Daemones then sets his slaves to guard the girls. Very soon Plesidippus and Trachalio enter. Plesidippus has Labrax bound and taken off to be indicted for fraud because he absconded with his deposit. Daemones takes the girls to his home under his protection.

Act IV

Daemones' slave Gripus enters. He has fished out of the sea a traveling trunk, and is carrying it on his shoulder tied round with a rope. Trachalio recognizes it as belonging to Labrax. He promptly claims a share of the contents, and the two tug back and forth at the rope. Finally they agree to let Daemones arbitrate the matter. Trachalio knows it contains Palaestra's casket of tokens. As Palaestra identifies the contents of the casket, Daemones discovers by the tokens that he is the girl's father. They are joyously reunited. Trachalio is sent to fetch his master, tell him the good news, and announce Daemones' consent to his marriage to Palaestra. Plesidippus hastens back to share the good fortune.

Act V

Labrax enters. The court has awarded Palaestra to Plesidippus, but he hopes to retrieve Ampelisca. When he hears from Gripus about the trunk, he deceitfully offers him a huge reward for its recovery. Daemones gives him the trunk, but Labrax refuses to pay the reward. Thereupon Daemones claims the reward money as his, and promptly declares that half will be counted as the purchase price to buy Ampelisca's freedom; the other half will be used to grant Gripus his freedom.

Labrax, no longer the villain, is invited to dinner by Daemones.

STICHUS
(From a play by Menander entitled *The Brothers*)

Act I

The scene is a street in Athens, before the houses of Epignomus, Pamphilippus, and Antipho. Panegyris and Pamphila, two sisters, are married to two brothers, Epignomus and Pamphilippus. Their husbands have been away for three years, and the wives yearn for them. Though they are loyal to their husbands, their father, Antipho, wants the women to divorce their husbands, who are poor men, and remarry.

Antipho enters. The sisters, desiring to win him over, shower him with affection. Despite his arguments they remain steadfast in their loyalty to their husbands.

The parasite Gelasimus enters, hungry. Crocotium, the maid of Panegyris, listens to him trying to auction off his possessions to the audience for a meal. She tells him that her mistress has sent for him.

Act II

Pinacium, slave boy of Panegyris, enters with good news. Panegyris' husband Epignomus has returned, and is now a rich man. Gelasimus anticipates a banquet. Panegyris is too excited to ask the parasite inside.

Act III

Epignomus enters with his slave Stichus and music girls. He has already met his father-in-law Antipho, who welcomed his rich son-in-law. Stichus is given the day off to enjoy himself. Gelasimus greets Epignomus, and tries to get a dinner invitation, without success.

Act IV

Pamphilippus enters with his father-in-law Antipho. He too has just returned, and is also prosperous. Epignomus greets his brother, and plans for dinner are settled. Antipho hints that he would like one of the flute girls for himself. Gelasimus returns and greets

Pamphilippus. He tries to get an invitation from the second brother, in vain. There is no more doleful parasite than Gelasimus.

Act V

Stichus is waiting for Sangarinus, slave of Pamphilippus, who is just returning from the harbor. They are going to celebrate their homecoming together. Like Stichus, Sangarinus' thoughts are on the slave girl Stephanium.

Sangarinus and Stichus, somewhat tipsy, come out laden with food. As they wait for their girl friend Stephanium, they drink, sing and dance. Finally Stephanium comes out, all dressed up for her boy friends. She joins them in dancing and general merriment.

THE THREE PENNY DAY
(Based on a Greek original by Philemon, *The Treasure*)

Prologue

The scene is before the houses of Callicles and Megaronides in Athens; nearby is the house of Philto. Luxury brings in her daughter Poverty, and, after sending her inside Lesbonicus' house, addresses the audience. Lesbonicus, the son of Charmides, has squandered his father's property during his father's long absence abroad.

Act I

Megaronides, an old Athenian gentleman, is troubled about the behavior of his friend Callicles. He reprimands Callicles because he has bought the house of his friend Charmides from his spendthrift son. It is the house in which Callicles is now living. Callicles tells his friend that, after Lesbonicus squandered his father's property, Charmides left on a trip abroad. Before going he entrusted to Callicles his unmarried daughter and his worthless son. He admits that he gave Lesbonicus a large sum for the house. Now, to protect his reputation, Callicles feels that he must entrust to Megaronides an important secret—that there is a large treasure in a room in the house. He bought the house to protect the treasure, which he plans to restore to Charmides, should he return, or to use as a dowry for his daughter. Megaronides apologizes and offers his assistance to his harassed friend.

Act II

Lysiteles, an Athenian youth, son of Philto and friend of Lesbonicus, presents a disquisition on love, whose disturbing effects he fears. His father Philto commends the uprightness of his son. Lysiteles informs his father that he wants to marry Lesbonicus' sister—without a dowry, in order to help out his penniless friend. Philto is aghast, but graciously consents.

Philto agrees to ask Lesbonicus for his sister's hand for his son. Lesbonicus and his slave Stasimus enter. Philto hears them discussing the tawdry details of the squandering of the money received from the sale of the house. He asks for the girl's hand for his son— without a dowry. Lesbonicus insists that his sister must have a dowry, and offers the family farm in the suburbs. Philto refuses the offer, and Lesbonicus, ashamed at the family's disgrace, reluctantly agrees to the betrothal. But Lesbonicus is determined that his sister shall have a dowry. He sends his slave to summon Callicles.

Act III

Callicles is troubled about the dowry problem, and goes to consult his friend Megaronides. Lysiteles is angry with Lesbonicus, for he thinks his offer to marry his sister was made out of pity. The family honor is at stake, and he is affronted because Lysiteles and Philto will not accept a dowry. Lysiteles insists that there is to be no dowry.

Callicles tells Megaronides that honor requires that the girl receive a dowry. Megaronides has an idea: they will take a part of the treasure concealed in the house, and hire some swindler who will pretend he is a foreigner bringing the gold from Charmides to provide a dowry for his daughter. In this way the secret of the treasure will be concealed from the spendthrift son.

Act IV

Charmides returns unexpectedly from abroad, a rich man. The swindler, hired for three pennies by Callicles and Megaronides, enters disguised as a foreigner. Charmides accosts him. The swindler, briefed on what he is to say, declares he has two letters from

the father of Lesbonicus, one for his son, one for Callicles. Charmides amuses himself with the swindler, and then announces that
he is Charmides. The swindler thinks Charmides is trying to swindle
him out of the gold. The swindler is driven off.

Stasimus enters in haste. He has been drinking and has lost a
ring. Now he moralizes on integrity and corruption. Charmides
greets his surprised slave, from whom he learns that the house was
sold to Callicles. Just then Callicles enters, and explains the truth
to Charmides.

Act V

Lysiteles has learned that Charmides has returned. Charmides
commends his friend Callicles for tending to his affairs with such
integrity and care. Callicles explains the deception of the swindler
to the amused Charmides.

Lysiteles greets his prospective father-in-law, who promises him
a fine dowry. Lysiteles begs Charmides to forgive his son. To this
Charmides agrees, and also announces that he has arranged for his
son to marry Callicles' daughter. Lesbonicus, chastened, promises
to lead a decent life henceforth.

TRUCULENTUS

(From a Greek original, by an unknown author)

Prologue

The scene is before the houses of Phronesium and Strabax's
father. The Prologue reveals that the courtesan Phronesium, a most
mercenary type, has pretended that she is the mother of a baby in
order to increase her plunder.

Act I

Diniarchus, a young Athenian, has bankrupted himself paying
for the favors of Phronesium. He is fully aware of the cause of his
ruination, but cannot help himself. Now she has given first place in
her affections to a soldier, Stratophanes. And she claims that she
has given birth to a baby and that the father is the soldier.

Astaphium, maid of Phronesium, is on her way to summon some-one for her mistress. Diniarchus accosts her, but gets a cold reception, for his money has run out. When he states that he still has some land and houses, she invites him in to see Phronesium, who, she declares, has just had a baby by the soldier.

Act II

Astaphium is very cynical about the ruin of Diniarchus. Phronesium has sent her to fetch the country youth Strabax, a generous giver. She knocks and is promptly greeted by Strabax's slave, the gruff, blunt Truculentus, who threatens he will inform Strabax's father about his son's attentions to the courtesan.

Diniarchus has not been able to see Phronesium, but soon she enters. She offers him a little attention, and frankly reveals to him the pretense about the baby and her plan to plunder more of the soldier's property. The baby, she says, was given to her by a hairdresser. She promises to come back to Diniarchus after her plan succeeds. He is overjoyed at her confidence in him and leaves.

Phronesium comes out again, playing the role of a new mother. Stratophanes the soldier returns to Athens after ten months' absence. He is told Phronesium had a baby just a few days ago. He offers her valuable gifts brought from abroad, but she is hardly satisfied with them.

Cyanus, Diniarchus' slave, arrives with a large quantity of food and some money sent by his master as a gift to Phronesium. Stratophanes is consumed with jealousy and departs angrily, proclaiming that he is through with her.

Act III

Strabax returns from the country. He has pilfered some money from his father, and immediately goes to see Phronesium. He is welcomed inside.

Truculentus, much softened, approaches Astaphium and offers her a purse to spend the night with her. They go in to the courtesan's house.

Act IV

Diniarchus is overjoyed at Phronesium's reception of his gifts, but he is now completely penniless. Astaphium comes out, and tells Diniarchus that Strabax is inside spending his money. Diniarchus is told he is not welcome, and is extremely bitter.

Just then Callicles, an old Athenian gentleman and Diniarchus' prospective father-in-law, arrives. He brings in Sura the hairdresser and a maid of his own, both in chains. It appears that Callicles' daughter had had an illegitimate boy and that the maid gave it to Sura, who turned it over to Phronesium. The maid reveals that Diniarchus is the man who fathered the baby by Callicles' daughter. Diniarchus is ordered to get the baby and marry the girl immediately.

Phronesium enters and Diniarchus demands his baby. She prevails upon him to let her keep the baby a few days in order to complete the swindle, and he agrees.

Act V

Stratophanes returns to offer Phronesium a large sum of money. She takes it, but demands more. Strabax comes out, and the two men vie for her favors in an utterly degrading fashion, "a fool and a madman competing for their own ruin." Phronesium promises to share herself between them, and as they all enter her house Phronesium offers her favors to the entire audience.

LOST PLAYS OF PLAUTUS

Acharistio; Agroecus; Artemo; Astraba; Bacaria; The Blind Man; The Bondsman; The Charcoal Woman; The Female Usurer; The Flatterer; The Grouch; Frivolaria; The Fugitives; The Little Garden; Nervolaria; The Parasite Doctor; The Lazy Parasite; Saturio; The Bucket Cleaner; The Suicide Pact; The Traveling Trunk; The Triplets; The Woman of Boeotia.

DRAMATIC TECHNIQUES AND STYLE OF PLAUTUS

1. Free adaptations from Greek New Comedy, with Roman allusions

2. Expository prologue; dramatic irony.

3. Broad farce, with song and dance elements.

4. Plots lively, gay, improbable; careless workmanship; many coincidences and improbabilities.

5. Farcical and grotesque treatment of characters; types frequently rogues.

6. Colloquial speech; speed and vivacity of dialogue.

7. Puns; comic coined compounds.

8. Moderate use of obscenity.

9. Boisterous, exuberant comic genius, full of gusto and robust vigor.

10. "He plays a whole gamut of comic effects, and manipulates to his liking the elements of comedy, farce, burlesque, operetta, pantomime, and extravaganza." (J. W. Duff, *A Literary History of Rome,* p. 193.)

CHAPTER ELEVEN

TERENCE

PUBLIUS TERENTIUS AFER (ca. 195-159 B.C.)

1. Slave boy from Carthage; freed in Rome.
2. Associated with Scipionic Circle in Rome, a group of phil-hellene aristocrats.
3. Wrote six plays, between 166 and 160 B.C., all extant, adapted from the plays of Menander and Apollodorus.
4. Originality of Terence: double plots and greater suspense.

TERENCE'S PLAYS

Andria (*Woman of Andros*)
Adelphoi (*The Brothers*)
Heautontimoroumenos (*The Self-Tormentor*)
Eunuchus (*The Eunuch*)
Phormio
Hecyra (*The Mother-in-Law*)

THE WOMAN OF ANDROS

Prologue

The prologue of this play is not the typical expository one of the New Comedy. In it Terence defends his dramatic art from criticisms directed against him. We learn that *The Woman of Andros* is a conflation, through *contaminatio,* of two plays of Menander—the *Perinthia* (*Woman of Perinthos*) and the *Andria* (*Woman of Andros*).

Act I

The scene is Athens. Simo, an elderly gentleman, tells his troubles to his faithful freedman Sosia. Simo had betrothed his son Pamphilus to Philumena, daughter of his friend Chremes, and the wedding was set for this very day. Simo is an indulgent father, but his son's behavior has begun to worry him. A woman from Andros, Chrysis by name, used to entertain young men in her house next door. Pamphilus was known to visit her. He is convinced, however, that his son did not become one of her lovers.

A few days ago Chrysis suddenly died. At the funeral Pamphilus was very much distraught, and showed tender solicitation for a lovely refined young girl, Glycerium, said to be Chrysis' sister. Chremes had come to him, asserting that it was obvious that Pamphilus was treating the foreign girl as his wife, and promptly broke off the marriage.

Now Simo decides to put his son to the test by pretending that the marriage will take place. One of his difficulties is to control the scheming slave Davus, who always meddles, and who favors Pamphilus. He asks Sosia's assistance in his plans.

Davus enters, and is warned by Simo not to interfere in the planned wedding. Davus is torn between fear of punishment and his devotion to Pamphilus. After Simo leaves, Davus, in an aside, tells that Glycerium is pregnant, and that Pamphilus has decided to recognize the baby as his own. He has also been told, though he does not believe it, that Glycerium is an Athenian citizen, who was taken from Athens on a sea voyage and shipwrecked on the Island of Andros. Here she was brought up by Chrysis' father. Davus goes off to find Pamphilus.

Mysis, a slave woman of Glycerium, comes out to get a midwife for her mistress. Pamphilus enters, very unhappy because he has been told that the marriage is actually to take place. He does not even know the girl Philumena, and supposes her to be ugly. He is torn between duty to his father and love for Glycerium, whom he regards as his wife. He tells Mysis how Chrysis on her deathbed had left all her property to Glycerium in his trust, and had blessed the couple as man and wife.

Act II

Charinus, Pamphilus' friend, is in love with Philumena. He tells his slave, the crude Byrria, his sadness at the announced marriage of his friend to his beloved. Pamphilus enters, and assures him he does not want to marry her. Davus rushes in to announce that he has learned that Chremes will not permit the marriage to take place. Charinus leaves overjoyed. Davus advises Pamphilus to pretend he will agree to Simo's "arrangements" for his marriage, in order to play for time. Byrria sneaks in to keep an eye on Pamphilus for his master Charinus. He overhears Pamphilus agree to Simo's wish that he marry Philumena today, and rushes off to tell Charinus. Simo is suspicious, fearing Davus' scheming.

Act III

Mysis returns with the midwife Lesbia. Simo hears that Glycerium is about to have a baby. When the baby's birth is announced, he thinks at first that everything was staged to deceive him, and he blames Davus. In any case, to save his son from disgrace, he decides to urge Chremes to agree once more to the marriage to Philumena. For friendship's sake Chremes reluctantly agrees. When Davus and Pamphilus hear of the change in plans, their gloom is profound.

Act IV

Charinus too has heard the news, and berates Pamphilus and Davus. Glycerium has been told, and she is heartbroken. Davus thinks of a new scheme: he takes the baby and places it on Simo's doorstep. Chremes enters to announce that all preparations for the wedding have been made. When he sees the baby, Davus slyly lets it be known that it is Pamphilus' child. He also plants the idea that Glycerium is an Athenian citizen, and that by law Pamphilus would be required to marry her. Chremes is aghast, and goes off to see Simo at once.

At this point Crito from Andros arrives. He is a cousin of the dead Chrysis, and has come to claim her property. When he hears that Glycerium still has not found her parents, he decides to let her keep the property.

Act V

Chremes has broken off the marriage again, despite Simo's pleas. Davus appears, elated with the news he has received from Crito— that Glycerium is an Athenian girl. Simo orders Davus put into chains. He calls Pamphilus from Glycerium's house and threatens to disown him.

Crito is summoned. Chremes recognizes him and vouches for his integrity. Crito tells how many years ago an Athenian ship was lost off Andros. A man and a girl were rescued and taken in by Chrysis' father. The man soon died, and the girl was brought up as Chrysis' sister. It turns out that the dead man, Phania, was Chremes' brother and that the girl is Chremes' long-lost daughter Pasibula.

Simo forgives Pamphilus and, of course, agrees to his marriage to his niece Glycerium (Pasibula). Davus is released from chains. Charinus enters overjoyed, and Pamphilus offers to intercede with Chremes for Philumena's hand. Chremes gives his consent.

THE BROTHERS

(Based on a play of Menander of the same name. It also contains a scene from a play of Diphilus, *The Suicide Pact*.)

Prologue

The scene is before the houses of Micio and Sostrata in Athens. The Prologue bespeaks the audience's goodwill, and defends Terence's dramatic methods against his critics.

Act I

Micio, an old Athenian gentleman, soliloquizes on his adoptive son Aeschinus. He himself is a bachelor, but was permitted by his brother Demea to adopt one of his two sons. He has brought up Aeschinus in a permissive fashion, being indulgent, generous, frank with him, and training him to do right by choice rather than through fear. By contrast, his brother Demea has brought up his son Ctesipho with stern discipline and the principle of obedience through fear. The brothers differ fundamentally in their concepts of the education of the young.

Demea enters from the country very much distressed. He has heard that Aeschinus has forcibly taken from a pimp named Sannio a courtesan, whom Aeschinus loves. He rebukes Micio for ruining Aeschinus. Micio is indulgent, but Demea is shocked at the affair. He is proud of having brought up his other son Ctesipho as an upright, obedient, hardworking boy. Micio goes off to find Aeschinus.

Act II

Aeschinus enters with a music girl, followed by the pimp Sannio, who demands his property. He tries to seize her but is beaten. The girl is then taken into Micio's house. Aeschinus brazens it out with Sannio. He will pay for the girl, he declares; if Sannio refuses the offer, he will claim her as freeborn, and keep her without paying. Sannio fears for his entire investment.

Syrus, slave of Micio and Aeschinus, offers Sannio half of the value of the girl. The pimp is willing to settle for just what he paid for her.

Ctesipho, Demea's son, enters, overjoyed. It is he who is really in love with the music girl, and his brother Aeschinus abducted the girl for his sake, taking upon himself the scandal to help his brother and to conceal the affair from the strict Demea. Aeschinus promises to get the money to pay Sannio, and Ctesipho goes in to his mistress.

Act III

Sostrata, a poor Athenian widow, enters in distress, accompanied by her slave Cathara. Her daughter Pamphila is in labor. Ten months before, Aeschinus seduced her, but continued to be interested in her and visited her frequently. Geta, Sostrata's slave, enters to report bad news: Aeschinus has brought a music girl home as his mistress. Sostrata is shocked, for Aeschinus promised to marry her daughter. She sends Geta to tell the story to Herio, her dead husband's best friend.

Demea is disturbed because he has heard that Ctesipho is somehow involved in the abduction. Syrus enters and, in an aside, tells that Micio was informed of the truth. He was indulgently pleased with the whole affair and gladly paid the money to Sannio for the girl. Demea is proud that his son would not have gotten into such a sordid affair. Syrus does not disabuse him, assuring him that Ctesipho is still in the country.

Just then Hegio, who is also a friend of Demea, arrives. He tells Demea that Aeschinus seduced Sostrata's daughter, promised to marry the girl, and now has brought home a music girl as his mistress. Demea promises to speak to Micio, and assures Hegio that all will be set right.

Act IV

Ctesipho comes out of Micio's house and expresses fear about what Demea may say when he discovers his absence from the farm. Just then Demea returns, having discovered that Ctesipho is not in the country. Syrus covers up for Ctesipho, and sends Demea off on a fool's errand after Micio.

Micio and Hegio enter. Micio has told Hegio the truth—that the music girl is Ctesipho's mistress. They go in to assure Sostrata about Aeschinus.

Aeschinus enters, very much troubled about the distress he has caused Sostrata and Pamphila. He is in a dilemma because he does not want to betray his brother. But he decides to clear his character with the women.

Micio comes out of Sostrata's house and decides to give his son a few uncomfortable moments because he concealed his private problems from him. Aeschinus bursts into tears and confesses his errors. Micio assures him he may marry Pamphila. Aeschinus is overjoyed and appreciative of having such a loving, understanding father.

Demea returns and informs Micio of the seduction of Pamphila by Aeschinus. Micio is amused, and tells him of the coming wedding. Demea is outraged, especially when Micio declares that the music girl has been bought from the pimp and will continue to stay with them in his house.

Act V

Syrus enters, drunk. Demea soon learns that Ctesipho is indoors. Micio enters from Sostrata's house. Demea, who now knows all, rebukes his brother for ruining both of his sons by extravagance and by permitting them to indulge in immorality. But Demea soon unbends and concedes he must go along with the fashions of the times.

Demea, after a little while in Micio's house, enters and declares that Micio's philosophy of life is superior to his stern, old-fashioned way.

Then he begins to put into practice his new amiability and generosity, practicing on Syrus and Geta. Soon he goes to an extreme of overindulgence with Aeschinus. It is Micio's turn now to be troubled by Demea's behavior. Demea suggests that the elderly bachelor Micio marry the widow Sostrata. Reluctantly Micio agrees. Demea also succeeds in getting Micio to give Hegio a plot of land in the suburbs, and obtains freedom for Syrus and his wife, together with a sum of money to start them off on an independent life. Finally, he agrees to permit Ctesipho to keep the music girl, and all ends well.

THE SELF-TORMENTOR

(Based on a comedy of the same name by Menander)

Prologue

The scene is before the houses of Menedemus and Chremes near Athens. Terence through the Prologue defends his methods and style of writing comedy against his critics. He begs the audience for a fair hearing.

Act I

Menedemus, an old gentleman of Attica, is reproached by his neighbor Chremes for working so hard on his land. He justifies his interference in his neighbor's affairs thus: "I am a human being; I am interested in everything human." Menedemus confesses that he is punishing himself by hard work. His only son fell in love with a girl, the daughter of a poor woman from Corinth, and was keeping her as his mistress. To break up the affair Menedemus talked his son into becoming a soldier. The young man, Clinia, secretly enlisted as a mercenary in the army of the king of Persia. This is why Menedemus is now tormenting himself. Chremes is deeply moved.

Clitipho, Chremes' son, greets his father, and informs him that his friend Clinia, Menedemus' son, has just returned from Asia and is now in their house. The young Clinia is still in love with his girl Antiphila, and has sent for her.

Act II

Clitipho soliloquizes about how fathers deny their sons the freedom they themselves had in their youth. He himself is concerned about how to keep his sweetheart, the courtesan Bacchis. As usual, the young lover has no money.

Clinia enters, and is informed by the slaves Syrus and Dromo that Antiphila will be here presently. She is coming, they say, with a troop of servants and much jewelry and clothing. Clinia is surprised; he fears that she has become a courtesan in his absence. Syrus assures him of Antiphila's integrity. It seems that the old woman who was said to be her mother was not really her mother. Moreover, she is now dead. The girl is still in love with Clinia. They reveal that the servants, clothes and jewelry really belong to Bacchis, Clitipho's mistress. Syrus, Chremes' slave, has a plan: Clitipho wants his mistress and has no money; therefore Bacchis is to be brought into the house on the pretense that she is Clinia's mistress. In this way they will conceal Clitipho's love affair from his father. Antiphila poses as one of Bacchis' servants, but is to be looked after by Clitipho's mother.

Bacchis and Antiphila enter. The contrast between the meretricious courtesan and the charming devoted Antiphila is obvious. Antiphila and Clinia are joyously reunited.

Act III

Chremes decides to tell Menedemus of his son's return. Despite Menedemus' desire to have his son home again at once, he is dissuaded by Chremes from going to him. Chremes warns him that Clinia's mistress has become a grasping courtesan. Still Menedemus is ready to give his son all his wealth to make up for his past treatment of him. Chremes advises him to spend his money through an intermediary rather than directly, for too much indulgence would spoil the young man and ultimately ruin him.

Syrus, who is now plotting to obtain money for Clitipho to give to Bacchis, greets Chremes. Chremes encourages him to hatch a plot to get the youth some money from Menedemus for his mistress.

Chremes discovers his son Clitipho making love to Bacchis, and rebukes him. Clitipho is cautioned by Syrus about his behavior. The slave tells Chremes that Bacchis owed a large sum of money to an old woman of Corinth, who is now dead. Her daughter was left in Bacchis' hands as security for the money. Bacchis, he declares, wants the money and will then hand over the girl to Clinia. Syrus plans to get the money from Menedemus.

Act IV

Sostrata, wife of Chremes, enters, and excitedly informs Chremes that one of the girls inside has a ring which was left with their daughter, who was supposed to have been exposed as a baby. Sostrata confesses she gave the baby to an old Corinthian woman. Chremes and Sostrata go in to see the girl.

Syrus is worried about his plans to get the money. He devises a new scheme. Clinia comes out and tells Syrus that it has been discovered that Antiphila is Chremes' daughter. It is now, says Syrus, Clinia's turn to help his friend Clitipho by continuing the pretense that Bacchis is his mistress, and by moving her into his own house. But Clinia is to tell his father the truth—that Bacchis is Clitipho's mistress and that Clinia wants to marry Antiphila. The same facts are to be told to Chremes. "I will deceive them both," says Syrus, "by telling the truth." The two old gentlemen will not believe the story. This will give Syrus time to obtain the money.

Bacchis enters with her maid Phrygia, complaining that Syrus has failed to obtain the money he promised. Her entourage moves over to Menedemus' house.

Chremes is sorry for Menedemus. Syrus tells Chremes that Menedemus has been told that Bacchis is Clitipho's mistress and that she has moved to his house, so as to conceal the truth from Chremes. Clinia, he says, will declare he wants to marry Antiphila. Chremes agrees to pay Syrus the money which is supposed to be owed to Bacchis for Antiphila. He brings out the money and gives it to his son Clitipho to bring to Bacchis to repay the supposed debt incurred for Antiphila.

Menedemus is happy because he has learned that his son wants to marry Chremes' daughter, but Chremes convinces him that it is part of Syrus' plot to get money. They decide, however, to pretend that a betrothal has been arranged. In this way Menedemus will be able to give his son some money without spoiling him.

Act V

Menedemus informs Chremes that his son wants no money. His only desire is to marry Antiphila at once. Chremes is told that Bacchis is really his son's mistress. He is furious that he has been deceived by his son, whose faults turn out to be more serious than those of Menedemus' son Clinia.

The two men then agree to the marriage of Clinia to Antiphila. Chremes asks Menedemus to pretend that the dowry is to be all of Chremes' property. In this way he will be able to punish his son. When Clitipho hears of this, he is heartbroken. Syrus advises Clitipho to play on his parents' sympathies by asking them whether, in view of Chremes' disposition of his property, he is really their son or not.

Sostrata pleads with Chremes not to disinherit Clitipho. Clitipho is contrite, seeks forgiveness, and promises to reform. Menedemus joins in urging Chremes to relent. He finally agrees on condition that Clitipho take a wife. Reluctantly Clitipho agrees. Chremes finally pardons Syrus, and all ends well.

THE EUNUCH

(Based on two plays of Menander, *The Eunuch* and *The Flatterer*)

Prologue

The scene is before the houses of Thais and Laches. Terence through the Prologue defends his dramatic methods against his critics.

Act I

Phaedria, in love with the courtesan Thais, is having the usual difficulties of the lovesick penniless young man with the calculating woman. He communicates his feelings to his slave Parmeno. Thais enters, and confides in Phaedria and Parmeno that her mother, while living in Rhodes, had been given a little girl by a slave dealer as a present. The girl had been kidnapped from Athens. Her mother brought her up as a daughter, and she was generally believed to be Thais' sister. When her mother died recently, Thais' uncle sold the girl in the slave market. By chance a soldier, Thraso by name, one of Thais' lovers, bought the girl as a present for Thais. He does not know the girl's identity. When he discovered that Thais was carrying on with Phaedria also, he decided to withhold the girl from her.

Thais begs Phaedria to help her recover the girl by letting the captain monopolize her affections for just two days. Phaedria petulantly informs Thais that he has just bought a eunuch for her. But he is charmed into agreeing to go away into the country for two days.

Act II

Phaedria instructs Parmeno to bring the two slaves he has bought to Thais, and departs for the country.

Gnatho, the soldier's parasite, brings Pamphila in. The soldier Thraso has sent her as a present to Thais.

Chaerea, Phaedria's younger brother, enters in distress. He has just fallen in love with a girl (it is Pamphila), followed her, but lost track of her. Parmeno reveals that she was given as a present to Thais by Phaedria's rival. Parmeno has a plan: Chaerea is to impersonate the eunuch, and thus be able to see his beloved Pamphila.

Act III

Thraso hears from Gnatho that Thais is pleased with the present of the girl. Thais in fact welcomes Thraso back. Parmeno now hastens to offer her Phaedria's gifts—a eunuch, impersonated by Chaerea, and a slave girl. Thais takes them indoors, and departs for dinner with Thraso and his parasite at the soldier's house.

Chremes, a young Athenian, has been summoned by Thais. She had previously questioned him about a sister of his who had been kidnapped as a little girl. Chremes is suspicious of her motives. Pythias, Thais' slave girl, greets him and has him taken to the captain's house to see Thais.

Antipho, Chaerea's friend, comes looking for him. He meets Chaerea coming out of Thais' house, and Chaerea tells him of his impersonation of the eunuch. He confides in him in detail how he was left alone with Pamphila—and ravished her. The two friends then go off to dinner.

Act IV

Dorias, Thais' maid, reveals that Thais and Thraso have quarreled because Thraso thinks that Chremes is another lover of Thais. As a result Thais is coming home presently.

Phaedria returns from the country, unable to stay away. Pythias enters sobbing, and informs Phaedria that the eunuch he gave Thais has raped the girl given to Thais by the soldier. Phaedria goes into the house to investigate.

Soon he drags out Dorus, the real eunuch, who is dressed in Chaerea's clothing. Pythias reveals that he is not the man, and Dorus declares that Chaerea, Phaedria's brother, took his clothes and impersonated him.

Chremes, somewhat tipsy, arrives, followed by Thais. Thais tells him that his sister is in her house, and that she wanted to restore the girl to him. The captain, however, is angry, and is threatening to take the girl away from Thais. She gives Chremes a box of tokens, which he is to offer as proof that she is his sister.

Thraso, followed by Gnatho and slaves, enters determined to retrieve the girl. Chremes declares that she is freeborn, a citizen of Athens, and his sister. Thraso and his "army" leave.

Act V

Thais rebukes Pythias for neglect of duty, because of the violence done to Pamphila. Pythias declares that the man was Phaedria's brother Chaerea.

Just then Chaerea, still dressed as the eunuch, returns. He tries to brazen it out, but declares that he did the deed out of love, and that he wants to marry the girl. Thais takes him in to her house.

Chremes enters with Pamphila's old nurse Sophrona, who has recognized the tokens and is to verify that Pamphila is Chremes' sister.

Parmeno enters, and is assailed by Pythias for his part in the deception. Chremes, when he heard about the rape, seized Chaerea, and is now threatening to unman him as if he were an adulterer. Just then Laches, the father of Phaedria and Chaerea, returns from the country. Parmeno tells him all that has happened, except the rape. Laches rushes in to save his son Chaerea.

Parmeno is in despair. He fears he will be punished for his part in the affair. Thraso and Gnatho return. The soldier is ready to surrender to Thais on her terms.

Chaerea enters overjoyed: Pamphila has been proven a citizen, and she has been betrothed to him. Phaedria is to be Thais' only love. Phaedria comes out rejoicing at the good fortune of his brother and himself.

Now Gnatho makes out a good case for his patron Thraso. It would, he argues, be to Phaedria's advantage to admit Thraso as his rival. The captain is dull and well-to-do. He will supply the funds for Phaedria's love affair with Thais. Phaedria agrees to share Thais with Thraso.

PHORMIO

(Based on Apollodorus' comedy *The Claimant*)

Prologue

The scene is Athens, before the houses of Demipho, Chremes and Dorio. Terence defends his comedies from the attacks of a literary rival.

Act I

Davus, a slave, comes out to repay a debt to his friend Geta, slave of Demipho. Geta needs the money as a marriage gift for his master's son. He tells Davus that his master departed on a journey to Cilicia in Asia Minor and left his son Antipho in his charge. At the same time Demipho's brother, Chremes, went to Lemnos, and entrusted his son Phaedria to him also.

Phaedria became enamored of a harp-girl belonging to the procurer Dorio, but did not have the money to enjoy her. One day the boys heard of a poor young girl who had just lost her mother, and went to see her. Antipho fell in love with Phanium at first sight. But his efforts to see more of the girl were rejected by the girl's elderly nurse, Sophrona, who asserted that the girl was respectable and the daughter of an Athenian citizen. Sophrona refused to let him have anything to do with her unless he married her legally. Antipho desired to marry her, but feared his father's wrath, because the girl had no dowry.

At this juncture a clever parasite Phormio entered the picture, and advised Antipho that according to Athenian law orphans must marry their next of kin. He offered to swear that Antipho is the girl's nearest relative. Antipho agreed, and married the girl. Phaedria's interest in the harp-girl is still frustrated by lack of money.

Act II

Antipho tells Phaedria how much he fears his father's return. Geta now enters very much frightened because his master has just returned to Athens. Antipho lacks the courage to face his father and runs off. Geta and Phaedria hide in the alleyway.

Demipho enters. He has already heard of his son's marriage and blames Geta. Phaedria tries to justify Antipho's behavior, attributing it to his youth and inexperience, and the legal provisions invoked to bring about the marriage. Geta comes out of hiding with renewed confidence. Demipho asks that Antipho and Phormio be brought to him.

Act III

Phormio and Geta plan their next step. Phormio offers to assume all responsibility. Meanwhile Demipho has called a few elderly friends together for advice—Hegio, Cratinus and Crito.

Phormio takes the offensive at once, accusing Demipho of falsely denying he knows the girl's father Stilpho, who, Phormio claims, is a relative of Demipho. The latter says he will not permit the marriage to continue, and offers Phormio a sum of money to take the girl away. Phormio threatens suit.

Demipho gets little concrete advice from his friends, and goes off to the harbor to wait for his brother Chremes. Antipho enters, feeling completely helpless in his troubles. Phaedria is seen with the procurer Dorio, pleading with him for the harp-girl. Dorio, it seems, has had a bonafide offer from a sea-captain, and has agreed to sell the girl to him. Phaedria begs him to wait three days until he can raise the money. Dorio gives him until the next morning. "First come, first served." The price for the girl is thirty minae. Geta promises to help raise the money with Phormio's help.

Act IV

Demipho enters with Chremes, who has been to Lemnos looking for a daughter and "wife" whom he had there under an assumed name. The mother and daughter had recently come to Athens, looking for him because of their poverty. When Chremes hears of Antipho's marriage, he is distraught, because he had planned to marry his daughter to Antipho, in order to conceal from his Athenian wife the existence of the other woman and her child.

Geta enters, and, while Antipho listens in despair, tells Demipho and Chremes that he has convinced Phormio to take Phanium off their hands and marry her for thirty minae. Phormio demands such a sum because he would have to break off his engagement to another girl, and, moreover, has incurred many debts in connection with his planned marriage. Demipho objects strongly, but Chremes, anxious to have Antipho marry his daughter, offers to pay the entire sum. The two brothers go into Chremes' house to obtain the money.

Antipho accosts Geta and berates him for destroying his marriage. Geta explains that Phormio does not intend to go through with the marriage, and is merely playing for time to secure the thirty minae for Phaedria. Chremes sends Demipho off to pay the money to Phormio under proper legal safeguards. He will have his wife Nausistrata go in to Phanium to prepare her for the dissolution of her marriage with Antipho and her coming marriage to Phormio.

Sophrona, Phanium's nurse, comes out of Demipho's house. Chremes at once recognizes her as his daughter's nurse. She too recognizes him as Stilpho, Phanium's father. Chremes learns that Antipho is already married to his own daughter.

Act V

Demipho has paid the thirty minae to Phormio. Geta goes inside to tell Phanium to fear nothing. Demipho and Nausistrata come out of Demipho's house. She has been cheering up Phanium. When Chremes hears that the money has already been paid to Phormio, he is furious. He does not want Phanium to leave any longer. Nausistrata's opinion is that Phanium should stay because she is an adorable girl. When Nausistrata leaves, Chremes tells Demipho the good news. They go into Demipho's house.

Antipho enters, happy that his cousin Phaedria has his harp-girl, but worried about his marriage.

Phormio enters with Antipho. Geta rushes out of the house to tell them what he has just overheard—that Phanium is Chremes' daughter, and that the marriage will not be dissolved. As Antipho and Geta go in to Phanium, Demipho and Chremes come out and demand of Phormio that he return the money. Phormio claims that he has spent the money to pay his debts, and that he has broken off his engagement to the other girl. When the brothers threaten him with legal action, he reveals that he knows the truth about Chremes. As they try to drag him off, Phormio shouts for Nausistrata and reveals everything to her.

Chremes is terrified about the consequences. Demipho tries to explain the circumstances of the other woman. Phormio tells that the thirty minae were used to buy her son Phaedria a harp-girl. When Nausistrata sees nothing wrong with her son's behavior in view of Chremes' escapade, Chremes consents. Nausistrata invites Phormio to dinner.

THE MOTHER-IN-LAW

(Based on a Greek original by Apollodorus, which was strongly influenced by Menander's play *The Arbitration*)

Prologue

The scene is before the houses of Laches, Phidippus, and Bacchis in Athens. The Prologue requests the audience to give this play a favorable reception. This is the third time it has been produced, having failed during the first two performances.

Act I

Philotis, a courtesan, tells Syra, an old bawd, that men are faithless to courtesans. A case in point is Pamphilus, who was in love with the courtesan Bacchis, but recently left her and married.

Parmeno, the slave of Pamphilus and his father Laches, enters, and greets Philotis and Syra. Parmeno informs them that Pamphilus' new marriage has proven to be a failure. The young man's father pressured him into marrying the daughter of their neighbor Phidippus. Pamphilus, he confides, has not consummated the marriage with Philumena, for he felt he could not go through with the marriage. Yet he gradually grew fond of his sweet wife, and felt more and more estranged from the mercenary Bacchis. A little while before, Pamphilus was sent abroad by his father on business. Pamphilus, having fallen in love with his wife, left her with his

mother. But after a few days Philumena announced she was unable
to live with her mother-in-law Sostrata, and returned to her parents,
unwilling to see anyone.

Act II

Laches blames his wife Sostrata for estranging his son's wife
Philumena. All mothers-in-law, he asserts, are alike. He and Sostrata have been made unwelcome in Philumena's house. When he
sees Phidippus, Philumena's father, he asks for an explanation of
his daughter-in-law's behavior, but is put off. He and Phidippus go
off to the market place.

Act III

Pamphilus returns from abroad and hears from Parmeno that his
wife has left his house. He is deeply distressed. Suddenly they hear
a cry of pain from Philumena inside. Pamphilus rushes in to learn
what is wrong.

Sostrata has heard that Philumena is ill. When Pamphilus returns
in tears, Sostrata rushes in to see Philumena. Pamphilus soliloquizes
on his unhappiness. Philumena is in labor. This explains her leaving
his house and returning to her parents. Inside, his mother-in-law
Myrrhina entreated his sympathy, telling him that Philumena was
violated by some scoundrel just before her marriage to Pamphilus.
He has promised to keep the matter secret, but refuses to take her
back, though he loves her.

Pamphilus sends Parmeno off on a wild goose chase, for his slave
is the only one who knows that he has not consummated his marriage with Philumena.

Laches and Phidippus return. They want Pamphilus to forgive
the supposed quarrel between Sostrata and Philumena and take his
wife back. Pamphilus firmly refuses.

Act IV

Myrrhina hoped to conceal the birth of the child from her husband, but Phidippus has discovered the truth. He cannot understand all the secrecy, and rebukes her for causing difficulties

between Philumena and Pamphilus because the latter had had a mistress before he married. Afraid that the baby may be exposed by the panic-stricken women, he rushes in to prevent this.

Sostrata pleads with Pamphilus to take his wife back. She offers to leave the city to live in the country if this will make her daughter-in-law happier. Laches offers to join her. But Pamphilus is stubborn, though half-willing to take Philumena back.

Phidippus tells them that Myrrhina is entirely to blame for the estrangement. He announces that a grandson has just been born. The two old men now urge Pamphilus to relent. Laches suspects that Pamphilus is still in love with the courtesan Bacchis. Pamphilus, in a dilemma, runs away from the situation. The fathers decide to plead with Bacchis.

Act V

Bacchis enters, and Laches asks if she is still his son's lover. She swears she has had nothing to do with him since his marriage, and agrees to go to the women to assure them of this. Phidippus thinks well of this idea.

Parmeno returns from the fool's errand he has been sent on. Bacchis comes out and tells him to fetch Pamphilus at once. Bacchis was wearing a ring which Pamphilus had given her. This ring had been taken by Pamphilus from a girl he violated while drunk just before his marriage. Myrrhina recognized it as belonging to her daughter. By coincidence, then, Pamphilus turns out to be the father of Philumena's baby. Bacchis is delighted at having been instrumental in clearing up the difficulties.

Pamphilus returns, and is overjoyed to hear the good news. He thanks Bacchis for her kindness, and is assured by her that his wife is indeed a charming woman.

DRAMATIC TECHNIQUES AND STYLE OF TERENCE

1. Great fidelity to Greek originals; no Roman allusions.
2. Subtle and artistic plays.
3. Intricate, skillfully constructed plots.
4. Integration of plot and character.

5. Double plots; greater suspense and surprise; use of *contaminatio*.

6. Personal, polemical prologues.

7. Character portrayal: subtle psychology; greater individualization; contrasts of characters; more humane, refined character types.

8. Greek purity of style—graceful, polished, urbane.

9. Quiet, tame humor (Julius Caesar said of Terence that he was "Menander halved").

10. Frequent epigrammatic sayings.

11 Little obscenity or coarseness.

CHAPTER TWELVE

SENECA

THE ROMAN EMPIRE (30 B.C.—A.D. 68)

1. Augustus (Julius Caesar's grandnephew) became the first Roman emperor. His reign (27 B.C.-A.D.14) ushered in the *Pax Romana* (Roman Peace) which was enforced through Roman armies and the collaboration of local aristocracies throughout the empire. He established an imperial civil service; stabilized the economy of the empire; reformed provincial administration; attempted to revive the old Roman religion; established emperor worship; attempted to limit the rampant individualism of the dying Republic by social and moral reforms.

2. Julio-Claudian Dynasty (A.D. 14-68)

   a. Tiberius (Augustus' stepson), Caligula, Claudius, Nero.

   b. Increasing despotism and suppression of freedoms.

   c. Disastrous consequences of palace intrigues and arbitrary whims of some of emperors, particularly Nero.

   d. First persecution of Christians, during reign of Nero.

   e. Revolt in A.D. 68; suicide of Nero.

GOLDEN AGE OF ROMAN LITERATURE— AUGUSTAN AGE

1. Imperial censorship; restricted freedom of expression.

2. Literary patronage; literature in the service of the new order of Augustus.

3. Great stress on perfection of form.

4. Decline in oratory and objective history; abandonment of sociopolitical scope of pre-Augustan literature.

5. Principal writers: Vergil; Horace; Livy; Ovid.

SILVER AGE OF ROMAN LITERATURE (A.D. 14-180)

1. Oppression and restraints on freedom.

2. Influence of increasing importance of the provinces: change from nationalism of Augustan Age to internationalism, cosmopolitanism, broad interest in all mankind.

3. Stagnation of thought; artificial showpieces; dilettantism; pedantic learning; epigrammatic style; rhetorical display.

4. Principal writers: Seneca; Petronius; Pliny the Elder; Pliny the Younger; Quintilian; Martial; Tacitus; Juvenal; Suetonius.

STOICISM AMONG THE ROMANS

1. Stoicism won widespread acceptance among the Roman ruling classes. It appealed to them because of its pantheistic view of the world, cosmopolitanism, concept of the brotherhood of man, justification of Roman imperialism, and, during the Empire, its support of monarchy.

2. Greek Stoicism (see p. 183) was gradually adapted to Roman needs. It served as a kind of religious creed which helped upper-class Romans face with fortitude and equanimity the chaotic world in which they lived and the sudden upheavals caused to their lives by the whims of despotic emperors.

LUCIUS ANNAEUS SENECA (ca. 4 B.C.—A.D. 65)

1. Born in Corduba, Spain, of eminent Roman family. His father was a famous teacher of rhetoric; his brother was Gallio, before whom St. Paul was brought for examination; his nephew Lucan, a famous epic poet, was the author of the *Pharsalia*.

2. Political career; exiled by the Emperor Caligula; became tutor of Nero and, later, one of his principal advisers; compelled to commit suicide by Nero because of suspicion of his complicity in the conspiracy of Piso against Nero.

3. Stoic philosopher.

4. Wrote philosophical and moral essays, scientific works, letters, satire, tragedies.

TRAGEDIES OF SENECA

BASED ON EURIPIDES	BASED ON SOPHOCLES
Medea	*Oedipus*
Phaedra	*Hercules on Oeta*
Phoenician Women	
Trojan Women	BASED ON AESCHYLUS
Mad Hercules	*Agamemnon*

Thyestes (source unknown)

(A tenth play, the *Octavia,* a *fabula praetexta* based on the tragic death of Nero's first wife Octavia, once attributed to Seneca, is by an unknown author.)

MEDEA

This play is based on Euripides' *Medea* (see pp. 76-80). But Seneca has introduced many innovations. The principal change is the shift of sympathy to Jason and the emphasis on the inhumanity of Medea. Seneca has transformed Euripides' play into a "blood and thunder" tragedy of revenge and a study in criminal psychology.

Act I

The scene is before the house of Medea in Corinth; nearby is the palace of King Creon. Medea, in a long monologue, shrieks for vengeance because Jason is deserting her to marry Creusa, the princess of Corinth. She prays to many gods and divine powers for death to the princess and Creon, and curses Jason, praying for a life of misery for him. She girds herself for horrible deeds of vengeance through her sorceress' skill.

The Chorus of Corinthian Men, sympathetic to Jason and hostile to Medea, sings a marriage song for Jason and Creusa. They pray for happiness for the bride and groom, and express their joy that Jason has been freed from wedlock with Medea.

Act II

Medea is stirred to heights of fury by the marriage song. She elaborates on all she has done for Jason, including the crimes she committed for his sake—her betrayal of her father, the slaying of her brother, the destruction of Pelias. She loves Jason, and blames him for weakness in submitting to Creon's royal will. It is Creon she must punish. The Nurse seeks to calm her wrath, but Medea's fury mounts.

Creon enters. He would have Medea out of his realm at once, but has yielded to Jason's plea on her behalf. Creon fears her powers of witchcraft. She defends herself before Creon, reminding him of her royal descent, her help to the famous Greeks among the Argonauts, who came seeking the Golden Fleece in Colchis with Jason, her services to Jason. She begs him to return Jason to her, and asks for asylum in his kingdom. Creon defends Jason from complicity in her horrible crimes, and orders her out of his kingdom. All fear her, he declares, because she combines woman's deceit with the strength of a man. He will permit her children to remain, and will care for them. She begs for time to say farewell to her children. Creon grants her one day, and departs to attend the marriage.

The Chorus comments on the boldness of man in inventing ships, and his daring in sailing the seas. The first ship, the Argo, brought the Argonauts across the seas in their perilous voyage. The prizes they brought back were the Golden Fleece—and Medea. Seafaring has expanded the horizons of man to the East and West. In time there will be no more unknown lands.

Act III

The Nurse tries to restrain Medea, who has been raging in mad fury. Medea wildly threatens terrible vengeance, and now begins to assail Jason.

Jason enters, declares his love for his children, and sincerely asserts they are his principal concern. Medea pours out her heart to Jason, pointing out the power and wealth she gave up to be with him, her difficult position as an exile, and all she has done for him. Then she vents her rage upon him as he defends himself from her charges that he was an accomplice in her crimes. Jason pleads with her to restrain herself for the sake of their children. She begs him to flee with her; he pleads it is necessary to submit to Creon's power. She asks that her sons accompany her in exile; he declares his deep love for them, and refuses to part with them. Thereupon Medea conceives a shattering vengeance upon Jason—she will kill the children. She requests permission to bid them farewell. When he departs, she fumes with wrath and formulates her plans to the Nurse: she will send the children with a robe and diadem as gifts to Jason's bride, but first she will poison them with magic spells.

The Chorus comments on the fury of a wife spurned by her husband. The daring of men who leave the beaten path is criticized as being counter to the laws of nature. So, of those who sailed on the Argo many suffered disastrous ends, among them Tiphys, Orpheus, Hylas, Idmon, Meleager, and Mopsus. They pray that Jason may be spared.

Act IV

The Nurse voices her fears of some coming disaster. She describes in elaborate detail Medea's resort to witchcraft—her concoction of a potent poison from serpent's venom, noxious herbs and other ingredients, such as unclean birds, a screech owl's heart, a vampire's vitals, and magic spells.

Medea appears, chanting her incantations and praying to diabolical supernatural forces for aid in her sorcery. In a savage frenzy she gashes her arm and lets the blood flow on the altar at which she is praying. Then she steeps in the potent drugs the robe and diadem to be sent as deadly gifts to Creusa, Jason's bride. She summons her sons and dispatches them abruptly to deliver the gifts.

The Chorus expresses horror at Medea's fury, and wishes she were already gone from Corinth.

Act V

A messenger enters to report the catastrophe—the horrible deaths of Creusa and Creon, both consumed by the poisoned gifts, and the destruction of the palace by flames.

Medea, in a long soliloquy, gloats over the deaths of the king and the princess, and promises an even more horrible crime. She recalls in mad ecstasy all her past crimes. On the verge of murdering her sons, she wavers momentarily, touched by mother love. She embraces them, but hate speedily conquers love, and she submits to her desire for consummate vengeance upon Jason. She utters the macabre wish that she had had fourteen children (twice as many as Niobe), so that she might have even greater vengeance. A vision of the Furies and her brother's ghost appear to her. In wild frenzy she kills one of her sons on stage, and, as the sound of the outraged Corinthians coming to seize her is heard, she picks up the corpse and drags her surviving son inside her house.

Jason enters to seize Medea for punishment, and to burn her house to the ground. Suddenly Medea appears on the housetop with her two sons, boasting of her powers. Momentarily she is again seized by remorse, but at once feels a wild joy in her deed. She is not satisfied, because Jason did not view the killing of his son. He entreats her to spare the other boy, and offers himself as a victim in his place. Ruthlessly she slays the second son. Suddenly a chariot drawn by dragons appears to carry her off to safety. She flings the bodies down to him, as she is borne away.

PHAEDRA

(Based on two of Euripides' plays, the extant *Hippolytus* and the lost *Hippolytus Veiled*)

Act I

The scene is before the palace of Theseus at Athens. The prologue is spoken by Hippolytus. He exuberantly assigns various duties to his fellow-huntsmen, as they prepare for the day's chase. He departs to the hunt with his followers.

Phaedra complains to her Nurse about her unhappy marriage to Theseus. He is unfaithful to her, and has finally deserted her, having descended to Hades to seize the queen of the underworld, Persephone, as his bride. She is lonely, cannot sleep, and is miserable. She feels akin to her mother Pasiphae, who was consumed by a monstrous passion for a bull.

The Nurse, who knows that Phaedra loves her stepson Hippolytus, counsels self-control and cognizance of the terrible shame. "Wouldst thou outsin thy mother?" It is, she says, an impious love that cannot be concealed.

Phaedra admits that her love is sinful, but she cannot control her passion. The Nurse rebukes the unrestrained license of the pampered rich. Phaedra, however, does not believe that Theseus will ever return. Even if he does, he might indulge her in her love. In any case, though Hippolytus hates women, she is confident that she will seduce him. When the Nurse stubbornly argues against her intentions, Phaedra artfully pretends she will commit suicide. The Nurse is taken in by the deception, and agrees to approach Hippolytus for Phaedra.

The Chorus of Athenian citizens sings of the universal power of love, which masters every living thing in the world.

Act II

The Nurse describes in realistic detail how Phaedra is consumed by her fierce passion for Hippolytus. Phaedra is ill and wasting away. Then Phaedra is revealed in a half-mad state. The Nurse prays to Diana, goddess of the hunt, for help in winning over Hippolytus.

Just then Hippolytus returns from the hunt. The Nurse invites the ascetic, chaste misogynist to seek a life of sensual pleasure in sophisticated urban society, seeking to seduce him for Phaedra. He glorifies the happiness to be found in the "silent places of the woods," away from the madding crowd. He delights in the peaceful life, without sin or guile, close to nature, a life such as existed before the corruption brought about by urban civilization. Besides, he hates all women.

At this point Phaedra enters, and conveniently faints in Hippolytus' arms. When she revives, she decides to employ direct methods. She begs him not to call her "mother" but "slave," and confesses her love for him. She offers him the royal power and herself. The-

seus, she is convinced, is dead. Hippolytus is horrified. Then she
throws herself at his feet, saying that he is the more ideal Theseus,
as she first knew him when he came to Crete to slay the Minotaur.

Hippolytus is revolted by her advances and rebukes her. As she
persists in her entreaties, he draws his sword and threatens to kill
her. When she pretends to swoon, he is frightened, throws away his
sword and flees to the forests.

The Nurse decides to throw the blame on Hippolytus by accusing
him of having made sinful advances to Phaedra. She cries for help
and denounces Hippolytus.

The Chorus tells of Hippolytus' flight, his extraordinary beauty
and strength. But tragedy awaits him, for Phaedra plans to destroy
him by false charges.

Act III

Theseus enters rejoicing at his escape from Tartarus with the aid
of Hercules. He hears sounds of wailing. The Nurse informs him
that Phaedra is about to commit suicide. Theseus demands of Phaedra to know the reason. She artfully refuses to tell her secret. When
he threatens to put the Nurse to torture to find out the secret, Phaedra asserts she was violated, but refuses to name Hippolytus. Instead she points to the sword.

Hastily Theseus denounces his son's behavior, his sinfulness concealed behind a mask of chastity, and prays to Neptune, who once
offered him three wishes, to destroy his son.

The Chorus comments on the orderly nature of the universe,
while man is the victim of chance. Why do the innocent suffer and
the sinful prosper so frequently?

Act IV

A messenger arrives to report to Theseus in detail the death of
Hippolytus. His chariot was miraculously overwhelmed by a tidal
wave. He was dragged headlong by the frightened steeds, and his
body was horribly shattered and mangled. The messenger presents
him with the parts of Hippolytus' body that were gathered up.
Theseus is remorseful.

The Chorus sings of the wheel of fortune, which harms the humble less frequently than the powerful. It is the great she strikes down. So Theseus, returning from Hades, was struck down by disaster.

Act V

Phaedra enters with a drawn sword. She curses and assails Theseus for causing Hippolytus' death. She grieves over the remains of Hippolytus, confesses her guilt and her false denunciation of Hippolytus, and declares his innocence. Then she commits suicide.

Theseus, overwhelmed with remorse, bewails his woes, curses himself, and wishes he were dead. He orders the remains of Hippolytus to be brought to him, and tries to arrange the bloody, shattered limbs one by one into the semblance of a human form. As he prepares the remains for burial, he curses Phaedra's corpse.

THE PHOENICIAN WOMEN

(This play is incomplete; it contains several scenes based probably on Euripides' play of the same name)

Act I

The scene is the country near Thebes; the time three years after Oedipus' discovery of his parentage.

Oedipus enters, led by the devoted Antigone. He is blind and in exile. He tells of his wanderings, and talks at length of suicide, being conscious of the enormity of his sins.

Antigone swears never to abandon her father. He bewails his suffering, and talks again of suicide and death, asking Antigone to aid him. He is overwhelmed with guilt because of his sins.

Antigone comforts him, offering him the counsel that " 'tis brave to face the greatest ills," and to endure adversity with fortitude. But he cannot, he says, flee from his conscience. He then relates his unhappy life: the oracle that he would kill his father and marry his mother; his exposure as a baby; his fulfillment of the oracle; his incestuous marriage with his mother; the terrible discovery of the truth. Now his sons Eteocles and Polynices are at war for the throne of Thebes, and new ills impend. Only Antigone loves him, and he will be guided by her.

Act II

A messenger arrives from Thebes and begs Oedipus to return and help stop the strife between his sons. Oedipus refuses, praying that the crime of his sons may be greater than his.

Act III

The scene is inside Thebes. Jocasta, mother of Eteocles and Polynices, tells how Polynices was exiled by Eteocles, took refuge with Adrastus, king of Argos, married his daughter, and organized the Seven Against Thebes to recover the throne. A Theban guard enters, followed by Antigone. He declares that the battle is about to begin, and begs her to hasten to her sons and urge them to cease the war. Antigone begs Jocasta to rush to the battlefield. She hastens away wildly, to plead with her sons.

Act IV

The scene is the plain before Thebes. Jocasta kneels between her sons and pleads with them. In an eloquent speech, she pours out her love for both of them, and implores them to end the fratricidal strife. Polynices states the justice of his case, but Jocasta counsels him not to fight injustice with the crime of attacking his native city.

Eteocles' reply is tyrannical and unyielding. He is willing to pay any price for royal power.

THE TROJAN WOMEN
(Based on Euripides' *Hecuba* and *Trojan Women*)

Act I

The scene is the seashore near Troy; in the background are the ruins of the burning city. Hecuba, attended by the Chorus of Trojan Women, speaks the prologue. She comments on the mutability of fortune—witness the fall and destruction of the once great and proud city of Troy. The Greeks have plundered the city, committing sacrilege. She bewails her dead, especially Hector and the aged Priam, who was brutally slain by Achilles' son Pyrrhus. She laments, too, the enslavement of the women of Troy.

The Chorus joins Hecuba in bewailing the ten years of suffering during the Trojan War, and the passing of glorious Hector and mighty Priam.

Act II

The herald Talthybius enters, and reports to the Chorus the horrifying details of the appearance of Achilles' ghost. Achilles demanded the sacrifice of Polyxena, Priam's daughter, as an offering to his shades. Pyrrhus soon appears, and recounts the glorious deeds of his father on behalf of the Greeks. He demands the immediate immolation of Polyxena as an offering to the spirit of Achilles. Agamemnon accuses Pyrrhus of having the same excessive pride as his father. He has scruples about such a barbarous act as sacrificing a human being. The Greeks, moreover, have already committed excesses and sacrilege. Agamemnon, therefore, commends restraint and reason, fearing also the whims of fortune, and harboring forebodings about the future. The two quarrel violently and abuse each other. Agamemnon summons Calchas for a ruling. The prophet at once orders the sacrifice of Polyxena, and of Astyanax as well. Otherwise, he declares the ships of the Greeks will remain becalmed at Troy.

The Chorus comments on death as a state of utter and final annihilation, with no hope beyond the grave. Humans must, therefore, resign themselves to fate.

Act III

Andromache, Hector's wife, enters leading little Astyanax. She is stoical, and prefers death, but lives only for Astyanax. She tells of the appearance to her of Hector's bloodstained ghost during the night. He warned her to save their son from death. She sees in her son a close resemblance to his father. Where can she hide him from the Greeks? She decides to conceal him inside Hector's tomb.

Ulysses enters, and demands the boy. He is direct, and informs her that the Greeks fear the rise of Astyanax as a future avenger. Andromache feigns ignorance of his whereabouts. He threatens her with torture unless she reveals where he is. She asserts that Hector's son is dead. The wily Ulysses is not easily deceived. When he threatens to demolish Hector's tomb in vengeance, Andromache's dilemma is unbearable. As his soldiers begin to destroy the tomb, she entreats the hard Ulysses for mercy, and finally decides to sacrifice Astyanax. She summons the boy and hands him over to Ulysses. Berating him for his unfeeling nature and deceitfulness, she bids a tearful farewell to Astyanax. Ulysses leads him away.

The Chorus speculates on where in Greece they will be taken in captivity.

Act IV

Helen has been assigned the role of bringing Polyxena to the Greeks. She is to pretend that Polyxena has been given in marriage to Pyrrhus. She bids Polyxena to put on marriage robes. Andromache assails Helen as the common curse of the Greeks and Trojans. Helen defends herself, seeking to win pity for her lot. Andromache suspects some terrible fate for Polyxena. Helen, with a sudden show of emotion, reveals that Polyxena is to be sacrificed at Achilles' tomb. Polyxena rejoices at the thought of death.

Hecuba bewails her daughter. Helen tells them to which of the Greek leaders each has been assigned: Andromache to Pyrrhus, Cassandra to Agamemnon, Hecuba to Ulysses. Pyrrhus comes to take Polyxena. Hecuba prophesies disaster for Ulysses and the other Greeks.

The Chorus comments that shared sorrows are lighter to endure.

Act V

A messenger relates in detail to Andromache and Hecuba the deaths of Polyxena and Astyanax. Both died like Stoics. Astyanax eluded his captors and hurled himself from the walls. Polyxena was bloodily slain at Achilles' tomb by heartless Pyrrhus.

Hecuba curses the Greeks, prophesying future disasters for them.

MAD HERCULES

(Based on Euripides' play of the same name)

Act I

The scene is before the palace of Hercules at Thebes. Juno, queen of the gods, speaks the prologue. She tells of Jupiter's many infidelities and the exalting of his illegitimate children. She harbors particular hate against Alcmena and her son by Jupiter, Hercules. She has imposed various labors on him, but he takes all this in stride. Recently he succeeded in capturing Cerberus, the three-headed dog, from Hades. He is proud, and she has decided to destroy him by driving him mad, thus causing him to do some dreadful deeds.

The Chorus of Thebans enters. They hail the dawn and the beginning of the day's activities in the peaceful country districts. The city is filled with fears and troubles: the worries of the rich, the envy and degradation of the poor, the gnawing of political ambitions, the tension of lawsuits. Happiness is possible for a few, while fate permits. Hercules voluntarily went to Hades. But destiny cannot be thwarted. Humility is best. Pride goeth before a fall.

Act II

Megara, wife of Hercules and daughter of Creon, enters with her children and Amphitryon, reputed father of Hercules. Amphitryon laments his woes: Juno's unrelenting hatred of Hercules from the moment of his birth; the horrible serpents which were sent to his cradle and which he promptly strangled; the twelve labors he has had to endure. Recently Megara's father Creon and her brothers were slain by a usurping tyrant, Lycus, an exile from another city. Amphitryon prays for Hercules' safe return from Hades. Megara joins in his prayer for the return of her husband.

Lycus enters, a proud and arrogant man. He has decided to bolster his regime by taking Megara as his wife. Declaring his desire for peace, he asks her to share his throne. Indignantly she rejects this offer by the murderer of her father and brothers. She declares her undying hatred of him, and scorns his shameful proposal.

Amphitryon commends her loyalty to Hercules, whom he declares to be the son of Jupiter.

Lycus threatens to take her by force, and compel her to bear him children. When she clings to the altars for protection, he decides to kill the entire family of Hercules. Amphitryon asks to die first. Megara then leaves to prepare her children for death. Lycus departs, and Amphitryon prays for the return of Hercules. Suddenly the earth shakes. Amphitryon is convinced that Hercules is on his way back from Hades.

The Chorus recounts the labors of Hercules. As Orpheus brought back Eurydice from Hades, so shall the mighty Hercules return.

Act III

Hercules enters, accompanied by Theseus, whom he had rescued from Hades. He is happy to be back in his native Thebes. Amphitryon joyfully welcomes him, and informs him of the slaying of Creon by Lycus, and of the tyrant's plans to destroy them all. Hercules is saddened by the failure of the Thebans to come to their aid. Theseus offers to kill Lycus, but Hercules claims the right, and departs.

Amphitryon desires to learn of Hercules' exploits in dread Hades. Theseus gives him a detailed account of the underworld, its waters, sights and horrors, its ruler, the judges of the dead, the punishments of the evil in Tartarus, and the blessed life of the pious in the Elysian Fields. He relates, too, how Hercules entered Hades, conquered the three-headed dog Cerberus, and released Theseus.

The Chorus rejoices at the liberation of Thebes from Lycus, whom Hercules has slain, together with the tyrant's henchmen.

Act IV

Hercules begins to offer sacrifices and prayers to the gods. Suddenly the madness planned by Juno begins to descend on him. He raves insanely. When he catches sight of his children, he imagines them to be the children of Lycus. He promptly slays one with an arrow, drags the other two inside, and slays them and Megara. Hercules then comes out, and falls into a deep sleep.

The Chorus laments the deaths of the family of Hercules, and is saddened by his madness.

Act V

Hercules returns to his senses. When he sees the four corpses, those of his children and his wife Megara, he is beside himself. Theseus and Amphitryon try to conceal the truth from him. When he learns that he himself killed them, he curses his lot and decides to commit suicide, before he can do any more harm.

Theseus counsels him to "meet adversity with your usual strength." When Amphitryon threatens to commit suicide, Hercules reassures him, and decides to live on and face responsibility. His only desire is to find some haven where he may be able to conceal himself. Theseus grants him asylum in Athens.

OEDIPUS

(This play, an adaptation of Sophocles' *Oedipus Rex,* pp. 51-55, presents the portrait of a suspicious tyrant consumed with a sense of guilt. Its emphasis is on horror, gruesome detail, and fate as the cause of suffering.)

Act I

The scene is before the palace of Oedipus at Thebes. Oedipus soliloquizes at length on the havoc caused by the plague ravaging Thebes, on Fate, and on the dangers of wielding power. He is overwhelmed by consciousness of guilt and by fear. He relates how he left Corinth for fear that he would slay his father and wed his mother, whom he believes to be Polybus and Merope, king and queen of Corinth. The horrors of the plague are described in detail by Oedipus, who feels that he is the guilty one infecting the city. He prays for his own death, as a sacrifice to the gods, to put an end to the pestilence.

Jocasta comforts her husband, and urges courage upon him. In answer, he relates his encounter with the dreaded Sphinx. He hopes the Delphic oracle of Apollo will light the path to safety.

The Chorus of Theban Elders gives a long detailed description

of the horrors of the plague—the deaths and funerals of the inhabi-
tants, the perishing of the flocks, the blight on all growing things.
A deadly epidemic is raging among the people.

Act II

Creon enters, having just returned from the Delphic oracle. He
reports that the oracle has ordered the banishment of the murderer
of Laïus. The oracle also foretold that the slayer will be responsible
for war, and will bequeath war to his children (Eteocles and Polynices are meant), and hinted at incest.

Oedipus pronounces a dreadful curse on the murderer, praying
that he live the life of an outcast forever, grieving over a shameful
marriage and monstrous offspring. Creon tells him how Laïus was
murdered by a band of robbers on the road to Delphi, at a fork in
the highway.

The blind prophet Teiresias is led in by his daughter Manto.
Teiresias is asked to reveal the name of the murderer. He tells
Oedipus that, because of his advanced age, he has lost the gift of
direct prophecy, but will seek the assistance of a sacrifice to discover the omens of Apollo. A bull and a heifer are led to the altar.
Manto acts as Teiresias' assistant in interpreting the omens evoked
by the incense cast upon the flames. Manto tells in horror how
when the wine was poured on the flames it changed to blood, and
the fumes surrounded Oedipus' head. Then the bull and heifer are
sacrificed. Teiresias, through Manto's eyes, tries to interpret the
omens. At Teiresias' bidding, she inspects the entrails of the animals, and describes all the meaningful signs. The deeds of Oedipus
—the slaying of his father, his unnatural marriage with his mother,
the incestuous children, Oedipus' self-blinding, Jocasta's suicide,
the Seven Against Thebes—are all darkly suggested by her interpretation of the signs revealed by the viscera of the animals. When
Oedipus requests the name of the murderer, Teiresias tells him that
only the ghost of Laïus can reveal it. Therefore a ceremony to raise
the ghost must be performed.

The Chorus sings a dithyramb. This long choral passage gives a
display of geographical and mythological erudition.

Act III

Creon returns from the necromancy performed by Teiresias. Reluctantly he describes to Oedipus the gloomy spot where the ceremony took place, the magic rites and chants, the sacrifices. In this weird atmosphere the earth suddenly opened, and Hades, with all its dread sights, was revealed. The ghosts of many famous persons appeared, and finally Laïus'. Compelled by Teiresias' exorcism, Laïus' ghost, covered with blood, names Oedipus as his murderer and the defiler of Jocasta's bed. The ghost shrieks out all the horrors of the family, declares that the plague will end only when Oedipus is exiled, and predicts his future as a blind beggar. Oedipus is terrified, but, believing his father and mother to be the king and queen of Corinth, he accuses Teiresias and Creon of a plot to deprive him of his throne. When Creon urges him to resign the kingship, he reveals his deep fears of everyone, and peremptorily orders Creon imprisoned in a dungeon.

The Chorus laments the woes of Thebes since its founding by Cadmus. It tells the legend of the dread exploits of Cadmus—the dragon, the armed men who sprang from the dragon's teeth sowed by Cadmus, their mutual slaughter. The fate of Actaeon, too, is related.

Act IV

Oedipus and Jocasta enter. He tells her of his fears, recounting his slaying of an older man at a place where three roads meet. Jocasta, by giving him details of the death of Laïus, confirms his fears.

A messenger from Corinth arrives to announce that King Polybus died a natural death, and that Oedipus is heir to his throne. When Oedipus expresses fear that he may yet marry Merope, the messenger assures him that she is not his mother. He tells how he received him as a baby from a shepherd of Laïus. The messenger seeks to deter Oedipus from pursuing the matter further, but Oedipus persists.

Phorbas, the head shepherd of Laïus, is brought in. He, too, tries to conceal the truth, but Oedipus must know. When the truth becomes known to Oedipus he curses his fate, and rushes into the palace.

The Chorus counsels moderation, citing the myth of Icarus.

Act V

A messenger comes from the palace, and describes the anguish of Oedipus and his desire for some dreadful self-imposed punishment. In a frenzy he tore his eyes from their sockets. The blood spurted out.

The Chorus philosophizes that all that happens is fated, and that we must resign ourselves to inevitable destiny, which not even the gods can change.

Blind Oedipus comes out. Jocasta appears, overcome with grief at the truth of her relationship with Oedipus and at his self-blinding. She seeks to comfort him with the view that all was fated. But desiring to atone for her own part in their relationship, she draws Oedipus' sword and thrusts it into her "capacious womb." Oedipus, assailing the Delphic oracle, gropes his way out into exile.

HERCULES ON OETA

(Based on Sophocles' *Maidens of Trachis;* see pp. 59-63)

Act I

The scene is in Euboea. Hercules speaks the prologue. He declares he has brought peace to men on earth, having fulfilled his mission on earth. He asks Jupiter to reward him with a place in heaven. He then recounts his labors and his victory over Juno's hatred. Finally he dispatches his herald Lichas to Trachis to announce his victory over Eurytus.

The Chorus of Oechalian Maidens enters, accompanied by Iole. The Chorus laments the fall of their city and their captivity, and sings of the might of Hercules. Iole has not enough tears to lament her father's death at Hercules' hands. She has been forced to become Hercules' concubine.

Act II

The scene shifts to Trachis, before the palace of Hercules. The Nurse of Deianira tells of the coming of the captive women, especially Iole, Hercules' beloved concubine. Deianira is consumed with jealousy and wrath, behaving like one insane. When Deianira enters, she utters wild threats and imprecations against Hercules. She wishes him dead. The Nurse seeks to console her, in vain. The offense to Deianira has been so great that she desires some dreadful revenge. The Nurse prevails upon Deianira to employ magic to win back Hercules' love. Deianira decides to abandon her intention of killing Hercules. She will seek to win back his love by anointing a robe with the blood of the centaur Nessus and sending it to Hercules as a gift. She tells how once, when she and Hercules desired to cross a river, the centaur Nessus offered to ferry her across. When he tried to molest her, Hercules shot him. Before he died he counseled Deianira to take up some of his blood and preserve it as a love charm which might some day help her regain Hercules' love.

Deianira prays to Cupid for aid in winning back Hercules' love. She smears the charm on a robe and gives it to Lichas to present to Hercules.

The Chorus of Aetolian Women sing of Deianira's unhappy marriage, praise the simple life, and ponder on the dangers of excess.

Act III

Deianira enters in terror. She suddenly has become apprehensive of Nessus' intentions toward Hercules. When she tested the charm he had given her, she discovered its deadly effects.

Her son Hyllus enters with terrible news. He describes in detail the harm done to Hercules by the poisoned robe as he was sacrificing. "The glory of the earth is gone." In his anger, Hercules seized the innocent Lichas and dashed him to death. Deianira is overwhelmed with profound remorse. She curses herself, prays for death, and threatens suicide. Hyllus seeks to dissuade her, but she rushes off, and Hyllus follows to prevent her.

The Chorus tells of Orpheus' descent to the underworld, his

enchanting music, his recovery and final loss of his wife Eurydice. Death is inevitable. The world will come to an end, now that Hercules is dying.

Act IV

Hercules enters, overwhelmed in an agony of pain. He laments his destruction at the hands of a woman, he who performed mighty feats of valor. "Death fled me everywhere that I might lack in death a glorious fate." Writhing in agony from poison, he relates his mighty labors, and begs Jupiter to destroy him with his thunderbolt.

His grief-stricken mother Alcmena enters to console him. He is stoically heroic in his suffering, as she gives way to unrestrained grief. Hyllus enters to declare Deianira's innocence of intent to harm Hercules. He tells how his unhappy mother committed suicide in remorse.

Hercules now recognizes his fate. He begins to face his end with superhuman strength and calm. He orders a funeral pyre to be built on Mt. Oeta. Philoctetes, his friend, is to place him on the pyre and set it ablaze. Hyllus is ordered to marry Iole. "Hercules conquered manfully all ill."

The Chorus laments Hercules' death. It glorifies the deeds of the savior of the world and his coming apotheosis.

Act V

Philoctetes recounts in detail the glorious end of Hercules on the funeral pyre. Before he died he gave to Philoctetes his famed bow and arrows as a legacy.

Alcmena enters carrying a funeral urn with Hercules' ashes. She bewails his passing. Even in death his ashes will protect her. Philoctetes consoles her. She recounts his great labors on behalf of mankind.

The voice of Hercules is heard on high. He declares that he has been taken to heaven. "My valor has made a way up to the stars." Virtue has again conquered death. The Chorus affirms that "the brave live forever."

AGAMEMNON
(Based chiefly on Aeschylus' *Agamemnon*)

Act I

The scene is before the palace of Agamemnon at Mycenae or Argos. The prologue is spoken by the ghost of Thyestes, father of Aegisthus. The ghost shrinks before the dread palace, which is the scene of many fearful crimes. He prefers Hades, with all its horrors, to this house of impious deeds, especially the feeding of the flesh of his sons to him by his brother Atreus, the birth of his son Aegisthus from his incestuous relationship with his own daughter. Now vengeance is at hand, for Agamemnon is returning from Troy. The ghost foretells the impending shedding of the blood of Agamemnon by Clytemnestra and Aegisthus.

The Chorus of Argive Women enters. They ponder on the cares and dangers that attend royal power. The mighty are brought low sooner than those who live in moderation.

Act II

Clytemnestra ponders on her next step. Now that she has committed adultery with Aegisthus, there is no way out but to commit an even greater crime—murder. Her Nurse urges her to abandon desperate measures, but Clytemnestra is consumed by hate of Agamemnon, because of his sacrifice of Iphigenia, his amours at Troy, and his current liaison with Cassandra, Priam's daughter. She is determined to slay both Agamemnon and Cassandra. To kill or be killed are for her the only alternatives. The Nurse warns her of the difficulties of attempting to kill the mighty hero who conquered Troy.

Aegisthus arrives, and asserts that the slaying of Agamemnon is ordered by the gods. Suddenly Clytemnestra weakens, and begs Aegisthus to desist from his plans. They bicker about the planned murders. She argues against them; he refutes her arguments. She is now conscious-stricken. In her anger she throws up to him his incestuous birth. He, in turn, is ready to commit suicide if she deserts him. Finally, she agrees to share his crime and fate.

The Chorus sings a hymn to Apollo, Juno, Minerva, Diana and Jupiter.

Act III

Eurybates, herald of Agamemnon, enters rejoicing to be home again. He proclaims the return of the conquering hero Agamemnon. Then he also describes in elaborate detail the sailing of the Greek fleet from Troy and the furious storm that shattered the ships and dispersed the remnants. Clytemnestra orders a festive celebration for the homecoming.

A second chorus of captive Trojan women enters, led by Cassandra. They praise death as a refuge from fate's blow and from the sorrows of life. They tell mournfully of the tragic fall of Troy, of the bloodshed, and the suffering that followed.

Cassandra describes her woes, and is suddenly overwhelmed by mad frenzy. As she is seized by prophetic inspiration, she foretells the horrors to come: the slaying of Agamemnon and herself. Finally she faints.

Act IV

Agamemnon arrives. Cassandra is revived, and she gives him a veiled warning before he enters the palace.

The Chorus sings of the labors of the hero Hercules. Among his achievements was the first overthrow of Troy. Now it has been destroyed for a second time.

Act V

Cassandra describes the scene within the palace: the feast, Agamemnon's donning of a robe which entraps him, the weak, futile effort of Aegisthus to deal the death blow, and Clytemnestra's severing of her husband's head with an axe.

Electra rushes out with her little brother Orestes, and urges him to flee for his life.

Strophius, King of Phocis, conveniently arrives with his son Pylades. He has come to greet the victorious Agamemnon. But when he learns of what has happened, he hastily departs, spiriting away the young Orestes, and leaving Electra to the fury of the murderers.

Clytemnestra, utterly heartless now, assails Electra and threatens to kill her too. Electra shrieks her hate at her mother and her paramour. Aegisthus orders her put into chains, imprisoned in a dungeon, and tortured until she reveals the whereabouts of Orestes. Clytemnestra orders Cassandra to be dragged away and killed. Cassandra goes calmly, predicting the vengeance that will be meted out by Orestes.

THYESTES
(Based on an unknown Greek source)

BACKGROUND

Atreus and Thyestes were the sons of Pelops and the grandsons of Tantalus. Upon the death of Pelops Atreus took the kingdom. Thyestes, seeking to gain the throne for himself, seduced Atreus' wife and stole a magical ram that had a golden fleece which was the key to the throne. Thyestes was then exiled by Atreus.

Act I

The scene is before the palace of Atreus. The ghost of Tantalus shrinks from the hated palace, the scene of many crimes in the past and of worse to come. The Fury Megaera grimly touches on all of the crimes, weaknesses and woes of the house of Tantalus: madness, murder, incest, exile, adultery, excessive ambition, lust. Soon Thyestes shall eat the flesh of his own sons fed to him by his brother Atreus. The ghost of Tantalus prefers Hades to this house. He hopes to restrain his kinsmen from new crimes, while the Fury is intent on stirring up new horrors. Crime passes from generation to generation.

The Chorus of Mycenaean men prays for an end to the crimes of the house of Tantalus. They review the atrocities committed by Pelops and Tantalus, and describe the punishment of Tantalus in Hades.

Act II

Atreus stirs himself into a fury of revenge against Thyestes. "A wrong is not avenged but by a worse wrong." Kill or be killed— that is the only way. As his attendant cautions restraint, Atreus'

tyrannical behavior is revealed more and more. His determination
for revenge is implacable. Moreover, he is merely following in the
path of Tantalus and Pelops. Now he plans the most monstrous
crime he can conceive: he will feed the flesh of Thyestes' children
to him. This he is sure he will be able to accomplish, because Thyestes is ambitious for power and desires revenge. To achieve his
purpose he will welcome back Thyestes, and offer him a share in
the throne. As emissaries he will send his own sons, Agamemnon
and Menelaüs, to lure back their uncle. Thus he will make them
accomplices in his crime.

The Chorus rejoices at the return of harmony to the brothers.
They praise the Stoic concept of the true king: one who has no
fears, no ambitions for wealth and power, no envy, who meets fate
calmly without fear of death, whose kingdom is within himself,
and who has complete control of himself.

Act III

Thyestes rejoices to be back again in his homeland. He means no
harm to Atreus. His three sons, including their spokesman Tantalus,
named for his famed ancestor, greet him. Thyestes is confused,
uncertain and fearful. He now rejects desire for power, and prefers
to return to the simple Stoic life of a poor exile. He fears the cares
and dangers of a palace, and prefers the peace of his present humble
circumstances. "He has a kingdom who can be content without a
kingdom." His son pleads with him to trust Atreus and help his
sons regain their positions of power and wealth.

Atreus greets Thyestes; he is scarcely able to curb his eagerness
for revenge. He pretends to be joyful at his brother's return. They
both know the deep hatred that exists between them, but talk in
civil terms. Atreus offers half his kingdom to Thyestes, and Thyestes gives his sons as pledges of his faith.

The Chorus sings of the strength of family ties, and of peace after
war. But fortune is not stable; the wheel of fortune turns swiftly.

Act IV

A messenger reports the gruesome events that have taken place in the dread palace. Atreus sacrificed Thyestes' sons at an altar, one by one. Then he cut the limbs apart, roasted some of the flesh, and boiled other parts. Finally he fed the meat to their father while he was drunk.

The Chorus sings of the unnatural darkness that has descended upon the world because of Atreus' crime. The sun has departed from its path in heaven. The universe appears about to be destroyed.

Act V

Atreus enters, and gloats over his revenge. He orders the gates of the palace opened, and we see the drunken Thyestes all alone, singing away his years of exile in the joys of the banquet. He feels, however, a strange uneasy premonition of disaster, and cannot restrain his tears.

Atreus approaches him, and offers Thyestes a cup of wine mixed with the blood of his sons. He cannot drink it, and begs his brother to spare his sons. Atreus brings in a covered platter. Then he uncovers it, revealing to his brother the heads of his three sons. Thyestes begs for the bodies of his sons so that he may give them decent burial. Atreus informs him that he has just banqueted on them, and mocks his brother brutally, cruelly describing how he slew them and prepared their flesh for the banquet.

Thyestes shrieks his woes to the skies, and utters a prediction of vengeance for Atreus' crimes.

TECHNIQUES AND VIEWS OF SENECA'S TRAGEDIES

1. The tragedies of Seneca are all adaptations of Greek plays of the Fifth Century B.C. Seneca was not a professional playwright. Whether his plays were written to be staged or were "closet dramas" intended as vehicles for his philosophic (Stoic) views and for political criticism is still a moot question.

2. "Blood and thunder" plays:

    a. Emphasis on violence, horror, gory details, gruesome scenes.

    b. Violence staged before the audience.

    c. Sensationalism and artificial theatrical effects.

    d. Emphasis on the supernatural: mysticism, ghosts, magic, divination, dreams.

  3. Structure:

    a. Five acts, divided by four choral lyrics.

    b. Euripidean expository prologue.

    c. Chorus takes no part in the action, sings interludes.

    d. Unities of time and place, but not action (irrelevancies).

  4. Characters: Seneca sought to give his characters universal, cosmopolitan scope, and psychological depth, but they remain unreal.

  5. Rhetorical display: declamation, long descriptive speeches, ciever epigrams, philosophic commonplaces, artificial dialogue, often formalized stichomythia.

  6. Pedantry: geographic, religious, and mythological learning for its own sake.

  7. Frequent soliloquies and asides.

  8. Artificial exits and entrances.

  9. Inconsistent tragic philosophy: the Stoic concept of Fate underlies Seneca's thinking, but this determinism is sometimes combined with free will and the concept of personal responsibility for suffering.

  10. Lack of true tragic feeling: Seneca is obsessed with death, which he regards as a good. True pity and fear are therefore not experienced.

OCTAVIA

This play, by an unknown author, is the only extant Roman historical play (*fabula praetexta*)

BACKGROUND

The Emperor Claudius killed his wife Messalina and married his niece Agrippina. At the some time he adopted Nero, her son by a former marriage. Claudius' daughter Octavia was married to Nero. When Claudius died in A.D. 54, Nero succeeded to the imperial power. Britannicus, Claudius' son, was put to death soon after. During the first "golden five years" of Nero's reign, his mad tend-

encies were restrained by his ministers, Seneca and Burrus. In A.D.
Nero decided to take the reins into his own hands. He had his
mother, Agrippina, slain, and gave his mistress Poppaea a position
of dominance.

Act I

The scene is before Nero's palace in Rome. Octavia, Nero's wife,
speaks the prologue. She grieves over the woes and crimes of her
family—the death of her mother, the cruelty of her stepmother,
the destruction of her father Claudius. Then she goes to her room.

Octavia's Nurse laments the crimes of the royal house. She fears
for Octavia. Octavia again bewails her woes, like another Electra.
The Nurse seeks to console her, in vain. Octavia cannot forget the
slaying of her mother and her father. She is outraged at being
scorned by her husband Nero, whom she hates profoundly. She
has dreamed that Nero killed her brother and herself. Moreover,
her rival, Nero's mistress Poppaea, now lords it over all.

The Nurse reviews again the crimes of the royal family. Octavia
thinks of slaying Nero himself, but the Nurse reminds her of her
weakness, and counsels Stoic resignation. Octavia has only violent
hate in her heart for Nero and Poppaea.

The Chorus of Romans expresses sympathy for Octavia, hoping
that rumors of her divorce from Nero are not true. They review the
crimes of Nero, especially his slaying of his mother Agrippina.

Act II

Seneca laments the high position into which Fate has thrust him.
Now he has no time for philosophic contemplation. He deplores the
growing corruption of men, who are debased by ambition for power
and wealth, by vice and lust.

Nero enters, and orders the execution of two of his kinsmen.
When Seneca rebukes him, Nero asserts, "A Caesar must be
feared." His tyranny is manifest. He threatens to kill his "hateful
wife" Octavia. Seneca urges moderation as the guide for rulers, but
Nero is filled with fear, and asserts he must rule by terror. Seneca
remonstrates with Nero when he declares his intention to marry

Poppaea. He warns him of the people's anger. Nero promptly announces the wedding will take place tomorrow.

Act III

The ghost of Agrippina appears, carrying a flaming torch symbolizing disaster. She desires vengeance for her murder by Nero, predicts the miserable death of her son, and vanishes.

Two days have elapsed. Nero has divorced Octavia and married Poppaea. Octavia warns the Chorus to exercise caution in the face of Nero's tyranny. They call on the Roman people to rise and overthrow Nero.

Act IV

Poppaea's Nurse wonders why her mistress is unhappy. Poppaea has had ominous dreams—of dead Agrippina, and of her former husband and her son, both of whom were soon to die violently. They go to sacrifice to the gods.

A Chorus of Women praises Poppaea.

A messenger enters, and reports a popular uprising on behalf of Octavia.

The Chorus sings of the invincible power of love.

Act V

Nero enters, enraged at the people. He threatens to slay Octavia and set fire to the city, in order to have his revenge on the people for supporting Octavia.

A prefect of the imperial guard declares that the uprising has been quelled and the leaders executed. Nero orders the death of Octavia.

The Chorus of Romans comments on the ruin brought about to many Romans in the course of their history because of the people's favor.

Octavia is dragged in by the palace guards. She laments her sorrows, as the Chorus counsels her to be stoical. "The race of men is by the fates controlled." She prays for vengeance on Nero. The Chorus denounces the brutality of Rome, which "delights to see her children bleed."

CHAPTER THIRTEEN

ARISTOTLE AND HORACE
ON DRAMA

ARISTOTLE'S POETICS

The *Poetics* of Aristotle contains not only his observations of Fifth Century drama and that of his own time (he lived from 384-322 B.C.), but also his personal preferences. In many aspects, the *Poetics* is a critique of Plato's views on art and poetry.

Chapters 1-5

GENERAL INTRODUCTION TO POETRY

1. Poetry, like all other arts, is a mode of imitation (*mimesis*). (The function of the poet or artist is to imitate, through media appropriate to the given art, not particular historical events, characters, emotions, but the universal aspects of life [form, essence, idea] impressed on his mind by observation of real life. Cp. Aristotle's *Politics* 3.11.4: "An artistic representation differs from ordinary reality in that elements which are elsewhere scattered and separate are here combined in a unity." Poetry is an act of creation, for it imitates mental impressions; it is therefore an idealization, not a direct copy of human life. It is closer to reality than the concrete situation, since the universal is truer than the particular.)

All arts, e.g., poetry, music, differ from one another in 1) the media they employ; 2) the objects they imitate; 3) their manner of imitation; 4) their proper function (end, purpose).

Media of Imitation: (Greek) poetry employs language, rhythm, and harmony (music). In dancing, rhythm alone is used; in playing an instrument, rhythm and harmony. Epic poetry employs language and rhythm; lyric poetry employs language, rhythm, and harmony; tragedy and comedy the same three media as lyric, but at times only language and rhythm (in the dialogue of the actors), at times all three combined (choral lyrics). It is not the use of meter that makes poetry, but rather the element of imitation of the universal. A person who writes on a scientific subject in verse is not a poet.

2. *Objects of Imitation in Drama:* human beings in action, their characters, acts, emotion. The persons imitated will be either higher than average (idealism), average (realism), lower than average (caricature). Tragedy imitates persons better than average, comedy those worse than average.

3. *Manner of Imitation:* 1) completely indirect imitation, as in straight narrative; 2) partly indirect and partly direct, as in epic, which contains both narrative and speeches of characters; 3) entirely direct action, as in the drama, where the entire incident is acted out before the audience. "Drama" means "action."

4. *Psychology of Artistic Creation and Enjoyment of Art:* Works of art are created because it is instinctive in man to imitate, and because of the human instinct for rhythm and harmony. People enjoy observing works of art for various reasons: 1) there is pleasure in seeing certain things and events imitated (e.g., murder, dead body, operation) which would be painful to observe in real life; 2) from art we often learn something new, and people take pleasure in learning; 3) if there is nothing new to be learned from the imitation, there can be pleasure in the recognition of what we know; 4) there is pleasure in observing the technical perfection of a work of art.

Origin and evolution of tragedy and comedy (see pp. 8, 138).

5. *Comedy:* This involves the imitation of lower types of men whose faults are ridiculous. What is ridiculous is ugly, and consists

of faults, acts, or deformities which do not cause pain to anyone (e.g., funny mask, pie throwing, slipping on a banana peel). The history of the development of comedy is obscure.

Epic vs. Tragedy: They have the same objects of imitation— actions of men of a higher type. But they differ in: 1) manner of imitation, which in epic is a combination of direct and indirect narrative, in tragedy direct action; 2) media of imitation, for epic does not have music or spectacle; 3) verse form, which in epic is single (dactylic hexameter), in tragedy varied; 4) length, which in epic is not fixed, in tragedy is approximately one day. Tragedy is more complex than epic, for it contains all the elements of epic, and in addition music and spectacle. Therefore a good judge of tragedy is also a good judge of epic.

Chapters 6-22

6. *Definition of Tragedy:* 1) objects: imitation of serious action, complete in itself, so far as size is concerned; 2) media: rhythm, language, and melody (Greek tragedy is poetic drama, employing alternation of dialogue and choral odes); 3) manner: direct action, not narrative; 4) purpose: to arouse pity and fear and effect a pleasurable catharsis (purging) of these two emotions.

(Interpretations of "catharsis": 1) Plato rejects tragedy on the ground that it arouses pity and fear and therefore makes men emotionally weak; Aristotle, on the other hand, believes that tragedy purges away these emotions and makes men stronger; 2) medical [or "vaccination"] theory: pity and fear are often present in persons to excess; by applying more of the same there will be a pathological release which will be pleasant and benefit persons by restoring proper emotional balance; 3) vicarious experience theory: we take pleasure in experiencing the emotions involved in such a fictitious scene without being personally harmed; 4) sadistic theory: we enjoy seeing others suffer, and there is added pleasure because we know it is only a play, not real life; we feel superior to the characters who suffer; 5) we tend to identify ourself with one of the characters in the play through empathy; when the drama is over, we take pleasure both because it has not really happened, and because we realize that our own troubles are minor as compared with what has happened in the tragedy; 6) in real life many sad occurrences happen that arouse pity and fear in people; but these events have no unity or inevitable logic, and therefore are intellectually frustrating, leaving us confused and emotionally imbalanced. In a drama that selects and arranges a series of events in a logical and inevitable order, the effect on the audience is a satisfying intellectual and emotional release.)

Six Elements of Tragedy: 1) *opsis*—spectacle (i.e., scenery, costumes); 2) *melos*—music; 3) *lexis*—language; 4) *ethos*—personality; 5) *dianoia*—views of characters; 6) *mythos*—plot. Order of importance of these elements: 1) plot (for tragedy is not mere character study, but a dynamic portrayal of life; good plot is necessary to produce the tragic effect of arousing and purging pity and fear); 2) personality (must be subordinated to action); 3) views of characters; 4) language; 5) music; 6) spectacle. The last two are the least important, since the tragedy may be read.

7. *Proper Construction of Plot:* it must be a complete whole, with a beginning, middle, and end, and have form, the events being ordered in a necessary and probably sequence. It must be neither too short nor too long, so that we may grasp both the separate parts and the unity of the whole in a single memory span. The natural limit in size is one that provides a change in the hero's fortunes (*peripetia*) with proper dramatic causation.

8. *Unity of Action* (the only one of the "three unities" which Aristotle insists upon). A unified plot does not consist of disconnected events about the same hero, but rather of organically unified events in which all the parts are absolutely necessary and in perfect order. There must be one central theme, as in the *Iliad* and the *Odyssey*.

9. *Philosophical Nature of Poetry:* The poet imitates not what actually happens, but what might happen, what is probable, and would befit a particular type of individual. The dramatist is not a historian, but a creative artist. He arranges events in an order that is likely, credible or inevitable. The poet therefore imitates ideal truth, the universal and typical. Hence "poetry is something more

philosophical and of graver import than history." Hence, too, plot, not verse form, is the heart of tragedy.

The worst plots are episodic ones, in which the sequence of events has no dramatic causation, since they are neither probable nor necessary. The best plot is one that arouses pity and fear, in the most powerful manner, through incidents that are unexpected but necessary and probable and linked together in sequence by cause and effect.

10. *Mechanism of the Tragic Plot:* 1) simple plot—single continuous movement of events without reversal (peripety) or discovery (*anagnorisis*); 2) complex plot—in which a change in the hero's fortune is attended by reversal or discovery or both.

11. *Parts of Plot:*

    a. Reversal (peripety)—change that occurs when opposite of what was intended turns out.

    b. Discovery (*anagnorisis*)—change from ignorance to knowledge, from love to hate, or vice versa. The best form of discovery is that which arouses pity and fear most, namely, that associated with peripety, being necessary or probable, dramatically caused, effecting love or hate, involving reversal which brings happiness or misery.

    c. Suffering (*pathos*)—murder, torture, injury, etc.

12. *Quantitative Elements of Tragedy:* prologue, episode, exodos, parodos, stasimon (see p. 11).

13. *Ideal Tragic Character and Plot:*

    a. Plot

        i. Complex.

        ii. Must arouse pity (what we feel when someone suffers more than he deserves for his faults and mistakes) and fear (what we feel when suffering happens to someone like ourselves).

    b. Character

        i. Must pass from happiness to misery (not the reverse).

        ii. Must not be perfectly virtuous and just, but basically of good character.

        iii. His downfall must not result from vice or baseness.

iv. His downfall must come about because of a flaw of character (*hamartia*—"tragic flaw") and error in judgment. The flaw is often an excess of a virtue.

v. Must belong to distinguished family, so that the fall will be all the greater.

The simple unhappy ending is best in tragedy. The double ending, happiness for the good and unhappiness for the evil, is less desirable, and is a concession to popular taste.

14. *Methods of Arousing Pity and Fear:* It is not artistic to effect this by staging (as a storm). The best means is through the incidents of the plot—when a murder or other horrible deed is about to be perpetrated by a person upon a blood relative who is unknown to him and whose identity he discovers just in the nick of time.

15. *Character (Ethos):* There are four things to aim at: 1) the character must be good (idealized); 2) true to type; 3) true to life; 4) consistent and unified throughout. All acts and words should be the probable or necessary outcome of the inner character. It is necessary to portray character flaws naturally, but the character as a whole must be made better than average (idealized).

The *deus ex machina* is not an artistic device. If it is used at all, it should be employed only to explain past events beyond the knowledge of the characters, or future events necessary to the story.

16. Types of Discovery (*Anagnorisis*): There are six types of discovery: 1) by signs, tokens, or marks on the person; 2) by arbitrary direct discoveries invented by the poet; 3) through awakened memory; 4) through logical reasoning; 5) through wrong sophistical reasoning which reaches the correct result; the best is 6) discovery that grows in a probable manner out of the incidents themselves (as in the *Oedipus Rex*).

17. *Practical Hints for Composition:* 1) visualize the scenes as they would be when performed; 2) get outside yourself, feel the emotions personally; act out the story yourself (the poet must be a good actor and have a touch of madness in him); 3) first make an outline of the plot (universal form), then fill in the necessary particular episodes.

18. *Complication and Denouément:* The complication is all that

precedes the crisis, the change in the hero's fortune; the denouément (unraveling) is all that follows the crisis to the end of the
drama.

There are four types of tragedy (viewed from the major emphasis): 1) complex (involving peripety and discovery); 2) of suffering; 3) of character; 4) of spectacle. All four should be properly
combined to achieve the best effect. Tragedy should not be too long
nor attempt to cover an epic story. The chorus should be an integral
part of the play, almost one of the actors, and not perform mere
unessential musical interludes.

19. General observations on thought and diction.

20. *Diction:* The parts of speech are analyzed.

21. *Types of Words in Poetry:* from the point of view of structure, simple or complex; in meaning—ordinary, foreign, metaphor,
ornamental; in form—coined, lengthened, shortened, altered
(poetic).

22. *Use of Diction in Poetry:* There must be clarity without
vulgarity, achieved by combination of the ordinary and the un-
familiar. It is bad to make excessive use of metaphors and foreign
words, nor must the language be entirely prosaic. Moderation is
necessary; otherwise the effect will be ludicrous. The most important element is mastery of metaphor.

Chapters 23-26

23-24. *Tragedy and Epic Compared:*

a. Likenesses: 1) epic, too, must be a complete whole and
possess unity of action (not, as in history, a chronicle of all events
in a given period, whether causally related or not); 2) epic has the
same types as tragedy—simple, complex, character, suffering; 3)
epic has the same parts, except melody and spectacle; 4) epic uses
peripety and discovery; 5) epic employs the same thought and
diction.

b. Differences: 1) length—epic is longer than tragedy; 2)
the epic meter is solely dactylic hexameter; 3) objectivity of epic
poet; 4) media—only language and rhythm; 5) combination of
indirect and direct manner (narrative and speeches); 6) more room

for the marvelous and improbable in epic, since it is listened to or read, not performed and seen.

25. *Solutions of Problems of Literary Criticism:*

a. The poet should not be expected to be scientifically correct. Apparent faults and impossibilities are permissible if they serve the ends of poetry and create a desired effect. They are not serious if the poet in describing something makes a technical error through ignorance.

b. Our impression of an impossibility or error may be wrong, for the poet may be treating things ideally or realistically, or vice versa.

c. We must not attribute to the poet errors that he puts into the mouths of his characters, for such error may be true to the character's type.

d. As for language, it must be remembered that a poet is permitted greater license.

e. We cannot criticize a supposed error, unless we know what the poet really intended.

f. Poetry often deals with probable impossibilities.

26. *The Highest Form of Poetic Imitation:* Which is the higher and more dignified form of imitation, epic or tragedy? The argument that, since tragedy appeals to the masses, it is vulgar is false. The degrading of tragedy is due not to the dramatic poet but to the overacting of the performers. For tragedy may produce its proper effect by being read. Hence the performance is not the criterion. Tragedy has everything that epic has—and more (music and spectacle); it can be both acted and read; it is more concentrated and more effective; it has greater unity. Thus tragedy is the highest form of poetic art.

HORACE'S ART OF POETRY

Horace's *Ars Poetica* (*Epistles* II.3), based on Greek canons of literary criticism, was directed at the deteriorated standards of Roman poetry, especially in the field of the drama. It was written between 16 and 8 B.C. Only the parts dealing with the drama are outlined here.

Lines 73-118

Each of the types of poetry has meters suitable to it established by the famous Greek poets. These meters must be mastered and followed. So also tone and style must be suited to the particular genre.

In dramatic poetry, comedy and tragedy must be kept distinctly separate in meter, style and tone. It is true, however, that they sometimes overlap. Poetry must have beauty, but must also touch the emotions of the audience. The language of the characters must be consistent with their personalities and the situations; otherwise they will appear ridiculous to the audience.

119-152

Either follow the traditional stories, or invent a plot that is consistent. If one of the traditional myths is employed, the characters must be portrayed as they are known in Greek literature. If a new character is created, it should be handled with a consistency of its own.

It is difficult to portray common human characteristics in an individualized way. It is more commendable to dramatize a theme from Homer than to attempt an original one. Yet one should make an effort to handle the Homeric material with originality. Otherwise, "mountains will labor and a ridiculous mouse will be born." Like Homer, employ a rapid, simple beginning, hurrying the audience *in medias res*. Omit unessentials, keeping beginning, middle and end consistent.

153-188

To write a successful play, one must study humanity, observing the distinctive characteristics of each age of man—childhood, youth, maturity, old age—so as to avoid confusing them. Events of the plot may be set forth through action or narrative. The latter is, in general, less desirable. Deeds of violence and revolting incidents, however, should not be acted out before the audience, but narrated.

189-219

A play should contain five acts. The *deus ex machina* should be employed only rarely. There should be no more than three speaking characters on stage at any one time. The Chorus should be integrated into the action, virtually like one of the actors. It should not sing irrelevant choral interludes. The chorus should give advice, support righteousness, praise moderation, justice, law, peace; should keep secrets, sympathize with the humble and shun the proud.

The musical accompaniment of the flute should be, as it was of old, simple and unembellished, not florid and sensational, as it has become. So, too, diction has become artificial and rhetorical.

220-250

Satyr plays are naturally gay and full of jesting, but they must be handled with delicacy and restraint. Neither gods nor heroes, in this dramatic genre, should use vulgar speech or be depicted in ridiculous scenes. Satyr plays should fuse the language of both tragedy and comedy.

251-274

With respect to the use of meter, avoid the crudeness and lack of precision of earlier Latin writers. Study the Greek models night and day. Judged by these standards, earlier generations overrated the rhythms and wit of Plautus.

275-294

Thespis invented tragedy; Aeschylus perfected it, giving it dignity and elevation. The license of Old Comedy resulted in its excesses being curbed by law. The abusive language of the Chorus was finally silenced.

Roman poets, besides imitating the Greeks, invented a national drama in both tragedy and comedy. They might have achieved greater heights had they been more painstaking. Every poem which has not been most carefully polished should be condemned.

BIBLIOGRAPHY

CHAPTER I

Agard, W. R., The Greek Mind (Princeton, 1957)

Agard, W. R., What Democracy Meant to the Greeks (Chapel Hill, 1942)

Bonner, R. J., Aspects of Athenian Democracy (Berkeley, 1933)

Bowra, C. M., The Greek Experience (Cleveland and New York, 1958)

Cambridge Ancient History, Vol. V (Cambridge, 1935)

Dickinson, G. L., The Greek View of Life. 7th Ed. (Garden City, 1936)

Festugière, J., Personal Religion Among the Greeks (Berkeley, 1954)

Freeman, K., Ancilla to the Pre-Socratic Philosophers (Cambridge, 1948)

Freeman, K., The Pre-Socratic Philosophers (Oxford, 1946)

Greene, W. C., Moira: Fate, Good, and Evil in Greek Thought (Cambridge, Mass., 1944)

Glover, T. R., Democracy in the Ancient World (Cambridge, 1927)

Glover, T. R., From Pericles to Philip. 4th Ed. (Cambridge, 1926)

Guthrie, W. W., The Greeks and Their Gods (London, 1950)

James, H. R., Our Hellenic Heritage. 2 Vols. (London, 1921-1924)

Jones, A. H. M., Athenian Democracy (Oxford, 1957)

Kerényi, C., The Gods of the Greeks (London, 1951)

Kirk, G. S., and Raven, J. E., The Presocratic Philosophers (Cambridge, 1958)

Kitto, H. D. F., The Greeks (Harmondsworth, 1951)

Mackenzie, C., Pericles (London, 1937)

Moore, C. H., The Religious Thought of the Greeks. 2nd Ed. (Cambridge, Mass., 1918)

Murray, G., Five Stages of Greek Religion. 3rd Ed. (Boston, 1952)

Nilsson, M. P., A History of Greek Religion. 2nd Ed. (Oxford, 1949)

Nilsson, M. P., Cults, Myths, Oracles and Politics in Ancient Greece (Lund, 1951)

Nilsson, M. P., Greek Popular Religion (New York, 1940)

Petrie, A., An Introduction to Greek History, Antiquities and Literature (London, 1932)

Robinson, C. A., Jr., et al., The Spring of Civilization: Periclean Athens (New York, 1954)

Rose, H. J., Ancient Greek Religion (London and New York, 1948)

Rose, H. J., Gods and Heroes of the Greeks (London, 1957)

Tucker, T. G., Life in Ancient Athens (New York, 1930)

Untersteiner, M., The Sophists (Oxford, 1954)

Webster, T. B. L., Greek Art and Literature 530-400 B.C. (Oxford, 1939)

Zimmern, A. E., The Greek Commonwealth: Politics and Economics in Fifth-Century Athens. 5th Ed. (Oxford, 1931)

CHAPTER II

Allen, J. T., Stage Antiquities of the Greeks and Romans and their Influence (New York, 1927)

Barnett, L. D., The Greek Drama. 4th Ed. (London, 1922)

Bieber, M., The History of the Greek and Roman Theater (Princeton, 1939)

Campbell, L., A Guide to Greek Tragedy for English Readers (London, 1891)

Flickinger, R. C., The Greek Theater and its Drama. 4th Ed. (Chicago, 1936)

Goodell, T. D., Athenian Tragedy (New Haven, 1920)

Haigh, A. E., The Tragic Drama of the Greeks (Oxford, 1896)

Harsh, P. W., A Handbook of Classical Drama (Stanford, 1944)

Hunnigher, B., The Origin of the Theater (The Hague, 1955)

Kitto, H. D. F., Form and Meaning in Drama (New York, 1957)

Kitto, H. D. F., Greek Tragedy: a Literary Study. 2nd Ed. (London, 1950)

Lattimore, R., The Poetry of Greek Tragedy (Baltimore, 1958)

Little, A. M. G., Myth and Society in Attic Drama (New York, 1942)

Lucas, D. W., The Greek Tragic Poets: Their Contribution to Western Life and Thought (London, 1950)

Lucas, F. L., Greek Drama for Everyman (London, 1954)

Matthei, L. E., Studies in Greek Tragedy (Cambridge, 1918)

Moulton, R. G., The Ancient Classical Drama. 2nd Ed. (Oxford, 1898)

Muller, H. J., The Spirit of Tragedy (New York, 1956)

Norwood, G., Greek Tragedy. 2nd Ed. (London, 1928)

Oates, W. J., and O'Neill, E., Jr., The Complete Greek Drama (New York, 1938)

Page, D. L., A New Chapter in the History of Greek Tragedy (Cambridge, 1951)

Pickard-Cambridge, A. W., Dithyramb, Tragedy and Comedy (Oxford, 1927)

Pickard-Cambridge, A. W., The Theatre of Dionysus in Athens (Oxford, 1946)

Prentice, W. K., Those Ancient Dramas Called Tragedies (Princeton, 1942)

Ridgeway, W., The Origin of Tragedy (Cambridge, 1910)

Sheppard, J. T., Greek Tragedy (Cambridge, 1911)

Webster, T. B. L., Greek Theatre Production (London, 1956)

Young, S. P., The Women of Greek Drama (New York, 1953)

MYTHOLOGY

Bulfinch, T., Mythology (Modern Library, 1934)

Fairbanks, A., The Mythology of Greece and Rome (New York, 1907)

Gayley, G. M., The Classic Myths. New Ed. (New York, 1911)

Graves, R., The Greek Myths. 2 Vols. (Harmondsworth, 1955)

Hamilton, E., Mythology (Boston, 1942)

Harrison, J. E., Myths of Greece and Rome (London and New York, 1928)

Howe, G., and Harrer, G., A Handbook of Classical Mythology (New York, 1929)

Rose, H. J., A Handbook of Greek Mythology (New York, 1928)

CHAPTER III

Murray, G., Aeschylus, The Creator of Tragedy (Oxford, 1940)

Murray, R. D., The Motif of Io in Aeschylus' Suppliants (Princeton, 1958)

Finley, J. H., Jr., Pindar and Aeschylus (Cambridge, Mass., 1955)

Owen, E. T., The Harmony of Aeschylus (Toronto, 1952)

Sheppard, J. T., Aeschylus and Sophocles: their Work and Influence. 2nd Ed. (New York, 1946)

Smyth, H. W., Aeschylean Tragedy (Berkeley, 1924)

Solmsen, F., Hesiod and Aeschylus (Ithaca, 1949)

Thomson, G. D., Aeschylus and Athens: a Study of the Social Origins of Drama (London, 1941)

CHAPTER IV

Adams, S. M., Sophocles the Playwright (Toronto, 1957)

Bowra, C. M., Sophoclean Tragedy (Oxford, 1944)

Ehrenberg, V., Sophocles and Pericles (Oxford, 1954)

Goheen, R. F., The Imagery of Sophocles' Antigone (Princeton, 1944)

Kirkwood, G. M., A Study of Sophoclean Drama (Ithaca, 1958)

Kitto, H. D. F., Sophocles: Dramatist and Philosopher (London, 1958)

Knox, B. M. W., Oedipus at Thebes (New Haven, 1957)

Letters, F. J. H., The Life and Work of Sophocles (London, 1953)

Linforth, I. M., Religion and Drama in Oedipus at Colonus (Berkeley, 1951)

Moore, J. A., Sophocles and Arete (Cambridge, Mass., 1938)

O'Connor, M. B., Religion in the Plays of Sophocles (Menasha, 1923)

Sheppard, J. T., Aeschylus and Sophocles: their Work and Influence. 2nd Ed. (New York, 1946)

Sheppard, J. T., The Wisdom of Sophocles (London, 1947)

Waldock, C. H., Sophocles the Dramatist (Cambridge, 1951)

Whitman, C., Sophocles: a Study of Heroic Humanism (Cambridge, Mass., 1951)

CHAPTER V

Appleton, R. B., Euripides the Idealist (London and New York, 1927)

Bates, W. N., Euripides: a Student of Human Nature (Philadelphia, 1930)

Blaiklock, E. M., The Male Characters of Euripides. A Study in Realism (Wellington, N. Z., 1952)

Carpenter, R., The Ethics of Euripides (New York, 1916)

Decharmé, P., Euripides and the Spirit of his Drama (New York, 1906)

Greenwood, L. H. G., Aspects of Euripidean Tragedy (Cambridge, 1953)

Grube, F. M. A., The Drama of Euripides (London, 1941)

Jones, W. H. S., The Moral Standpoint of Euripides (London, 1906)

Lucas, F. L., Euripides and his Influence (Boston, 1928)

Murray, G., Euripides and his Age. New Ed. (Oxford, 1946)

Norwood, G., Essays on Euripidean Drama (Cambridge, 1954)

Verrall, A. W., Euripides the Rationalist (Cambridge, 1913)

CHAPTER VI

Cornford, F. M., The Origin of Attic Comedy (London, 1914)

Croiset, M., Aristophanes and the Political Parties at Athens (London, 1909)

Ehrenberg, V., The People of Aristophanes: a Sociology of Old Attic Comedy. 2nd Ed. (Oxford, 1951)

Hugill, W. M., Panhellenism in Aristophanes (Chicago, 1936)

Lever, K., The Art of Greek Comedy (London, 1956)
Lord, L. E., Aristophanes: his Plays and Influence (Boston, 1925)
Murray, G., Aristophanes and the War Party (London, 1919)
Murray, G., Aristophanes: a Study (New York, 1933)
Norwood, G., Greek Comedy (London, 1931)
Pickard-Cambridge, A. W., Dithyramb, Tragedy and Comedy (Oxford, 1927)

CHAPTER VII

Dunkin, P. S., Post-Aristophanic Comedy. Studies in the Social Outlook of Middle and New Comedy at both Athens and Rome (Urbana, 1946)
Ehrenberg, V., Alexander and the Greeks (Oxford, 1938)
Glover, T. R., From Pericles to Philip. 4th Ed. (Cambridge, 1926)
Jouguet, P. F. A., Macedonian Imperialism and the Hellenization of the East (New York, 1928)
Laistner, M. L. W., A History of the Greek World from 479-323 B.C. (London, 1936)
Lever, K., The Art of Greek Comedy (London, 1956)
Webster, T. B. L., Art and Literature in Fourth Century Athens (London, 1956)
Webster, T. B. L., Studies in Later Greek Tragedy (Manchester, 1953)

CHAPTER VIII

Bevan, E. R., Stoics and Sceptics (Oxford, 1913)
Bury, J. B., A History of the Greek World from 323 to 146 B.C. 2nd Ed. (London, 1951)
Cary, M., The Legacy of Alexander: A History of the Greek World from 323 to 146 B.C. (London and New York, 1932)
Couat, A., Alexandrian Poetry under the First Three Ptolemies (New York, 1931)
De Witt, N. W., Epicurus and his Philosophy (Minneapolis, 1954)
Dunkin, P. W., Post-Aristophanic Comedy. Studies in the Social Outlook of Middle and New Comedy at both Athens and Rome (Urbana, 1946)

4314 BIBLIOGRAPHY

314BIBLIOGRAPHY

4Hicks, R. R., Stoic and Epicurean (London, 1910)

Jouguet, P., Macedonian Imperialism and the Hellenization of the East (New York, 1928)

Legrand, P. E., The Greek New Comedy (London and New York, 1917)

Lever, K., The Art of Greek Comedy (London, 1956)

Tarn, W. W., and Griffith, G. T., Hellenistic Civilization. 3rd Ed. (London, 1952)

Webster, T. B. L., Studies in Menander (Manchester, 1950)

CHAPTER IX

Bailey, C., The Legacy of Rome. 7th Ed. (Oxford, 1947)

Barrow, R. H., The Romans (Harmondsworth, 1949)

Chapot, V., The Roman World (London, 1928)

Duff, J. W., The Literary History of Rome. Vol. I: From the Origins to the Close of the Golden Age. Rev. and ed. by A. M. Duff (London and New York, 1953)

Fowler, W. W., Rome. 2nd Ed. rev. by M. P. Charlesworth (Oxford, 1947)

Frank, T., Life and Literature in the Roman Republic (Berkeley, 1940)

Hanson, J. A., Roman Theatre-Temples (Princeton, 1959)

Marsh, F. B., A History of the Roman World from 146 to 30 B.C. 2nd Ed. (London, 1953)

Greene, W. C., The Achievement of Rome (Cambridge, Mass., 1933)

Grenier, A., The Roman Spirit in Religion, Thought and Art (London and New York, 1926)

Jones, H. S., Companion to Roman History (Oxford, 1912)

MacKendrick, P., The Roman Mind at Work (Princeton, 1958)

Petrie, A., An Introduction to Roman History, Literature, and Antiquities (London, 1918)

Rose, H. J., A Handbook of Latin Literature. 2nd Ed. (London, 1949)

Scullard, H. H., A History of the Roman World from 753 to 146 B.C. 2nd Ed. (London, 1951)

Stobart, J. C., The Grandeur That Was Rome. 3rd Ed. (New York, 1935)

CHAPTER X

Beare, W., The Roman Stage; a History of Latin Drama in the Time of the Republic. 2nd Ed. (London, 1955)
Collins, W. L., Plautus and Terence (Philadelphia, 1880)
Duckworth, G. E., The Complete Roman Drama (New York, 1942)
Duckworth, G. E., The Nature of Roman Comedy: A Study in Popular Entertainment (Princeton, 1952)
Norwood, G., Plautus and Terence (New York, 1932)

CHAPTER XI

Beare, W., The Roman Stage: a History of Latin Drama in the Time of the Republic. 2nd Ed. (London, 1955)
Collins, W. L., Plautus and Terence (Philadelphia, 1880)
Duckworth, G. E., The Complete Roman Drama (New York, 1942)
Duckworth, G. E., The Nature of Roman Comedy: A Study in Popular Entertainment (Princeton, 1952)
Norwood, G., The Art of Terence (Oxford, 1931)
Norwood, G., Plautus and Terence (New York, 1932)

CHAPTER XII

Arnold, E. V., Roman Stoicism (Cambridge, 1911)
Charlesworth, M. P., The Roman Empire (1951)
Duckworth, G. E., The Complete Roman Drama (New York, 1942)
Gummere, R. M., Seneca the Philosopher and his Modern Message (Boston, 1922)
Hicks, R. R., Stoic and Epicurean (London, 1910)
Holland, F., Seneca (London, 1920)
Mendell, C. W., Our Seneca (New Haven, 1941)
Murray, G., The Stoic Philosophy (London and New York, 1915)
Nilsson, M. P., Imperial Rome (New York, 1926)

Pratt, N. T., Dramatic Suspense in Seneca and His Precursors (Princeton, 1939)

Salmon, E. T., A History of the Roman World from 30 B.C. to A.D. 138. 3rd Ed. (London, 1957)

Starr, C. G., Civilization and the Caesars: The Intellectual Revolution in the Roman Empire (Ithaca, 1954)

Stevenson, G. H., The Roman Empire (London, 1930)

Stock, St. G. W. J., Stoicism (New York, 1908)

Wenley, R. M., Stoicism and its Influence (Boston, 1924)

CHAPTER XIII

Butcher, S. H., Aristotle's Theory of Poetry and Fine Arts. 4th Ed. (New York, 1955)

Bywater, I., Aristotle on the Art of Poetry (Oxford, 1909)

Cooper, L., Aristotle on the Art of Poetry (Boston and New York, 1913)

Else, G. F., Aristotle's Poetics. The Argument (Cambridge, Mass., 1958)

Fyfe, W. H., Aristotle's Art of Poetry (Oxford, 1940)

House, H., Aristotle's Poetics (London, 1956)

Lucas, F. L., Tragedy in Relation to Aristotle's Poetics (London, 1927)

Owen, A. S., Aristotle on the Art of Poetry (Oxford, 1931)

Potts, L. J., Aristotle on the Art of Fiction (Cambridge, 1953)

INFLUENCES OF GREEK AND ROMAN DRAMA

Allen, N. B., The Sources of Dryden's Comedies (Ann Arbor, 1935)

Boas, F. S., Aspects of Classical Legend and History in Shakespeare (London, 1942)

Bullough, G., Narrative and Dramatic Sources of Shakespeare. 2 Vols. (New York, 1957-1958)

Chapman, P. A., The Spirit of Molière. An Interpretation (Princeton, 1940)

Charlton, H. B., The Senecan Tradition in Renaissance Tragedy (Manchester, 1946)

Coggin, P. A., The Uses of Drama. A Historical Survey of Drama and Education from Ancient Greece to the Present Day (New York, 1956)

Cunliffe, J. W., The Influence of Seneca on Elizabethan Tragedy (London and New York, 1893)

Dickinson, G. L., The Contribution of Ancient Greece to Modern Life (London, 1932)

Gordon, G. S., Ed., English Literature and the Classics (Oxford, 1912)

Grismer, R. L., The Influence of Plautus in Spain before Lope de Vega (New York, 1944)

Herrick, M. T., The Poetics of Aristotle in England (New Haven, 1930)

Highet, G., The Classical Tradition: Greek and Roman Influence on Western Literature (New York, 1949)

Jones, E., Hamlet and Oedipus (New York, 1949)

Lindberger, O., The Transformations of Amphitryon (Stockholm, 1956)

Lord, L. E., Aristophanes: his Plays and Influence (Boston, 1925)

Lucas, F. L., Euripides and his Influence (Boston, 1928)

Lucas, F. L., Seneca and Elizabethan Tragedy (Cambridge, 1922)

Lumley, E. P., The Influence of Plautus in the Comedies of Ben Jonson (New York, 1901)

MacCallum, M. W., Shakespeare's Roman Plays and their Background (London, 1910)

Magnus, L., English Literature in Its Foreign Relations (London, 1927)

McArthur, J. R., Ancient Greece in Modern America (Caldwell, 1943)

Moore, R. W., The Root of Europe. Studies in the Diffusion of Greek Culture (New York, 1952)

Parker, W. R., Milton's Debt to Greek Tragedy in 'Samson Agonistes' (Baltimore, 1937)

Root, R. K., Classical Mythology in Shakespeare (New York, 1903)

Sheppard, J. T., Aeschylus and Sophocles: their Work and Influence. 2nd Ed. (New York, 1946)

Stapfer, P., Shakespeare and Classical Antiquity (London, 1880)

Theobald, W., The Classical Element in Shakespeare's Plays (London, 1909)

Thomson, J. A. K., Classical Influences on English Prose (London, 1956)

Thomson, J. A. K., Shakespeare and the Classics (London, 1952)

Thomson, J. A. K., The Classical Background of English Literature (New York, 1948)

Tucker, T. G., The Foreign Debt of English Literature (London, 1907)

Watt, L. M., Attic and Elizabethan Tragedy (London, 1908)

Wheatley, K. E., Molière and Terence. A Study in Molière's Realism (Austin, 1931)

Wilson, P. C., Wagner's Dramas and Greek Tragedy (New York, 1919)

GLOSSARY

To avoid uninstructive duplication, this glossary has been prepared with several restrictions. Characters in tragedies are listed, but those who appear in comedies are not. The latter, usually limited to the action of a single play, can readily be located with the aid of the Index. Similarly, the Index should be consulted for titles of plays.

Accius, Roman author (170-ca. 86 B.C.) of tragedies and historical plays, none of which is extant.

Achaeus, Greek author (Fifth Century B.C.) of tragedy, none of which is extant.

Achilles, famed Greek hero, son of Peleus and Thetis; character in Euripides' *Iphigenia in Aulis.*

Admetus, king of Pherae; husband of Alcestis; character in Euripides' *Alcestis.*

Adrastus, king of Argos; father-in-law of Polynices, whom he aided in "Seven Against Thebes;" character in Euripides' *Suppliants.*

Aegeus, king of Athens; father of Theseus; character in Euripides' *Medea.*

Aegisthus, son of Thyestes; lover and second husband of Clytemnestra; character in Aeschylus' *Oresteia,* Sophocles' *Electra,* Euripides' *Electra,* Seneca's *Agamemnon.*

Aeneas, Trojan prince, second in command to Hector at Troy; character in tragedy *Rhesus.*

Aeschylus, Athenian author (525-455 B.C.) of tragedy; real creator of tragedy; seven of his plays are extant; character in Aristophanes' *Frogs.*

319

Aethra, mother of Theseus, king of Athens; character in Euripides' *Suppliants.*

Afranius, leading Roman writer of comedy in native dress (*fabula togata*); none of his plays is extant.

Agamemnon, king of Mycenae; husband of Clytemnestra; father of Iphigenia, Electra, Orestes, Chrysothemis; commander-in-chief of Greek forces in Trojan War; character in Aeschylus' *Oresteia,* Sophocles' *Ajax,* Euripides' *Hecuba, Iphigenia in Aulis,* Seneca's *Agamemnon, Trojan Women.*

Agathon, Greek author (Fifth Century B.C.) of tragedy; none of his plays has survived; character in Aristophanes' *Thesmophoriazusae.*

Agave, mother of Pentheus, king of Thebes; character in Euripides' *Bacchae.*

Agon, dramatized debate in Old Comedy.

Agrippina, mother of Emperor Nero, slain by him; her ghost appears in the tragedy *Octavia.*

Ajax, Greek hero who committed suicide at Troy; character in Sophocles' *Ajax.*

Alcestis, wife of Admetus; character in Euripides' *Alcestis.*

Alcmene, beloved of Zeus; mother of Heracles, wife of Amphitryon; character in Euripides' *Children of Heracles,* Plautus' *Amphitryon,* Seneca's *Hercules on Oeta.*

Amphitryon, king of Thebes; husband of Alcmene; character in Euripides' *Mad Heracles,* Plautus' *Amphitryon,* Seneca's *Mad Hercules.*

Anagnorisis, the "discovery" or "recognition;" a frequent element in the plot of classical drama involving recognition by long-parted persons.

Andromache, wife of Hector; mother of Astyanax; character in Euripides' *Andromache, Trojan Women,* Seneca's *Trojan Women.*

Angiportum, alley between two houses representing scene in Roman comedies; here characters concealed themselves to eavesdrop.

Antigone, devoted daughter of Oedipus; punished with death for burying her brother Polynices; character in Aeschylus' *Seven Against Thebes,* Sophocles' *Antigone, Oedipus at Colonus,* Euripides' *Phoenician Women,* Seneca's *Phoenician Women.*

Antistrophe, division of a choral ode, a "countermovement."

Aphrodite (Venus), goddess of love and beauty; character in Euripides' *Hippolytus.*

Apollo (Phoebus), god of prophecy, music, sun, medicine, archery;

his oracle at Delphi much frequented; character in Aeschylus' *Eumenides*, Sophocles' *Trackers*, Euripides' *Alcestis, Ion, Orestes.*

Apollodorus, leading Greek writer of New Comedy; none of his plays is extant.

Areopagus, council of aristocrats in Athens; tried murder cases in Fifth Century B.C.; form jury in Aeschylus' *Eumenides* which tried Orestes.

Aristarchus, Greek author (Fifth Century B.C.) of tragedy; none of his plays has survived.

Aristophanes, greatest writer of Old Comedy (446-385 B.C.); eleven of his plays are extant.

Aristotle, famous Greek philosopher (384-322 B.C.); author of numerous works; wrote *Poetics.*

Artemis (Diana), goddess of hunting, moon, maidens; sister of Apollo; character in Euripides' *Hippolytus, Iphigenia in Aulis.*

Astyanax, son of Hector and Andromache; slain by Greeks after fall of Troy; character in Euripides' *Trojan Women*, Seneca's *Trojan Women.*

Astydamas, Greek author (Fourth Century B.C.) of tragedy; none of his plays is extant.

Atë, goddess of infatuation; supposed to assail those guilty of sin of *hybris* (excess, pride, arrogance).

Athena (Minerva), patron divinity of Athens; goddess of wisdom, defensive war, household arts; character in Aeschylus' *Eumenides,* Sophocles' *Ajax,* Euripides' *Ion, Iphigenia in Tauris, Suppliants, Trojan Women*; also appears in the tragedy *Rhesus.*

Atossa, queen of Persia; mother of Xerxes; character in Aeschylus' *Persians.*

Atreus, king of Mycenae; father of Agamemnon and Menelaüs; character in Seneca's *Thyestes.*

Atta, leading Roman writer of comedy in native dress (*fabula togata*).

Bacchantes, female worshippers of Dionysus; chorus in Euripides' *Bacchae.*

Bacchus: see Dionysus.

Cadmus, king of Thebes; father of Pentheus; character in Euripides' *Bacchae.*

Caecilius Statius, leading Roman writer (ca. 219-166 B.C.) of comedies; none of his plays is extant.

Calchas, soothsayer of Greek expedition to Troy; character in Seneca's *Trojan Women.*

Carcinus, Greek author (Fourth Century B.C.) of tragedy; none of his plays survives.

Cassandra, prophetess daughter of King Priam of Troy; concubine of Agamemnon; slain by Clytemnestra; character in Aeschylus' *Agamemnon*, Euripides' *Trojan Women*, Seneca's *Agamemnon*.

Catharsis, "purging;" according to Aristotle, the purpose of tragedy is to arouse pity and fear in such a way as to effect a pleasurable catharsis of these emotions.

Chaeremon, Greek author (Fourth Century B.C.) of tragedy; none of his plays survives.

Choerilus, Greek author (523-468 B.C.) of tragedy; none of his plays survives.

Choregus, wealthy citizen at Athens selected to pay for cost of training and costumes of chorus in Greek dramas.

Chorus, group which sang and danced between the episodes of a Greek play.

Chrysothemis, sister of Electra and Orestes; character in Sophocles' *Electra*.

Cloudcuckooland, name of fantastic utopia in Aristophanes' *Birds*.

Clytemnestra, wife of Agamemnon; mother of Iphigenia, Electra, Orestes, Chrysothemis; sister of Helen of Troy; slew her husband on his return from Troy; character in Aeschylus' *Oresteia*, Sophocles' *Electra*, Euripides' *Electra*, *Iphigenia in Aulis*, Seneca's *Agamemnon*.

Contaminatio, practice of Roman dramatists of combining parts of two or more plots from Greek New Comedy to form new play.

Copreus, herald of Eurystheus of Argos; character in Euripides' *Children of Heracles*.

Cothurnus, buskin, the high-soled boot worn by tragic actors to give them added dignity.

Crates, leading Greek writer of Old Comedy; none of his plays is extant.

Cratinus, leading Greek writer of Old Comedy; none of his plays is extant.

Creon, king of Corinth; slain by Medea; character in Euripides' *Medea*, Seneca's *Medea*.

Creon, king of Thebes; uncle of Oedipus, brother of Jocasta, father of Haemon; character in Sophocles' *Antigone*, *Oedipus the King*, *Oedipus at Colonus*, Euripides' *Phoenician Women*, Seneca's *Oedipus*.

Creusa, 1. Wife of Xuthus; mother of Ion; character in Euripides' *Ion*.

2. Daughter of Creon, married to Jason, slain by Medea; character in Seneca's *Medea*.

Cyllene, nymph, foster-mother of Hermes; character in Sophocles' *Trackers*.

Danaïds, fifty daughters of Danaüs; leading characters and chorus in Aeschylus' *Suppliant Women*.

Danaüs, father of the Danaïds; character in Aeschylus' *Suppliant Women*.

Darius, king of Persia; father of Xerxes; his ghost appears in Aeschylus' *Persians*.

Deianira, wife of Heracles; unwittingly causes his death; character in Sophocles' *Maidens of Trachis*, Seneca's *Hercules on Oeta*.

Delphic Oracle, shrine at city of Delphi, sacred to Apollo; consulted by Greeks and Romans to secure prophecies of the future.

Demophon, king of Athens; son of Theseus; character in Euripides' *Children of Heracles*.

Deus ex Machina, "god from the machine;" a dummy suspended from the top of skene in Greek theater representing a god who unraveled all the unsolved problems of the play.

Deuteragonist, actor who had supporting roles in Greek drama.

Diomedes, Greek hero; character in the tragedy *Rhesus*.

Dionysia: see Great Dionysia; Rural Dionysia.

Dionysus (Bacchus), god of wine and reproductive forces in life; patron divinity of the drama; character in Euripides' *Bacchae*, Aristophanes' *Frogs*.

Dioscuri (Castor and Pollux), minor divinities; brothers of Helen and Clytemnestra; characters in Euripides' *Electra, Helen*.

Diphilus, leading Greek writer of New Comedy; none of his plays is extant.

Dithyramb, hymn to Dionysus, sung by chorus of fifty men representing satyrs.

Dolon, a Trojan; character in the tragedy *Rhesus*.

Dramatic Foil, a character used as sharp contrast with another character to highlight personality; favorite device of Sophocles.

Dramatic Irony, a device involving double meanings in what is said or done in a drama; the audience, having foreknowledge of the situation, understands what is said or done in a different way from the characters.

Eccylema, movable platform rolled out from skene building into orchestra to depict events which take place inside the building in front of which the action occurs.

Economy of Roles, limitation of number of actors in a Greek play; from Sophocles' time a maximum of three was used, each of whom might take several roles.

Electra, daughter of Agamemnon and Clytemnestra; sister of Orestes; character in Aeschylus' *Choëphoroe,* Sophocles' *Electra,* Euripides' *Electra, Orestes,* Seneca's *Agamemnon.*

Ennius, outstanding Roman author (239-169 B.C.) of tragedies, comedies, historical plays. None of his plays is extant.

Episode, a sort of act—action in a classical drama between choral odes.

Epode, a division of a choral ode, an "afterpiece."

Erinyes: see Furies.

Eteocles, son of Oedipus and Jocasta; slew and was slain by his brother Polynices; character in Aeschylus' *Seven Against Thebes,* Euripides' *Phoenician Women,* Seneca's *Phoenician Women.*

Eumenides, "Kindly Ones," benevolent protecting divinities of Athens; figure importantly in Aeschylus' *Eumenides,* Sophocles' *Oedipus at Colonus.*

Eupolis, leading Greek writer of Old Comedy; none of his plays is extant.

Euripides, Athenian author (480-406 B.C.) of tragedy. Eighteen of his plays are extant; character in Aristophanes' *Acharnians, Thesmophoriazusae.*

Eurybates, herald of Agamemnon; character in Seneca's *Agamemnon.*

Eurydice, wife of Creon; mother of Haemon; character in Sophocles' *Antigone.*

Eurysaces, son of Ajax by Tecmessa; character in Sophocles' *Ajax.*

Eurystheus, king of Argos; character in Euripides' *Children of Heracles.*

Evadne, wife of Capaneus, Argive chieftain; character in Euripides' *Suppliants.*

Exodos, the action of a Greek play after the last choral ode.

Fabula Atellana, early Italian popular pre-literary dramatic form—a rustic farce with song and dance, featuring stock characters.

Fabula Palliata, Roman adaptation of Greek New Comedy.

Fabula Praetexta, native Roman historical play.

Fabula Togata, Roman comedy in native dress.

Fescennine Verses, early Italian popular pre-literary dramatic form consisting of improvised rude banter by masked entertainers.

Furies (Erinyes), forces of conscience; horrible divinities thought to pursue murderers, especially of close relatives; chorus in Aeschylus' *Eumenides*.

Gamos, male-female union, frequent concluding scene in Old Comedy.

Great (City) Dionysia, annual dramatic festival honoring Dionysus in Athens during March/April.

Haemon, son of Creon; betrothed of Antigone; character in Sophocles' *Antigone*.

Hamartia, "tragic flaw," the weakness in a character's personality that affects his fortunes.

Hector, famed Trojan hero; son of Priam and Hecuba; husband of Andromache; father of Astyanax; character in the tragedy *Rhesus*.

Hecuba, queen of Troy, wife of Priam; character in Euripides' *Hecuba, Trojan Women*, Seneca's *Trojan Women*.

Helen, daughter of Zeus and Leda; wife of Menelaüs, Paris; mother of Hermione; character in Euripides' *Helen, Orestes, Trojan Women*, Seneca's *Trojan Women*.

Hephaestus (Vulcan), smith of the gods; character in Aeschylus' *Prometheus Bound*.

Hera (Juno), queen of the gods, wife of Zeus; patron goddess of married women; character in Seneca's *Mad Hercules*.

Heracles (Hercules), son of Zeus and Alcmene, national hero and benefactor of Greeks; famed for his Twelve Labors; character in Sophocles' *Maidens of Trachis, Philoctetes*, Euripides' *Alcestis*, Aristophanes' *Frogs, Birds*, Seneca's *Hercules on Oeta, Mad Hercules*.

Hermes (Mercury), messenger of the gods; god of speed, commerce; character in Aeschylus' *Prometheus Bound*, Sophocles' *Trackers*, Euripides' *Ion*, Aristophanes' *Peace, Plutus*, Plautus' *Amphitryon*.

Hermione, daughter of Menelaüs and Helen; character in Euripides' *Andromache, Orestes*.

Hippolytus, son of Theseus; stepson of Phaedra; character in Euripides' *Hippolytus*, Seneca's *Phaedra*.

Histrio, Roman word for "actor."

Horace, Roman author (65-8 B.C.) of many works, including *Art of Poetry* (*Ars Poetica*).

Hybris, the sin of excess in Greek thought which was believed to cause pride and arrogance and to be punished by Nemesis sent by the gods.

Hyllus, son of Heracles and Deianira; character in Sophocles' *Maidens* *of Trachis,* Euripides' *Children of Heracles,* Seneca's *Hercules on Oeta.*

Hypokrites, Greek word for "actor."

Io, beloved of Zeus; suffered because of Hera's jealousy; character in Aeschylus' *Prometheus Bound.*

Iolaüs, friend and war-comrade of Heracles; character in Euripides' *Children of Heracles.*

Iole, concubine of Heracles; character in Sophocles' *Maidens of Trachis,* Seneca's *Hercules on Oeta.*

Ion, 1. Greek author (Fifth Century B.C.) of tragedy; none of his plays is extant. 2. Son of Apollo and Creusa; character in Euripides' *Ion.*

Iphigenia, daughter of Agamemnon and Clytemnestra; supposedly sacrificed at Aulis; rescued by Orestes from the Taurians; character in Euripides' *Iphigenia in Aulis, Iphigenia in Tauris.*

Iphis, father of Evadne and Eteoclus; character in Euripides' *Suppliants.*

Ismene, daughter of Oedipus; character in Aeschylus' *Seven Against Thebes,* Sophocles' *Antigone, Oedipus at Colonus.*

Jason, famed Greek hero who obtained the Golden Fleece; loved by Medea; character in Euripides' *Medea,* Seneca's *Medea.*

Jocasta, wife and mother of Oedipus; character in Sophocles' *Oedipus the King,* Euripides' *Phoenician Women,* Seneca's *Oedipus, Phoenician Women.*

Juno: see Hera.

Jupiter: see Zeus.

Kommos, responsive lyric exchange between chorus and actors in Greek tragedy; usually a lament.

Komos, revelry in honor of Dionysus.

Laius, father of Oedipus; his ghost appears in Seneca's *Oedipus.*

Lenaea, annual festival of Dionysus in Athens during January/February; only comedies performed.

Lichas, herald of Heracles; character in Sophocles' *Maidens of Trachis,* Seneca's *Hercules on Oeta.*

Livius Andronicus, Roman author (ca. 284-ca. 204 B.C.) of tragedies and comedies adapted from Greek originals. None of his plays has survived.

Lycus, tyrant of Thebes; slain by Heracles; character in Euripides' *Mad Heracles,* Seneca's *Mad Hercules.*

Macaria, daughter of Heracles; character in Euripides' *Children of Heracles.*

"Machine," mechanical device in classical Greek theater used to raise and lower flying figures, and to introduce and remove gods.

Magnes, leading Greek writer of Old Comedy; none of his plays survives.

Manto, daughter of Teiresias; character in Seneca's *Oedipus.*

Medea, sorceress princess of Colchis; loved Jason; character in Euripides' *Medea,* Seneca's *Medea.*

Megara, wife of Heracles; character in Euripides' *Mad Heracles,* Seneca's *Mad Hercules.*

Menander, famed Greek writer (ca. 342-291 B.C.) of New Comedy; only one complete play of his and extensive portions of three others are extant.

Menelaüs, king of Sparta; husband of Helen; father of Hermione; brother of Agamemnon; character in Sophocles' *Ajax,* Euripides' *Andromache, Helen, Iphigenia in Aulis, Orestes, Trojan Women.*

Menoecus, son of Creon, king of Thebes; character in Euripides' *Phoenician Women.*

Mercury: see Hermes.

Middle Comedy, transitional Greek dramatic form (400-338 B.C.) between Old and New Comedy.

Mime, popular Italian dramatic form—a farce including dancing and gesticulation.

Mimesis, Greek word for creative artistic process of "imitation," or "representation."

Molossus, son of Andromache and Neoptolemus; character in Euripides' *Andromache.*

Moschion, leading Greek writer (Fourth Century B.C.) of tragedy; none of his plays survives.

Naevius, leading Roman writer (ca. 270-ca. 201 B.C.) of comedies, tragedies, and historical plays; none of his plays survives.

Nemesis, goddess thought by Greeks to be sent by gods to punish those guilty of *hybris* (excess, pride, arrogance).

Neophron, leading writer (Fifth Century B.C.) of tragedy; none of his plays survives.

Neoptolemus, son of Achilles; character in Sophocles' *Philoctetes,* Euripides' *Andromache.*

Nero, Roman Emperor (A.D. 54-68); character in the tragedy *Octavia.*

New Comedy, dramatic genre of Hellenistic Age (330-150 B.C.); realistic Comedy of Manners, with stock characters, dealing with private lives of leisure class.

Oceanids, daughters of Oceanus; chorus in Aeschylus' *Prometheus Bound.*

Oceanus, a Titan; character in Aeschylus' *Prometheus Bound.*

Octavia, first wife of Nero; character in tragedy *Octavia.*

Odysseus (Ulysses), king of Ithaca; Greek hero famed for his cunning; character in Sophocles' *Ajax, Philoctetes,* Euripides' *Cyclops, Hecuba,* the anonymous tragedy *Rhesus,* Seneca's *Trojan Women.*

Oedipus, king of Thebes; son of Laïus and Jocasta; killed father and married mother; character in Sophocles' *Oedipus the King, Oedipus at Colonus,* Euripides' *Phoenician Women,* Seneca's *Oedipus, Phoenician Women.*

Old Comedy, dramatic form written in Fifth Century B.C.; involves satire on contemporary life and persons; most of Aristophanes' plays belong to the Old Comedy.

Orchestra, originally circular "dancing place" of Greek theater where chorus and actors performed; in Hellenistic and Roman times it was semicircular and not used.

Orestes, son of Agamemnon and Clytemnestra; slays mother to avenge father; character in Aeschylus' *Oresteia,* Sophocles' *Electra,* Euripides' *Andromache, Electra, Iphigenia in Aulis, Iphigenia in Tauris, Orestes,* Seneca's *Agamemnon.*

Pacuvius, leading Roman writer (ca. 220-ca. 130 B.C.) of tragedies; none of his plays has survived.

Pantomime, acting and dancing in dumb show; popular dramatic form during period of Roman Empire.

Parabasis, "coming forward" of the chorus which addresses the audience giving the author's views on various topics.

Parascenia, "wings" of Greek and Roman stage structure.

Paris, prince of Troy; son of Priam and Hecuba; husband of Helen; character in the tragedy *Rhesus.*

Parodos, entering dance of the chorus in classical drama; also passageway in theater through which chorus entered and exited from orchestra.

Pelasgus, king of Argos; character in Aeschylus' *Suppliant Women.*

Peleus, king of Phthia in Thessaly; father of Achilles; grandfather of Neoptolemus; character in Euripides' *Andromache.*

Peloponnesian War, disastrous war between rival imperialisms of Athens and Sparta (431-404 B.C.). Most of extant Greek tragedies and comedies were written during this period.

Pentheus, king of Thebes; character in Euripides' *Bacchae.*

Pericles, head of Athenian government during Golden Age of Athens (461-429 B.C.). The theater flourished during his régime.

Peripetia (Peripety), Greek word for "reversal"—the sudden change in the fortunes of the hero of a play.

Phaedra, wife of Theseus; stepmother of Hippolytus; character in Euripides' *Hippolytus,* Seneca's *Phaedra.*

Pherecrates, leading Greek writer (Fifth Century B.C.) of Old Comedy; none of his plays is extant.

Pheres, father of Admetus; character in Euripides' *Alcestis.*

Philemon, leading Greek writer of New Comedy; none of his plays is extant.

Philoctetes, Greek hero; character in Sophocles' *Philoctetes,* Seneca's *Hercules on Oeta.*

Phrynichus, 1. Greek writer (Fifth Century B.C.) of tragedy; none of his plays survives. 2. Leading writer (Fifth Century B.C.) of Old Comedy; none of his plays survives.

Platon, Greek writer (Fifth Century B.C.) of Old Comedy; none of his plays survives.

Plautus, greatest Roman writer of comedy (254-184 B.C.); twenty of his plays are extant.

Poetics, Aristotle's famed work on literary criticism, dealing with poetry in general and tragic drama in particular.

Polydorus, son of Hecuba and Priam; his ghost appears in Euripides' *Hecuba.*

Polyidus, leading Greek writer (Fourth Century B.C.) of tragedy; none of his plays survives.

Polymestor, king of Thrace; character in Euripides' *Hecuba.*

Polynices, son of Oedipus; slew and was slain by his brother Eteocles; buried by his sister Antigone; character in Aeschylus' *Seven Against Thebes,* Sophocles' *Oedipus at Colonus,* Euripides' *Phoenician Women,* Seneca's *Phoenician Women.*

Polyphemus, a Cyclops; character in Euripides' *Cyclops.*

Polyxena, daughter of Priam and Hecuba; sacrificed to Achilles' spirit at Troy; character in Euripides' *Hecuba,* Seneca's *Trojan Women*

Poppaea, second wife of Nero; figures in the tragedy *Octavia.*

Poseidon (Neptune), god of the sea; character in Euripides' *Trojan Women.*

Pratinus, leading Greek writer (Fifth Century B.C.) of tragedy; none of his plays survives.

Prologue, action before entrance of chorus in classical Greek tragedy and Old Comedy; later conventionalized introduction to a play.

Prometheus, a Titan, benefactor of man; punished for giving man fire; character in Aeschylus' *Prometheus Bound,* Aristophanes' *Birds.*

Proscenium, the façade of the skene building in Greek and Roman theaters which depicted the scene of the play.

Protagonist, actor in Greek drama who took the leading role, the "star" of the play.

Pylades, cousin and best friend of Orestes; character in Aeschylus' *Choëphoroe,* Sophocles' *Electra,* Euripides' *Electra, Iphigenia in Tauris, Orestes.*

Pyrrhus (or Neoptolemus), son of Achilles; character in Seneca's *Trojan Women.*

Rhesus, king of Thrace; ally of the Trojans; character in the tragedy *Rhesus.*

Rural Dionysia, annual dramatic festival honoring Dionysus in Attica, December/January.

Satura, early Italian popular pre-literary dramatic form; possibly a musical medley consisting of dialogue, gestures, music.

Satyr Play, mock-heroic tragicomedy which regularly followed trilogy of tragedies in Athenian drama.

Satyrs, minor woodland divinities; followers of Dionysus; chorus in Euripides' *Cyclops,* Sophocles' *Trackers.*

Seneca, famed Roman author (ca. 4 B.C.-A.D. 65); Stoic philosopher; nine of his tragedies, based on Greek plays, are extant; character in the tragedy *Octavia.*

Silenus, woodland divinity; follower of Dionysus; character in Sophocles' *Trackers,* Euripides' *Cyclops.*

Skene, building of Greek theater containing dressing rooms for actors; Roman equivalent—*scaena.*

Soccus, sandal worn by actors in Greek comedy.

Socrates, Athenian philosopher (469-399 B.C.); "Father of Ethics;" character in Aristophanes' *Clouds.*

Sophocles, Athenian writer of tragedy (497-405 B.C.); eight of his plays are extant.

Sphinx, mythical monster whose riddle was solved by Oedipus; figures importantly in Sophocles' *Oedipus Rex.*

Stage, apparently none in Greek theater of classical times; the Hellenistic Greek theater and the Roman theater had a raised stage.

Stasimon, a choral ode sung and danced after the chorus has entered the orchestra.

Stichomythia, rapid conversation in which characters speak alternate lines.

Strophe, a division of a choral ode, a "movement."

Strophius, king of Phocis; father of Pylades; character in Seneca's *Agamemnon.*

Talthybius, herald of the Greeks at Troy; character in Euripides' *Hecuba, Trojan Women,* Seneca's *Trojan Women.*

Tecmessa, concubine of Ajax; character in Sophocles' *Ajax.*

Teiresias, blind prophet of Thebes; character in Sophocles' *Antigone, Oedipus the King,* Euripides' *Bacchae, Phoenician Women,* Seneca's *Oedipus.*

Terence, leading Roman writer of comedy (ca. 195-159 B.C.); all of his plays, six in number, are extant.

Terpsichore, muse of dancing; mother of King Rhesus of Thrace; character in tragedy *Rhesus.*

Tetralogy, group of four plays, consisting of trilogy (three tragedies) and a satyr play.

Teucer, Greek hero; brother of Ajax; character in Sophocles' *Ajax,* Euripides' *Helen.*

Thanatos (Death); character in Euripides' *Alcestis.*

Theater of Dionysus, at foot of Acropolis in Athens; seating capacity ca. 17,000.

Theatron, the place where the audience sat in Greek theater.

Theodectes, leading Greek writer (Fourth Century B.C.) of tragedy; none of his plays is extant.

Theoklymenus, king of Egypt; character in Euripides' *Helen.*

Theologeion, a platform on the skene from which gods and heroes spoke from on high in classical Greek theater.

Theonoë, prophetess sister of Theoklymenus; character in Euripides' *Helen.*

Theoric Fund, theater fund from which admission fees to theater in Athens were paid for needy citizens.

Theseus, king of Athens; son of Aegeus; father of Hippolytus; character in Sophocles' *Oedipus at Colonus,* Euripides' *Mad Heracles, Suppliants,* Seneca's *Mad Hercules, Phaedra.*

Thespis, "Father of the Drama" (ca. 550-500 B.C.); created first actor.

Thetis, sea-goddess; wife of Peleus, mother of Achilles; character in Euripides' *Andromache.*

Thinkery, name of Socrates' school in Aristophanes' *Clouds.*

Thoas, king of the Taurians; character in Euripides' *Iphigenia in Tauris.*

Three Unities: see Unity of Time; Unity of Place; Unity of Action.

Thyestes, brother of Atreus; father of Aegisthus; appears in Seneca's *Agamemnon, Thyestes.*

Thymele, altar of Dionysus in orchestra of classical Greek theater.

Titinius, leading writer of Roman comedy in native dress (*fabula togata*); none of his plays survives.

Tragoedia, "goat-song" or dithyramb in honor of Dionysus which evolved into tragedy.

Trilogy, group of three tragedies, originally on unified theme, later on separate subjects.

Tritagonist, actor in Greek drama who performed the minor roles.

Tyndareus, of Sparta; father of Clytemnestra; character in Euripides' *Orestes.*

Unity of Action, concentration on one single action in a play, with no irrelevancies or subplots.

Unity of Place, one unchanged scene throughout the play.

Unity of Time, limitation of the action of a play to a time period not exceeding one revolution of the sun.

Xerxes, king of Persia; character in Aeschylus' *Persians.*

Xuthus, king of Athens; husband of Creusa; character in Euripides' *Ion.*

Zeus (Jupiter), king of the Olympian gods; god of sky, heavenly phenomena, hospitality; husband of Hera; figures importantly in Aeschylus' *Prometheus Bound*; character in Plautus' *Amphitryon.*

INDEX

333